D0829147

The Essential
Catholic Handbook
of the Sacraments

The Essential Catholic Handbook of the Sacraments

A SUMMARY OF BELIEFS, RITES, AND PRAYERS

A REDEMPTORIST PASTORAL PUBLICATION

Liguori
LIGUORI, MISSOURI

Imprimi Potest
Richard Thibodeau, C.Ss.R.
Provincial, Denver Province
The Redemptorists

Written and Edited by Thomas M. Santa, C.Ss.R.
Published by Liguori Publications
Liguori, Missouri
www.liguori.org
www.catholicbooksonline.com

Library of Congress Cataloging-in-Publication Data

Santa, Thomas M., 1952
  The essential Catholic handbook of the Sacraments : a summary of beliefs, rites, and prayers : with a glossary of key terms / written and compiled by Thomas M. Santa.—1st ed.
      p.   cm.— (A Redemptorist pastoral publication)
      Includes bibliographical references.
      ISBN 0-7648-0781-1 (pbk.)
      1. Sacraments—Catholic Church. 2. Catholic Church—Doctrines. I. Title.
II. Series.

BX2200 .S29 2001
234'.16'08822—dc21   2001029367

All scriptural citations are taken from the *New Revised Standard Version of the Bible*, copyright 1989 by the Division of Christian Education of the National Council of the Churches of Christ in the USA. All rights reserved.

Excerpts from the English translation of the *Catechism of the Catholic Church* for the United States of America, copyright © 1994, United States Catholic Conference, Inc.—Libreria Editrice Vaticana; English translation of the *Catechism of the Catholic Church: Modifications from the Editio Typica* copyright © 1997, United States Catholic Conference, Inc.—Libreria Editrice Vaticana. Used with permission.

Contents

Contents

Part Three: The Sacraments of Healing 65

I. *Penance and Reconciliation* 67

II. *Anointing of the Sick* 81

Part Four: The Sacraments of Communion and Mission 91

Contents

Contents

VI. *Prayers for the Sacrament of Matrimony* 198

VII. *Prayers for the Sacrament of Holy Orders* 203

Introduction

Catholics are a sacramental faith community. They are identified by the celebration of the seven sacraments. Most Catholics understand that celebration of the sacraments is the primary way to experience the grace that comes from God. An understanding of sacrament is essential to the identity of Catholics, who they are and how they see themselves. This sacramental identity is also understood by most other Christians and even by members of other religious traditions as the defining focus of the Catholic spiritual tradition.

The significant moments of life and of death are celebrated in the Catholic practice of the sacraments. Most Catholics probably will not be able to recall their own baptism, but certainly they understand the emphasis and the concern expressed by parents and godparents that baptism is celebrated after the birth of a new baby. The celebration of a person's first holy Communion and first confession (sacrament of penance) is often a "special event," complete with a party and gift giving, in the life of Catholic children. The celebration of confirmation also receives a special emphasis, and, depending on the age at which it may be celebrated in a particular local church, it often marks the passage from childhood to the beginning of adult life in the church.

As a child grows into adulthood and often prepares to marry, the expectation of the family is that they will be married in church, with an exchange of vows witnessed by a priest, and often within the celebration of a nuptial Mass. After marriage, the process begins again, this time for the children of the newly created and blessed family. Some Catholic families also have an opportunity to celebrate the ordination to the priesthood of a son or grandson and, occasionally, are able to celebrate the ordination to the diaconate of their father or perhaps a favorite uncle or close family friend. Finally, the anointing of the sick is celebrated, not only at the moment of impending death but also on those occasions when there is a serious illness or even when the advancing signs of the inevitable process of simply growing old are evident.

Catholics are a sacramental people, from the moment of their birth, through all the stages of their life, up to the moment of death. Even in death, family and friends at the funeral Mass usually celebrate a final sacrament in the memory of the deceased.

Sacraments, however, are more than simple rituals that mark significant steps in the spiritual journey. They are the life-giving celebration of the love and power of God that freely flows from Jesus Christ as a result of his passion, death, and resurrection. Understood in this sense, sacraments are an opportunity for the individual to encounter the saving action of God and the salvation promised to all who believe in Jesus Christ.

Most Catholics have been taught a simple definition of what a sacrament is from their first experience of religious education. It is not unusual to hear a Catholic answer, when asked to explain what a sacrament is, that "a sacrament is a sign, instituted by Christ, to give grace." This simple definition learned long ago in a now forgotten time and place serves as a summary of extensive and detailed Catholic dogma and a shorthand understanding of sacramental theology. The ability to name all seven sacraments and to explain the "matter and form" of a sacrament and the "sacramental character" is not beyond the ability of many Catholics of a prior time and age.

The ability of Catholics of a certain period to quickly define the basic components of the sacraments should come as no surprise. This training in the basics of the Catholic faith, reflects a concern, rooted deep in the Protestant Reformation, of the need for the Catholic faithful to understand and explain an important foundation of their faith. Uniform answers, dutifully learned, to a set of uniform questions became a defining experience of Catholic life and education.

It is also true, however, that since the Vatican Council II there has been a change in emphasis and a change in sacramental training. Some perceive that these changes have produced a whole generation of Catholics who no longer understand the fundamentals of sacramental theology. This handbook may help to provide a small answer to these concerns.

The Essential Catholic Handbook of the Sacraments is envisioned as a helpful resource and a practical tool for understanding our Catholic sacramental tradition and belief. The text is presented in a popular style, with an emphasis on a clear and practical presentation of Catholic faith and dogma. The historical development of the sacraments is not ignored, but speculative theology, the argument for further development and change in sacramental theology from different theological starting points, is not included. The decision to omit presentation of possible scenarios for future avenues of sacramental theology has been made, not because of a lack of interest or perspective, but rather because it seems to be beyond the scope of what is essential. There are other fine resources available that discuss what may be possible or even required in future expressions of Catholic sacramental practice.

Also included in this handbook is a glossary of words, expressions, and key concepts that are useful in the study of the sacraments, along with a selection of prayers, both traditional and contemporary. Particular emphasis has been placed on the Eucharist, the core and summit of Catholic sacramental worship. Eucharistic meditations are included, as well as a selection of other prayers suitable for meditation and reflection. Whenever possible, *The Essential Catholic Handbook of the Sacraments* has been cross-referenced to the *Catechism of the Catholic Church* (paragraphs cited from this book are indicated by the letters CCC).

Finally, the reader should be advised that as part of *The Essential Catholic Handbook* series, this handbook on the sacraments should be understood as an introduction to the sacraments but by no means a complete presentation. Readers who desire to know more about the sacraments are directed to Joseph Martos's book, *Doors to the Sacred: A Historical Introduction to Sacraments in the Catholic Church.* This is the most complete work on the sacraments to date. It is very readable, easily understood, and is highly recommended. Of course, readers are also directed to the *Catechism of the Catholic Church.* Further information on both of these valuable resources may be found in the bibliography section of this *Essential Catholic Handbook of the Sacraments.*

The Essential
Catholic Handbook
of the Sacraments

PART ONE

Discovering the Sacraments

1. Christ Is the Sacrament

The Catholic understanding of sacraments is rooted in the personal experiences and encounters of the faithful with the person of Jesus. This understanding arises from a personal encounter with the Lord, as a historical person in a specific space and time. These encounters are experiences of normal, everyday people who witnessed the preaching of Jesus and who interpreted this encounter as an "experience of God." Not only did they experience the preaching of Jesus but also they experienced Jesus healing, Jesus listening to their needs, Jesus responding to their questions, and Jesus filling up their hearts and souls with a sense of completeness. In each of these human experiences of God, in the person of Jesus, we have the beginning of what is today understood as "sacramental theology."

In a very real sense, Jesus was the sacrament of God for the people. He was a sign of the presence of God among them. He was a sign of the desire of God to both heal and forgive his people. And, perhaps more than anything else, Jesus was a sign that the people were not abandoned and forgotten, unloved and uncared for. Although it would be a stretch to suggest that the people of his time experienced Jesus as "sacrament," it would not be a stretch to say that people may well have felt the same way about Jesus as we today when we celebrate one of his sacraments.

Although Jesus no longer physically walks among us, we believe that he is nevertheless alive and active in our lives. We celebrate the presence of Jesus in the Word of God; we celebrate the presence of Jesus in our observance of sacred liturgies and rituals, in hymns, religious art, and in a variety of other ways. For Catholics, however, the primary experience of the presence of God is found in our encounter with Jesus through the sacramental life of the Church.

3

2. Church Is Sacrament

The conviction and understanding that it is through the Church that we may encounter Christ in our world today is rooted in Scripture. In the Gospel of Matthew, Jesus promises his disciples and, by extension, each of us that he would be with us, "always, to the end of the age" (Mt 28:20). In John's Gospel (14:15–16) and in the Acts of the Apostles (1:4–5) Jesus promises us that he would send the Holy Spirit to help build up the Church, and Saint Paul in his letter to the Christian community at Colossae proclaims that Christ "is the head of the body, the Church" (Col 1:18).

But perhaps the most powerful statement that it is in the Church that we encounter the Body of Christ can be found in 1 Corinthians 12:12–13:

> For just as the body is one and has many members, and all the members of the body, though many, are one body, so it is with Christ. For in the one Spirit we were all baptized into one body— Jews or Greeks, slaves or free—and we were all made to drink of one Spirit.

The Church, which is the Body of Christ, demonstrates that it is filled with the Spirit of God, just as Jesus was filled with the Spirit, whenever it preaches the just word, calls upon the people of God to open their hearts and minds to conversion, and when it celebrates the healing, forgiving, and saving ministry of the Lord.

When Jesus walked among us, it was his words and his saving actions that demonstrated to those who were willing to "see and believe" that the Spirit of God was active in him. After his death and resurrection, and after the experience of Pentecost, the same Spirit of God was alive and active in his apostles and disciples. Again, for those people who were willing to "see and believe," the "spirit-filled" lives and activity of the followers of Jesus reminded them of the person of Jesus and the kingdom that he preached.

Another way of understanding this development in relation to the sacramental theology of the Church is to understand that just as people came to understand and appreciate that Jesus was a sign of the presence of God in the world, people also came to understand that the community of believers, the Church, was also the sign of the presence of God in the world. It is this understanding and appreciation of the activity of the Spirit of God that prompted Saint Paul to clearly identify the Church as the Body of Christ.

Whenever the Church, or any individual member of the Body of Christ, acts in the spirit of Christ, they continue the saving ministry of the Lord in the world. When individuals love as Jesus loved, when they forgive as Jesus forgave, or when they reach out to another, especially those who are poor, alienated, or marginalized, they become the sign and, indeed, the presence of God in the world.

The Second Vatican Council in the Dogmatic Constitution on the Church, §18, recognized this understanding of the Church as sacrament. The council perceived that whenever the saving message of Jesus was proclaimed, whenever people experienced the truth and love of God in the myriad number of ways that this has been manifested in our lives and in our choices, the Church is a sacrament for them. The Church is a sacrament because it is a sign and instrument of the presence of God in the lives of the faithful and a sign of the kingdom that has been promised (CCC 774–776).

3. Seven Sacraments of the Church

Even though, as we have seen, the basic approach to sacramental theology begins with an understanding that Christ is the primary sacrament, and the Church, as the Body of Christ, is the essential sign and instrument of Christ in the world, the Church nevertheless celebrates seven specific "encounters with God"—seven special "signs" of the activity of God and the Spirit of the Lord in the lives of the people of God.

Each sacrament, each sign of God's presence in our lives, has been traditionally understood as a ritualistic celebration of God's saving activity and encounter with the people of God. Each sacrament is understood as both directly and indirectly instituted by Christ in his ministry and in his proclamation of the kingdom of God.

Upon reflection, it should come as no surprise to anyone that the Church celebrates specific rituals that remind the people of God of the presence of Christ in the world. It should also come as no surprise that the Church celebrates such rituals, confident that such celebrations have been given to us directly by the Lord himself who participated and celebrated essential moments in the lives of the people whom he served.

Readers of the Scriptures can see, for example, that Jesus, when he appeared early in his ministry at the Jordan River, celebrated baptism with John the Baptist. Still later, Jesus instructed his disciples to "go therefore and make disciples of all nations, baptizing them in the name of the Father and of the Son and of the Holy Spirit" (Mt 28:19). The celebration of the Last Supper, in which Jesus instituted the sacrament of his body and his blood (Lk 22:19), is another obvious example. We also understand and appreciate that the Church, acting as the Body of Christ, and intent on being a visible sign and symbol of the presence of God in the world, developed other ritual celebrations that remind us of the ministry of the Lord.

4. Sacraments Are Necessary for Salvation

Central to the idea of sacrament in the thinking of the Church is the conviction that the sacraments are not only celebrations of the presence of God in the world but also necessary experiences in human believers' encounters with God so that they may enjoy the fullness of this life and the eternal life that is to come. This teaching, promulgated by the Council of Trent in 1547, and repeated in the *Catechism of the Catholic Church* (CCC 1129), forcefully illustrates both the intent and the commitment of the Church to the ongoing mission of Jesus in the world.

In a sense, in this understanding of sacrament, the Church is proclaiming that it is impossible to imagine how a person who claims to be committed to a relationship with the Lord would not also desire to often celebrate that commitment through an encounter with the Lord in his sacraments. For it is only through the sacraments that a person is united "in a living union with the only Son, the Savior" (CCC 1129) and experiences "life for God in Christ Jesus" (CCC 1134). Perhaps, in this simple yet profound statement of belief, we may understand and appreciate the essential role of the sacraments in the life of the Church and in the lives of the people of God.

5. A Process of Revelation and Discernment

The *Catechism of the Catholic Church* (CCC 1117) acknowledges that the way in which the sacraments are practiced and the way in which the sacraments have been understood has been one of a gradual development. Although this recognition may come as a surprise to some people who may never have been inclined or challenged to reflect on the development of faith within themselves and within the Church, it is totally understandable within the context of the process of divine revelation. Clearly, the plan of salvation for God's people is a process. God's plan has been slowly revealed to us (1 Cor 2:7–13; Eph 1:9–10). Each layer of the plan has been implemented in a pattern and within a time frame known only to the Lord—whose people are newly forming and re-forming each day into the kingdom of God.

In cooperation with divine revelation and the Holy Spirit who directs the process of revelation, the Church has "discerned over the centuries" that there are seven sacraments, in the strict sense of the term, and that these seven sacraments were instituted by Christ. The Church has discerned this truth from three specific sources of the revelation of God: from the holy Scriptures, from the tradition of the apostles, and from an agreement of the majority of the Fathers of the Church (CCC 1114).

Holy Scriptures: Examples of the institution of the sacraments that are found in Scripture are as follows: the baptism of the Lord by John the Baptist (Mt 3:13) and the apostolic commission to baptize all nations (Mt 28:19–20; Mk 16:15–16); the celebration of the Last Supper and the Institution of the Eucharist and Holy Orders (Lk 22:7–20; Mt 26:17–29; Mk 14:12–15; 1 Cor 11:23–26); the presentation of the "keys of the kingdom" to Saint Peter and the apostles, the ministry of "binding and loosing" (Mt 16:19; 28:16–20); countless references to the compassion of Christ toward the sick (Mt 25:36; Lk 6:19; Jn 1:29).

Apostolic Traditions: In the Acts of the Apostles and the letters of the apostle Paul, three specific sacramental actions are consistently referred to: baptism (Acts 2:22–36; 8:34–39), the laying on of hands (Acts 8:14–17; 19:4–6; Gal 5:22–23), and the sharing of the Lord's supper (1 Cor 11:23–27; 10:16–17). References to healing and the mutual confession of sins can also be discovered (Acts 3:1–10; Jas 5:14–15; 5:16).

Consensus of the Fathers: The following members of the early Church articulated the practice and theology of the sacraments and were instrumental in developing a consensus: Tertullian (160–230 A.D.), who first introduced the general term of *sacramentum* to describe the rituals and practices of the Christian community, Cyprian of Carthage (200–258 A.D.), Theodore of Mopsuestia (314–368 A.D.), John Chrysostom (347–407 A.D.), and, of course, the great Augustine (354–

430 A.D.), among many others. However, it was the bishops who gathered in the Second Council of Lyons in 1274 who declared that there are seven sacraments in the Church and the bishops of the Council of Trent (1545–1547) who clarified and defined the core of our sacramental theology, which finalized much of our current practice and understanding.

6. The Sacraments As Sign and Symbol

"A sacramental celebration is woven from signs and symbols," says the *Catechism of the Catholic Church* (CCC 1145). In other words, even though they are profound expressions of the mystery of the relationship between God and humanity, sacraments are nevertheless experienced in a form with matter (material) that can be communicated, experienced, and appreciated. Humankind uses many different signs and symbols to "communicate with others, through language, gestures, and actions" (CCC 1146). The sacraments are not an exception to normal human experience because God has consistently spoken to his people in and through creation (Wis 13:1; Rom 1:19; Acts 14:17).

In the Scriptures, for example, numerous examples can be found where the people of God have encountered God in light and darkness (Gen 1:4; Mt 4:16; Lk 12:3), in wind and fire (1 Kgs 19:11; Zech 2:5), in water and earth (Job 5:10; Gen 1:1). These exist, along with other examples of common experiences familiar to the daily lives of human beings, as illustrations used by God as a symbol of an encounter with mystery, such as washing (Acts 9:37), anointing (Ex 40:9; 1 Jn 2:20), and the sharing of food and a meal (Isa 29:8; Mk 14:22).

The Church, consistently open to the promptings of the Holy Spirit, uses, integrates, and sanctifies elements from creation and from human culture (CCC 1149) in the sacramental encounters that it celebrates. These include signs of the covenant and signs taken up by Christ.

9

Signs of the Old Testament Covenant (CCC 1150): The people of the Old Testament and the original covenant received specific signs from God which identified their spiritual journey and which confirmed their identity as the chosen people of God. These signs included circumcision (1 Mac 1:15), anointing and consecration of kings and priests (Ex 29:33; 2 Chr 29:17), laying on of hands (Lev 16:21), sacrifices (Gen 31:54; Lev 7:12), and, above all, the Passover (Ex 12:27; Lev 23:5).

Signs Used by Christ (CCC 1151): In his public ministry, Jesus used many different signs and symbols in his preaching and in his healing ministry. However, Jesus also, because he is the Son of God and the ultimate fulfillment of the Old Covenant, perfectly completes two of the central symbols of the presence of God: the Exodus and the Passover (Jn 9:6; Mk 7:33; 8:22). The Church teaches that, for a full understanding and appreciation of these two pivotal events in the salvation history of the people of God, reference to the person of Jesus is essential; for it is Jesus who perfectly completes and fulfills both of these signs and symbols.

Signs of the Sacraments (CCC 1152): Central to the Church's understanding of sacrament is the understanding and appreciation that the signs and symbols of the Old Covenant have given way to the sacramental signs of the New Covenant. This is not to say that the signs and symbols of the Old Covenant are no longer important or worthy of reflection but rather it is to say that since Pentecost, and by means of the activity of the Holy Spirit, the mission of Jesus is made actively present in our world through them (CCC 1152).

7. Sacraments Celebrate a Lived Reality

Buried, it almost seems, in the theology and dogma of the sacramental theology of our own historical time and place and also in the pages and experiences of history lived throughout the entire Christian world is the central experience of what the sacraments celebrate. In each of the sacramental encounters that were celebrated by the Christian community and which continue to be celebrated today is the desire, the openness, and the willingness of the people of God to encounter and enter into relationship with Jesus, their Lord and Savior.

When the Fathers of the Church discussed the essential elements of the sacrament of baptism, they were concerned not only with the understanding that baptism was necessary for salvation, but they were also concerned with the recognition that the lives of the people who received the sacrament were changed as a result of the experience. When they discussed the essential components of the sacrament of penance, they were also profoundly aware of the experience and awareness of sin among the people of God and the conversion and acceptance experienced by all who celebrated the sacrament with devotion. This experience of an individual person's encounter with the Lord in the sacrament was the lived reality, the ultimate sign and symbol of the continued and active presence of the Holy Spirit.

In the period of Church history marked by the presence of the early Church Fathers, a time commonly understood as comprising the second to the sixth century, the primary sources for an understanding of the sacraments were Scripture and personal experience. There was no sacramental system yet in place, and so the Fathers of the Church "took their time" in developing the sacraments into the full-blown celebrations of today. That is not to say that they "invented" the sacraments, but it is to illustrate the fluidity of the process and the important role that personal experience and reflection contributed to the developmental process. During this period of time, the meaning, the number, the rituals, and the practice of the sacraments had not yet been defined and sometimes varied widely from one region of the Church to another.

From the sixth to the eleventh century, the Church experienced great hardship and difficulties. The Roman Empire had collapsed and much of Europe, for example, was experiencing the turmoil and the change associated with the migration of peoples from one place to the next. This constant change and challenge left very little time for theological development. In addition, the missionary efforts of the time were centered in monasteries, populated by practical men and women, who knew what was needed to survive and who understood the difference between what was essential and what was not. The sacramental developments and practices of the period reflected the times, and so we see the idea of the sacraments gradually move toward the celebration of seven specific rituals and practices. It had not yet been definitively defined that there were seven sacraments, and only seven sacraments, but it was becoming an increasingly more common belief and practice.

The twelfth and thirteenth centuries seem to be highlights in the development of the Church's understanding of the sacraments. During this period of time, the unrest and the challenges of the previous centuries seem to have settled down, and relative calm descended upon the people. Time for theological reflection was provided and there was a corresponding desire among the people of God for clarity, fuller explanations, and uniform practice.

Perhaps the clearest statement of belief that emerged from this period in the development of sacramental theology was the understanding that the seven sacraments were not only an experience of the grace of God but, in a very real sense, they "caused" God's grace to be given. This was an essential change in the theology of the sacraments and enabled the Church, for the first time, to make a clear distinction in its presentation and teaching about the sacraments.

Another point that emerged during this time was the understanding of the necessity of the seven sacraments for salvation. Seven was understood as a powerful number and an obvious "spiritual remedy" for such things as the "seven deadly sins." God had given his Church the tools to combat evil and to build the kingdom; God gave the Church not only the tools, but also, it would seem, the necessary confidence and authority to proceed to do so.

8. *Ex Opere Operato*

A major development in the theology of the sacraments that also emerged during the Middle Ages was the concept of *ex opere operato*. This concept promoted the belief that all that was necessary for the sacraments to "cause the grace" to be transmitted was that they be performed correctly. In other words, as long as the proper "matter" of the sacrament was present and as long as the proper "form" of the sacrament was celebrated, the sacrament automatically and, in some unfortunate sense, "magically" accomplished what was needed for salvation.

The commonly held belief of the people was that as long as the waters of baptism were poured over the head of the baby and the proper words were used, the baby was then automatically "snatched from hell" and placed on the path of salvation. If the bishop anointed the head of the person being confirmed, that person was confirmed in the Spirit. If two people pronounced their marriage vows accompanied by the witness of a priest, they were bound together for life and considered married. Each sacrament "caused" some specific grace, and all that was required and all that was necessary was that it was properly celebrated. God would then somehow take care of all of the details, difficulties, and challenges; nothing more was necessary or required.

This simple understanding of how the sacraments worked was never sanctioned or promoted as the "official" and "accepted" doctrine of the Church. However, there is no doubt that this simple concept took root deep within the core experience of what was commonly understood as Catholic. Because of this unfortunate, and by no means deliberate, understanding, it was only a matter of time before this concept would develop far-reaching consequences.

The "automatic" concept encouraged by *ex opere operato* "spilled over" into other areas of Church practice and devotion. If the sacraments automatically accomplished the grace that was desired, certainly there could be other automatic causes of the grace of God in the lives of individuals. For the people of the Middle Ages, other instances of "automatic" grace soon appeared in common devotion and practice, for instance, specific prayers and novenas that guaranteed a particular result or a pilgrimage to a specific shrine or church that would automatically produce a specific indulgence (grace). There was an abundance of other similar instances.

9. The Council of Trent

The Council of Trent, meeting in twenty-five sessions from December 13, 1545, until its close on December 13, 1563, was the Catholic answer to Martin Luther and other reformers who had posed a series of questions and concerns beginning on October 31, 1517. Although a discussion of all of the reform issues that faced the council is well beyond the purpose of this explanatory discussion, the council did define and clarify Catholic belief and dogma concerning the sacraments of the Church.

The council addressed the Church's understanding of the sacraments in general but it also discussed particular issues regarding each of the seven sacraments. As important as this clarification and teaching was, the council's most far-reaching contribution to sacramental understanding and practice was the fact that the council established uniform liturgical ritual and practice for each of the sacraments. These standards were to be followed for the next four hundred years. In addition, the council established seminaries for the training of priests so that the uniform practice and teaching of the theology of the Church could be assured. Sacramentaries, which outlined the specific rubrics and directions for the celebration of the sacraments, were also promulgated by this council. The effect of these decisions was to firmly identify and establish a Catholic sacramental practice with a uniformity that was to take root so deeply that the uniformity itself became a source of pride and distinction for Catholics all over the world. No matter where you went in the world, no matter what country you might find yourself in, the sacraments were normally celebrated identically to the experience of sacraments that you would have had in your home parish and diocese.

The singular effect of the Council of Trent was the establishment of Catholic understanding, ritual, and practice for the sacramental life of the Church. The council firmly, and it was believed completely and finally, defined all that was needed by the Church for the celebration of the sacraments. All the questions had been settled, and all had been prescribed, directed, and established. All that was left to be accomplished was to faithfully follow that which had been determined and promulgated, from that moment on until the end of time.

10. The Second Vatican Council

The Second Vatican Council (1962–1965) concluded deliberations almost four hundred years after the close of the Council of Trent. The Church, before the Second Vatican Council opened, was very much the Church formed by the Council of Trent, although pushed, pulled, and strained in different directions as a result of the times and the culture. However, by the end of the Second Vatican Council, it was obvious to most people that the Church after this council would be a much different Church.

Many, many significant events, encounters, and experiences contributed to the Second Vatican Council, but perhaps two specific events should be isolated as essential for our reflection on the sacramental life of the Church: liturgical renewal and biblical renewal.

15

Liturgical Renewal was the result of scholarly research, perhaps set in motion by Pope Pius XII in 1947 with his encyclical "Mediator Dei." Scholars were slowly learning that many of the rubrics and rituals associated with the sacramental life and worship of the Church were not, as it had been assumed, a uniform and seamless whole. For example, the Tridentine Mass was a composite of prayers, readings, and rubrics that had been accumulated through the centuries and did not always agree with each other. The other sacramental rituals reflected the same process of accumulation and formation.

Biblical Renewal was also the result of scholarly research, and it, too, was given the necessary "stamp of approval" by Pope Pius XII in 1943 when he stimulated discussion about the literary form and analysis of the Bible with his encyclical "Divino Afflante Spiritu." For most Catholics, and for most Christians up until the mid-twentieth century, it was simply assumed that the Bible was to be understood literally; however, this understanding was slowly beginning to change. Once Pope Pius XII permitted Catholic scholars, with prudence and discernment, to apply the new methods of research to biblical studies, they soon learned that some of the assumptions that had been made about the sacraments, for example, and their biblical foundation, could not be fully supported. Biblical renewal suggested that there was sometimes a difference between a biblical statement and a doctrinal statement of belief. The history, the place, and the culture all contributed to the final interpretation.

But perhaps the most significant contribution of the Second Vatican Council was the implicit acknowledgment by the bishops that the world in which we lived was changing and that it was necessary for the Church to also change. While the bishops of the Council of Trent concluded that their work would stand forever, unchanged and eternal in both scope and purpose, the bishops of the Second

Vatican Council understood that although some truths were eternal and unchanging, the expression of those truths was not. The Church, and the sacramental expressions of the Church, are encountered in a modern world, and that world was and is changing continually.

11. Contemporary Sacramental Theology

Contemporary sacramental theology emphasizes four essential components which are necessary to a proper understanding and appreciation of the sacramental life of the Church. The four essential components are as follows: (1) the sacraments as efficacious signs of grace; (2) celebrated by a priestly community; (3) formed by the Holy Spirit and the Word of God; (4) which give personal and ecclesial life to those who celebrate them.

Efficacious Signs of Grace (CCC 1131): The sacraments, instituted by Christ, are efficacious because it is in the sacrament that Christ is at work. It is Christ who baptizes, who acts in all of the sacraments and communicates the grace of the sacrament to the individual person and the community who is celebrating it. It is most certainly not the righteousness of the celebrant or that of the recipient but rather it is Christ, through the power of the Holy Spirit, who calls upon his Father to act on our behalf, and the Father always hears the prayer of his Son.

Celebrated by a Priestly Community (CCC 1132): Through the sacraments of baptism and confirmation the people of God are formed into a priestly community, and some members of the community, through the sacrament of holy orders, receive the "Spirit of Jesus to act in his name and in his person" (CCC 1120). Through the reception of these sacraments, the individual person is configured to Christ and to the Church and becomes properly disposed to receive grace and the vocation to worship and service.

Formed by the Holy Spirit and the Word of God (CCC 1133): Because the people of God have been baptized in the name of the Father, the Son, and the Holy Spirit, they have received the promise of the Holy Spirit to heal and transform them, opening their hearts so that they may hear and act upon the preached Word of God. It is through the power of the Holy Spirit that the people of God are enabled to receive the nourishment that they need for worship and service.

Gifted With Personal and Ecclesial Life (CCC 1134): The sacraments are necessary for salvation, and it is only through the sacraments that the fullness of life, both for the individual person and the Church, may be experienced. At the same time, this fullness of life is not meant simply to be received but it is also meant to be lived so that all of the people of God are called to a life of witness of the power of God working within them.

Contemporary sacramental theology emphasizes that the sacraments are to be understood primarily as gifts, gratuities of Christ's love, efficacious signs of salvation through which dignity, grace, and commitment to a Christian life come to the people of God. The sacraments cannot be understood in the abstract, or as bare precepts. Christ is the Word Incarnate, flesh and blood, fully visible and attractive, and the sacraments must be understood as experiences of his incarnate love.

The proper place and task of sacraments are to show, in a human way, the expanse and primacy of God's love and the loving response we are expected to give. Sacraments bring a visible and fascinating presence of God's love in Christ Jesus, which manifests itself in the Church and its members through the work of the Holy Spirit. The following premises may be essential to a Catholic understanding of the sacraments:

The Sacraments Are Unique: Even in speaking of the seven sacraments, the point of view remains always the unique sacramentality of Christ, the Word Incarnate. Sacraments are signs of the presence of Jesus in the world.

The Sacraments Are Signs of Grace: The sacraments are true symbols of God's gracious presence in the world, but this does not mean that the sacraments hold a monopoly on grace. As privileged signs of salvation, the sacraments open and direct the attention of God's people to all the other ways in which God shows graciousness. Sacraments demand vigilance to the signs of the times, and great respect and reverence for the wonderful ways in which God works.

The Sacraments Are the Celebration of the Universal Priesthood of the People of God: Although it is true that sacramental theology emphasizes the role of the minister in the celebration of the sacraments, since the Second Vatican Council, much more attention is given to the active participation of the faithful.

12. The Sacraments As Experiences of Grace

Grace (*charis*) means the graciousness of God in turning the divine countenance to us. It is a sign of God's nearness, a word of love, which arouses in us an answering love. Grace means gentleness, the attractive energy of true love; it means alliance, a reciprocal relationship, which, however, remains wholly the gift of God. On our part, it is received with the awareness that it is an undeserved gift, and this awareness energizes us, teaches us, disciplines us, and gives orientation to our whole lives.

The sacraments are divine signs that provoke human initiatives of authentic love, of true mercy, and of new dimensions in personal relationships. As long as we continue to speak of the sacraments and of grace in a language of causality, we fail in two respects. First, we neglect the human hunger for personal meaning, for more humane and intimate relationships: and second, we fail to stress grace, the divine initiative that encourages human openness, spontaneity, and initiative.

The scholastic doctrine expresses the primacy of grace in the sacraments by the phrase *opus operatum*: The sacrament is the work of God. But the work of God always has the character of Word, of message. When we speak of *opus operatum*, therefore, we speak of the Word in whom all things are created, and of the new creation in the Word Incarnate, whom by all that he does, speaks to our minds and our hearts.

We are unworthy of God's grace. The sacramental economy reminds us that it is only because we are redeemed—through Christ's passion, death, and resurrection—that we have access to God; only because we are redeemed do we receive the signs of God's graciousness and goodness. The sacraments, precisely because they make us aware of the gratuitousness of redemption, transform us and constitute us as signs of the reign of God.

A full understanding of the sacraments teaches us to accept all things with a spirit of gratitude for the goodness of God. Through the sacraments, Christ continually reminds us: "You did not choose me but I chose you. And I appointed you to go and bear fruit, fruit that will last, so that the Father will give you whatever you ask him in my name" (Jn 15:16).

When we become fully conscious of being redeemed and elected by divine mercy, then we bear the fruits of mercy, of goodness, of thanksgiving. The farewell discourses teach this sacramental reality, which is continued in the Church: "I am the true vine, and my Father is the vinegrower. He removes every branch in me that bears no fruit. Every branch that bears fruit he prunes to make it bear more fruit. You have already been cleansed by the word that I have spoken to you. Abide in me as I abide in you. Just as the branch cannot bear fruit by itself unless it abides in the vine, neither can you unless you abide in me. I am the vine, you are the branches. Those who abide in me and I in them bear much fruit, because apart from me you can do nothing" (Jn 15:1–5).

Authentic catechesis, and the sacramental celebration itself, transform us precisely because they make us all the more conscious that, "[God] destined us for adoption as his children through Jesus Christ" (Eph 1:5).

PART TWO

The Sacraments of Initiation

The sacraments of initiation are understood as the "foundations" of the Christian life. Baptism, confirmation, and Eucharist are the essential "stepping stones" on the spiritual journey that will eventually lead a person to the fullness of the divine life with Christ and the perfection of charity (CCC 1212). These sacraments are also understood by the Church as the necessary "first steps" in the ongoing sacramental life of the Christian who will most likely celebrate the sacraments of healing and the sacraments of service and mission as he or she grow and develop in the Christian life.

For the majority of Catholics, the sacrament of baptism will be received as an infant and the sacraments of confirmation and Eucharist will be received sometime during the elementary school experience, although this is not always the case. Increasingly, probably as a consequence of societal and cultural influences within a secularized environment, not all Catholics can be referred to as "cradle Catholics"; there are more and more adults who present themselves to the Church for initiation into the Church, who have no previous experience or tradition of a religious or spiritual life. As a result of this growing trend, the Rite of Christian Initiation of Adults (RCIA) has been rediscovered. Often the RCIA experience in a Catholic parish is an experience of grace, not only for the individual initiates, but also for the entire community which celebrates the process with them.

I. Baptism

Holy Baptism is the basis of the whole Christian life, the gateway to life in the Spirit...and the door which gives access to the other sacraments. Through Baptism we are freed from sin and reborn as sons of God; we become members of Christ, are incorporated into the Church and made sharers in her mission: "Baptism is the sacrament of regeneration through water in the word" (CCC 1213).

1. Jesus and Baptism

One of the most vivid stories of the gospels is the story of the baptism of Jesus in the Jordan River by John the Baptist. Archeologists and other scholars have told us that the ritual baptism that John was performing was not at all unusual in the Jewish culture of that time and place. Water had played a significant role in the salvation history of the Jewish people in times of transition and change in their history as a people. The Red Sea, for example, had figured prominently in the escape of the people from Egypt, and the Jordan River had also come into play earlier, since it was the river the people had to cross in order to enter the Promised Land. For this reason, the use of water as a sign and symbol of a transition in a person's personal life and spiritual journey could be connected to the journey of faith experienced by the Jewish community.

When Jesus appeared at the Jordan to be baptized by John, he was on the cusp of a significant change in direction in his life. The traditional way of understanding this change is that Jesus was moving from his "hidden life" to his "public life." However it is understood, the baptism of Jesus, although certainly not required as a sign of his willingness to convert but perhaps partaken of as a sign of his "self-emptying" (CCC 1224), was definitely a transition and a change. Why he chose to present himself to John at this specific moment and place is not known; what is known is that immediately after he emerged from the river a voice from the heavens declared that "this is my Son, the Beloved, with whom I am well pleased" (Mt 3:17).

Although it is documented that Jesus was baptized at the beginning of his ministry, it is not clear if Jesus and his disciples baptized people during the years of his public ministry; the gospels do not agree on this point. However, the gospels do agree that Jesus, after his Resurrection, instructed his disciples to use this sign and symbol of conversion and change: "Go therefore and make disciples of all nations, baptizing them in the name of the Father and of the Son and of the Holy Spirit" (Mt 28:19).

The community of the apostles took this command very seriously and from the day of Pentecost on the Church administered baptism to all those who wished to be regenerated and renewed by the Holy Spirit (CCC 1213). The apostle Peter, preaching to the crowds who had gathered to hear the apostles, proclaimed, "Repent, and be baptized every one of you in the name of Jesus Christ so that your sins may be forgiven; and you will receive the gift of the Holy Spirit" (Acts 2:38).

2. The Practice of the Early Church

At first, flush with the Holy Spirit, the early Church offered baptism to all who desired to follow Jesus, almost upon request. An example of this can be found in the story in the Acts of the Apostles in which a servant of the queen of Ethiopia requested baptism from Philip with the words, "Look, here is water! What is to prevent me from being baptized?" (Acts 8:36). Another example of the swiftness in which the early Church offered baptism can be found in the story of Saint Paul and one of his jailers in Philippi whom he challenged by saying, "Believe on the Lord Jesus, and you will be saved," and immediately as the narrative continues, the jailer and his entire family were "baptized without delay" (Acts 16:31–33). But later, as the Church became more established and possibly also as a result of the persecutions of the Church that sometimes occurred, it became the practice to introduce a time of waiting and preparation before baptism was celebrated.

As the period of preparation and initiation developed, certain elements emerged that seemed to be seen as necessary for the celebration of the sacrament. These elements included the proclamation of the Word of God, the acceptance of the gospel and some obvious change in lifestyle (even, in some instances, a requirement to change jobs if a person was a gladiator, a soldier, or a maker of idols, for example), a profession of faith in Jesus Christ, the baptism itself, the outpouring of the Holy Spirit, and then, finally, admission to eucharistic communion (CCC 1229).

Men and women who were preparing to enter the Church were *catechumens* (a word from the Greek which means "to be instructed") and their period of training and instruction could last for as long as three years. Baptisms were normally celebrated only once a year, on the feast of Easter, and those who were preparing to be baptized prepared themselves for this commitment to Jesus Christ through a period of prayer and fasting. The entire baptized community prepared and waited with them, a situation that prompted a second-century writer named Tertullian to observe, "Christians are made, not born."

This process served the Church well until around the fifth century when, as a result of the pressures and the changes that were experienced in the society of the time as a result of the collapse of the Roman Empire, the practice began to change.

3. Before the Council of Trent

Two developments in the middle centuries influenced the practice of the sacrament of baptism with far-reaching consequences: the baptism of infants and suspension of the rite of immersion. Primarily, both of these developments were driven not so much because of a change in the theological understanding of baptism but rather as a practical matter, reflective of the lived experience of the times.

As more and more people became Christians, and it became obvious that the anticipated imminent return of Jesus was probably going to be delayed, there was a growing desire among Christian families that the sacrament of "new life" be celebrated as quickly as possible instead of being delayed to adulthood and after the period of the catechumenate. With a high infant mortality rate there was also a great concern about "what might happen to the souls of infants who were not baptized, were they to be denied eternal life?" Saint Augustine seems to have argued that the unbaptized could not merit eternal life and would suffer some sort of eternal damnation, although not as severe as that of the unrepentant sinner. Obviously, Saint Augustine's opinion on the matter and the concern for a child's eternal happiness and well-being became a persuasive and a driving force.

The second development was the perceived need of the Church to convert the Germanic tribes that were in the process of migrating into the Roman Empire. The Church took seriously the challenge of evangelizing the migrating peoples and was quite successful in its efforts. The conversion of a tribal leader (the normal emphasis and practice) usually dictated that the entire tribe, a very large and potentially unwieldy number, would also convert to Christianity. The climate in Northern Europe was much colder than the climate in the south and so baptism by immersion seemed to be less and less practical; baptism by pouring or sprinkling the water soon became the norm.

The baptism of infants and the mass baptisms of the Germanic tribal people meant that the period of instruction, usually associated with the catechumenate period of preparation, was now delayed until after the reception of the sacrament. As the period of preparation was delayed, so also was the reception of what today is known as the sacraments of confirmation and Eucharist. With the exception of the Orthodox churches, which continue to celebrate the entire sacraments of initiation as a single whole, the Roman Catholic Church began the practice of distinct and separate celebrations of each component of initiation and over a longer period of time and preparation.

By the time of the Council of Trent, the sacrament of baptism was understood as the single act of pouring water (matter) over the head of the person to be baptized, while at the same time repeating the words (form) of the sacrament, "I baptize you in the name of the Father, and of the Son, and of the Holy Spirit. Amen."

4. The Council of Trent

The Council of Trent did not have much to say about the sacrament of baptism. Although the Protestant reformers had specific opinions about the sacramental theology and practice of the Church, the reformers did not doubt the necessity of the sacrament of baptism. As a result, the bishops of the council did not have to teach much about the sacrament and rather concentrated their efforts on clarifying issues directly related to baptism: justification (primarily a work of God through the sacraments) and original sin (transmitted to the entire human race but removed by baptism). These clarifications in addition to affirming the teaching of the Church that there were seven sacraments comprised the bulk of their efforts.

5. Contemporary Practice

The most common experience of baptism in the Church today is infant baptism. Until the reforms of Vatican Council II, baptism was usually celebrated on Sunday, within a few days after the birth of a child. The only people present at the celebration were the priest/ deacon, the immediate family of the child, and perhaps a few close friends. However, since the council, it is not unusual to celebrate baptism within the celebration of a Sunday Mass, with much of the parish community present and participating in the rite. Although baptism may be celebrated outside of Mass, at almost any time and as often as necessary, the common practice of most parish communities is to celebrate the sacrament once a month, on a specific Sunday, within the context of the parish celebration of the Eucharist. Of course this means that children are at least a few weeks old and most are usually a few months old.

6. The Rite of Baptism

The celebration of the sacrament of baptism within Mass begins with the priest or celebrant greeting the parents of the child who are present for baptism (it is not unusual to have more than one child presented for the celebration of the sacrament). He asks each of the parents the name that they have chosen for their child and what do they ask of God's Church for their child? The parents answer, "Baptism." He then asks the godparents of the child if they are ready and willing to help the parents in their task of forming and nurturing the child in the Christian community, to which they answer, "We are." The priest then traces the Sign of the Cross (CCC 1235) on the forehead of those to be baptized, and he invites the parents and godparents to do the same.

The Scripture readings for the Mass are proclaimed, the homily is preached—with a special emphasis on the necessity (CCC 1257) and importance of the sacrament that is to be celebrated. The prayers of the faithful are offered with the entire parish community joining in with their response of praise and petition. The parents and godparents then present the child for baptism.

At this point, all move to the baptismal font and, if the water being used has not been blessed during the Easter Vigil, the water is then blessed. The purpose of this ritual act is to remind all present that the water of baptism is water that has been blessed through the outpouring of the Holy Spirit, thus fulfilling the sacred words of Scripture that those who are to be baptized are "born of water and Spirit" (Jn 3:5; CCC 1238).

The priest prays a traditional and ancient prayer of exorcism and anoints the child with the oil of the catechumens, a gesture that explicitly renounces Satan and prepares the child (or in this case the parents and godparents in the name of the child) to confess the faith of the Church (CCC 1237). "Do you reject sin, so as to live in the

31

freedom of God's children? Do you reject the glamour of evil, and refuse to be mastered by sin? Do you reject Satan, father of sin and prince of darkness?" To each question those gathered respond, "I do."

All those gathered are then asked not only to *renounce* the power of evil but also to *renew* the grace of their own baptism (Rom 6:17) through their person and communal assent to the Creed. "Do you believe in God, the Father almighty, creator of heaven and earth? Do you believe in Jesus Christ, his only Son, our Lord?" and other creedal statements of belief. To each statement the people gathered respond, "I do."

After assuring himself and the gathered congregation that the parents desire to baptize their child in the faith that they have just professed, the priest then moves to perform the essential rite of the sacrament, either the triple immersion of the child in the water or pouring water three times over the head of the child while praying, "I baptize you in the name of the Father, and of the Son, and of the Holy Spirit. Amen" (CCC 1239–1240).

After the baptism with water, the priest then prays a prayer that recalls the fact the Christians are the anointed people of God, and he then anoints the newly baptized with sacred chrism, a perfumed and blessed oil (blessed by the bishop of the diocese on Holy Thursday) which signifies the gift of the Holy Spirit. In the Roman Catholic Church, this anointing with oil "announces a second anointing with sacred chrism to be conferred later by the bishop" (CCC 1242) which is the celebration of the sacrament of confirmation. In the liturgy of the Eastern Church, this anointing is understood as chrismation (the sacrament of confirmation).

Two symbols are now introduced into the sacred ritual, the white garment and the candle. The white garment, which may be bought or made for the occasion, is a reminder of the white robe that the newly baptized received in early Christian communities as a symbol that they have now "put on Christ." The candle, lit from the Easter Candle, and presented with the words, "Receive the Light of Christ," signifies that Christ has enlightened the newly baptized person and that they are to go forth as the "light of the world" (Mt 5:14; Phil 2:15; CCC 1243).

The newly baptized are now presented to the Christian community and the eucharistic liturgy continues in the normal way. This is the most common form of the celebration of the sacrament of baptism in the Church today.

7. The Effects of Baptism

As the first sacrament and as the beginning of the initiation process, the sacrament of baptism marks the person who receives it as being born "into the new life of Christ," or in contemporary understanding, as being "born anew" (CCC 1277). The primary effect of this experience of rebirth is grace, a rich reality of the presence of God in the life of the person, marked by the forgiveness of original sin and all other personal sin, and incorporation into the Church, the Body of Christ, the priesthood of the faithful (CCC 1279).

Baptism configures the person who receives the sacrament to the person of Christ. In a very real sense, the person becomes "marked" with the "seal" of Christ. Catholics understand that this indelible spiritual mark, which is called the "character" of the sacrament, is a way of proclaiming their belief that once they have been baptized into the Body of Christ, there is no need to ever repeat the sacrament again. Nothing can erase the fact that Christ has claimed us as his own. Nothing can change the fact that the Holy Spirit has marked the Christian with "the seal of the Lord for the day of redemption" (CCC 1272–1274).

8. The Rite of Christian Initiation

Although infant baptism is the most common form of baptism in the Church, there are people who seek membership in the Church as adults (for example where the gospel is still new, that is, missionary territory) and for whom the faith journey more closely resembles the faith journey of adults who wished to join the Christian community in earlier times. In response to the need to support and encourage the process of adult conversion, the Church established a revised process for faith formation and development (CCC 1247–1248).

The historical roots of the RCIA (Rite of Christian Initiation of Adults) or CIC (Christian Initiation of Children), often called "the catechumenate," is a process of faith development and catechetical instruction which culminates in full membership in the Christian Roman Catholic community, the reception of the "sacraments of initiation": baptism, confirmation, and Eucharist. This journey of faith is similar to the one people made when joining the early Church communities. Today's revised process, promulgated in 1972, calls on the entire parish community to be involved and to offer prayerful support.

The RCIA is understood as a process, and during the first stage in the faith journey, inquirers begin to form relationships with one another and with their catechists. Sessions are informal, with life stories shared and curiosities about "things Catholic" answered. When a decision to continue in the process is made, inquirers obtain sponsors or godparents to mentor them along the way. Then, the Rite of Acceptance Into the Order of Catechumens is celebrated within the parish community's Sunday Mass.

With the Rite of Acceptance, those who have not been baptized officially become catechumens, while those who are baptized become candidates. Now they learn specifics about the Catholic faith, especially information about the sacraments. Sessions become more instructional, with an emphasis on breaking open the Word of God in the Sunday readings. Several optional rites may be celebrated during this period, which precedes the season of Lent.

The Rite of Election takes place on the first Sunday of Lent. This rite is celebrated by the bishop or his representative and marks a major transition. Catechumens and candidates now become the elect, and their names are inscribed in the diocese's Book of Enrollment. On the third, fourth, and fifth Sundays of Lent, the Rites of the Scrutinies are celebrated at a Sunday Mass. As Lent draws to a close, the elect will be invited to participate in a day of reflection and, in the case of those already baptized, their first reception of the sacrament of penance. There may also be a Rite of Preparation before the Easter Vigil is celebrated.

The Rites of Initiation take place at the Easter Vigil, immediately after the homily. First comes the Liturgy of Baptism, then the Rite of Confirmation. The elect are now neophytes (new Catholics). They lead the parish community of Church to the sacrificial altar/banquet table and receive their first Eucharist. Neophytes' final stage of preparation, during the season of Easter, centers on the practical learning of their Church's specific ministries and their personal commitment to at least one of these.

9. The Rights and Obligations of the Baptized

I have a baptism with which to be baptized, and what stress I am under until it is completed! (Lk 12:50).

Christian baptism is understood as initiation into the priesthood of believers (CCC 1268). This primary sacrament of the Church is the plunging of the baptized into the life, death, and resurrection of Christ. The baptized are gifted with both the right and the obligation to offer the sacrifice that Christ offered: prayers, works, their very lives. Baptism is not an event in life but a process of life. It is the process of being ordered and conformed to the will of Jesus Christ, the High Priest.

Christians are responsible for each other by virtue of their baptism. At baptism, the entire community enters into a relationship with the one being baptized, and all are responsible for that person's spiritual well-being. That is why the Church teaches that baptism imprints an indelible spiritual mark upon the person who receives it (CCC 1272), configuring them to Christ. Baptism also calls the baptized to a life that is rooted in grace and which is marked by the theological virtues of faith, hope, and charity.

Although there are many different definitions of grace, one definition is that grace is God sharing the divine life with us. When a person receives grace, they experience real change; they move toward oneness with God. Such radical change is accompanied by forgiveness of actual sins (CCC 1263). The Christian call is rooted in a foundation that is the direct work of grace. By virtue of baptism, Christians are ordered into a life of eternal hope. Their call is to change the world, and the theological virtues of faith, hope, and love provide a key to these expectations. "And now faith, hope, and love abide, these three; and the greatest of these is love" (1 Cor 13:13).

10. Pastoral Concerns

Because baptism is operative at the parish level, it is vital for Catholics to identify and actively participate in the life of a specific parish. Just as it is important that medical and dental records be on file, so also it is vital that one identifies with a parish that keeps one's sacramental records.

Active Catholics need to reach out to those who have been baptized Catholic and have not been practicing their faith. All they may need is a caring invitation to join in worship and be welcomed warmly into a parish community of faith.

11. Essentials

Name: Sacrament of Baptism.

Sacramental Identification: Sacrament of initiation.

Minimum Age: No minimum age for reception.

Can Be Repeated? No.

Sacramental Character Imparted? Yes.

Matter: Natural water that is poured on the head of the person or water in which a person may be immersed.

Form: "I baptize you in the name of the Father, and of the Son, and of the Holy Spirit. Amen."

Ordinary Minister: Bishop, Priest, Deacon.

Extraordinary Minister: In the case of an emergency, any person who carries out the rite of baptism and who intends to baptize according to the intent of the Church may do so.

II. Confirmation

By the sacrament of Confirmation, [the baptized] are more perfectly bound to the Church and are enriched with a special strength of the Holy Spirit. Hence they are, as true witnesses of Christ, more strictly obliged to spread and defend the faith by word and deed (CCC 1285).

1. Jesus and the Holy Spirit

Throughout his earthly ministry, Jesus acted with courage and compassion; he stretched out his hand to nourish and to heal, and to give new life where there was once only death. This ministerial action was an activity that Jesus identified to his followers as something that was enabled in him by the fact that he was filled with the Spirit, "the Spirit of the Lord is upon me, / because he has anointed me / to bring good news to the poor" (Lk 4:18). It was only after the Resurrection that the apostles came to understand that the same Spirit that filled Jesus was also to be given to them, "stay here in the city until you have been clothed with power from on high" (Lk 24:49). The Acts of the Apostles (2:2–4) describes the experience of the apostles and those others who had gathered in the upper room, waiting as they had been instructed to do so. "And suddenly from heaven there came a sound like the rush of a violent wind, and it filled the entire house where they were sitting.... All of them were filled with the Holy Spirit...."

It was probably not until the experience of the feast of Pentecost that the apostles were able to comprehend and understand that Jesus intended that the Spirit, which Christians today call the Holy Spirit, be his gift to the Church. Just as the Holy Spirit had worked within Jesus, that same Spirit would now work within the Church, enabling all that Jesus had promised, and slowly guiding and directing the baptized in the way of the kingdom.

2. The Practice of the Early Church

For at least the first three centuries of the Church, confirmation, the sacrament of the Holy Spirit, was not a distinct sacrament, but rather an essential component of the sacrament of baptism. Immediately after the candidates had emerged from the baptismal water, they were anointed with oil to signify the fact that they had been filled with grace by the Holy Spirit. In those places where a bishop was in attendance, it was not at all unusual for the bishop to anoint the newly baptized with oil and impose his hands upon their head, praying for an outpouring of the Holy Spirit upon them. Each member of the Christian community would then embrace the new Christian and they would all proceed to celebrate a thanksgiving Eucharist, a sharing in the body and blood of Christ.

Although this anointing and imposition of hands by the bishop was common, it did not take place in a uniform manner throughout the entire Church. In some places, there was no anointing at all, but simply baptism by immersion, and in those places it was understood that the gift of the Holy Spirit had nevertheless been imparted to the newly baptized. In still other places, the anointing was quite extensive: the assisting deacon would anoint the entire body of the male Christian and a deaconess would anoint the females. And in still other places, the anointing and imposition of hands was performed if a bishop was in attendance but routinely omitted if a bishop could not be present. Some would insist that later, if the opportunity presented itself, those baptized but not anointed by a bishop should take an opportunity to do so in order to "perfect" the reception of the sacrament, but again this practice and requirement was inconsistent.

By the fourth century, when the Church had completed the transformation from a small persecuted sect within the pantheon of the religious practices of the Roman Empire to a position where it now enjoyed official and protected status, the situation had changed again. The sheer number of people requesting baptism made it all the more difficult for a bishop to be present, but by now the preference that the bishop somehow formally approve all baptisms was also seemingly established. As a result of this development, and because of the changing political circumstances in the empire, two distinct practices emerged.

In the eastern part of the empire, the priest would use oil previously blessed by the bishop during the baptismal rite. In this way, the oil signified the bishop's witness and acceptance of the person into the Christian community. In Rome and the western part of the empire, the newly baptized would seek the blessing and approval of the bishop in a separate and distinct ceremony. It was not unusual for the bishop to visit local communities, "parishes," expressly for this purpose. This distinct rite was called the blessing, the signing, the perfection or completion, and in some places, it was even identified as confirmation, because the bishop was "confirming" that which had been celebrated in the local church.

The sacrament of confirmation was to experience one other significant change, as a result not so much of a change in theological understanding, but again as a result of changes in the surrounding society. In the fifth century, when the Roman Empire had collapsed and the infrastructure of the empire had fallen into disrepair, it became very dangerous to travel from the outlying districts to the place where the bishop was in residence. As a result, people were very reluctant to risk the necessary travel in order to have their baptism, and the baptism of their children, confirmed by the bishop. Despite some vigorous efforts, most notably the efforts of Bishop Faustus of Riez, France, in 460 A.D., to convince the people that baptism was completed by the laying on of hands by the bishop, the sacrament gradually fell into a state of disuse in much of the Church.

3. Before the Council of Trent

Around the year 850 A.D., the sacrament of confirmation enjoyed a revival, as the result of a series of very complicated maneuverings by the French bishops who were attempting to consolidate their power and define their authority. Although the situation was very complicated and is very difficult to explain, one of the unintended results of this maneuvering was that the practice of the bishop confirming baptisms became once again accepted in most of the Church. Practical obstacles still made the reception of the sacrament difficult, but it was accepted by most members of the Church as necessary, and was celebrated as much as possible.

By the year 1274, the Council of Lyons named confirmation as one of the seven sacraments of the Church and necessary for salvation. However, the bishops of the Church, well aware of the fact that so few actually celebrated the sacrament, did wrestle with trying to come to an understanding of why the sacrament was essential. They also wrestled with the matter and form of the sacrament, trying to determine if it was the laying on of hands or the anointing with oil that was the matter and determining which ritualistic words were the actual form of the sacrament, since there seemed to be so many different variations available and used.

The Council of Florence in 1439 clarified the medieval understanding of the sacrament of confirmation. The council taught that the sacrament strengthened individual Christians in faith and fortified them against temptation. It determined that the matter of the sacrament was the anointing with chrism and that the form of the sacrament at that time was found in the words, "I sign you with the sign of the cross, and I confirm you with chrism of salvation, in the name of the Father, and of the Son, and of the Holy Spirit. Amen." In addition, the council defined the bishop as the ordinary minister of the sacrament but priests could be delegated (given permission) to perform the sacrament in the name of the bishop.

4. The Council of Trent

The Protestant reformers dismissed the sacrament of confirmation because there was no firm scriptural foundation for the sacrament. They dismissed the Catholic scriptural references, such as Jesus breathing on the apostles with the Holy Spirit (Jn 20:22) or Jesus resting his hand on the heads of the children who were brought to him (Mk 10:13) as inadequate.

The Council of Trent made no doctrinal statement on confirmation, but it did clearly affirm to all that it was a sacrament and that it was not, as the reformers claimed, "a useless ceremony." The Catechism of the Council of Trent, issued in 1566, basically reaffirmed the teaching of the Council of Florence, which has been noted in the previous section.

One practical change in the reception of the sacrament of confirmation was that after Trent it became commonplace in the Church that the sacrament was received after the age of seven and before the age of twelve if at all possible. The primary reason for this was so that the person who was receiving the sacrament might understand the importance and significance of what they were celebrating.

5. Contemporary Practice

Most Catholics are confirmed in their early teen years, but in some dioceses confirmation may occur at a much younger age and, in still others, it is not celebrated until the middle teen years. Of course, there are those who are confirmed as part of the RCIA, during the Easter Vigil on Holy Saturday, but for most Catholics, confirmation is celebrated at a sacramental liturgy distinct from other sacraments. Since the ordinary minister of the sacrament is the bishop, it is for many of the candidates the first time that they encounter him, and experience the direct ministerial and teaching office of the bishop in their lives.

The sacrament is normally celebrated after an extended period of special preparation and review of Catholic dogma and practice which more and more includes the expectation that those who are about to be confirmed participate in some experience of Christian service, such as volunteer work for the sick and the elderly or perhaps hours spent working at a soup kitchen. The candidates come to the special eucharistic celebration with the understanding that they will be asked to renew their baptismal promises, and with personally chosen sponsors (often their baptismal godparents but it can be any adult Christian with whom they have a special relationship). The candidates also come to the celebration with a new name of a Christian saint chosen which will remind them of their reception of the sacrament and which may also be a source of inspiration and example to them in their daily lives. The bishop will use this new name when he seals the candidates with the gift of the Holy Spirit.

6. The Rite of Confirmation

Ordinarily, confirmation takes place within the Mass. The rite of confirmation begins after the readings from Scripture are proclaimed. The candidates are presented to the bishop and after he receives them in the name of the community, he then teaches them about the meaning of the sacrament and the power of the Holy Spirit. The bishop encourages the candidates to be open to the gifts of the Holy Spirit in their lives and to permit the Spirit to mold and form them each day into the sons and daughters of God.

After the homily, the bishop invites the candidates to renew their baptismal promises, the same promises made on their behalf by their parents and godparents at their baptism, but now renewed in their own name and from their own faith conviction. When the candidates finish their renewal of the promises, the bishop confirms what they have promised by proclaiming, "This is our faith. This is the faith of the Church. We are proud to profess it in Christ Jesus our Lord."

The bishop then extends his hands over all of the candidates and invokes the outpouring of the Holy Spirit (CCC 1299):

All-powerful God, Father of our Lord Jesus Christ,
by water and the Holy Spirit
you freed your sons and daughters from sin
and gave them new life.
Send your Holy Spirit upon them
to be their helper and guide.
Give them the spirit of wisdom and understanding,
the spirit of right judgment and courage,

the spirit of knowledge and reverence.

Fill them with the spirit of wonder and awe in your presence.

We ask this through Christ our Lord.

The essential rite of the sacrament follows this prayer. The candidates file up to the bishop and the bishop lays his hand on the head of the person to be confirmed, anoints them with chrism on their forehead (matter), and then prays these words (form): "N., be sealed with the Gift of the Holy Spirit" (CCC 1300). The sign of peace concludes the ritual, which is a sign of the communion of all of the people with the bishop and the bishop with all of the faithful (CCC 1301).

It is interesting to note that in the Eastern Church, the sacrament features a much more extensive anointing. Not only the forehead, but also the eyes, nose, ears, lip, breast, back, hands, and feet are also anointed.

At the conclusion of the celebration of the sacrament, the Eucharist continues in the normal way. All present are encouraged to give thanks and praise to the Lord for the newly confirmed, to reflect on their own spiritual journey and the acceptance and practice in their own lives of the gifts of the Holy Spirit, and finally, to celebrate through their reception of holy Communion their membership in the Body of Christ.

7. The Effects of Confirmation

The primary effect of confirmation is the full outpouring of the gifts of the Holy Spirit (CCC 1302). Confirmation increases and deepens the roots of grace that were first experienced at baptism and enables those confirmed to become fuller witnesses to the power of God working within them. In the words of Saint Ambrose, quoted in a reference in the *Catechism of the Catholic Church*, confirmation gifts the person who receives the sacrament with "a spiritual seal, the spirit of wisdom and understanding, the spirit of right judgment and courage, the spirit of knowledge and reverence, the spirit of holy fear in God's presence" (CCC 1303).

Like baptism, confirmation also imprints a special character, an indelible spiritual mark, upon the person. Confirmation completes the process, first experienced through baptism, by which the Lord claims the individual person for his kingdom and sends each one forth as a witness to this kingdom. As such, confirmation, once received, may never be repeated.

8. The Rights and Obligations of the Confirmed

People confirmed in the faith are tremendously important to God's plan for the world. They are members of the priesthood of the faithful and called to build God's kingdom. For Christians, the whole world is full of opportunities to do God's work.

Married persons have a primary responsibility to be living signs of Christ's love for the Church through their sacramental relationship of marriage. Single persons generally have more time to devote to youth ministry, the care of the elderly or sick, evangelization, religious education, or administration of programs. The widowed have a special place in the life of the Church due to their ability to help others who experience grief and loss, and to share their wisdom and experience.

Central to the ministry of the priesthood of the faithful is intercessory prayer. There are always opportunities to pray for the needs of others. Through prayer, God can open hearts to the reception of God's healing gospel.

At Home: Since many members of the priesthood of the laity are called to the vocation of married life, they are also called to family life. Thus, their primary responsibilities revolve around spouses and children. Other kinds of service in the Church come second.

At Work: Sharing Christ in the workplace is a sensitive issue because Christian charity demands we respect the beliefs of others. In no way ought Christ be pushed upon others. Christ himself invited people to believe in him and let the Spirit do the rest. But there will be times when an explicit explanation of the life and work of Jesus will be in order.

At Church: While liturgical ministries, such as lector, extraordinary eucharistic minister, and greeter, are visible for all to see, they are no more important than visiting with residential or hospital shut-ins, setting up the hall for parish socials, or stocking shelves in the parish outreach center. Administrative help is also needed, both at parish and diocesan levels.

All Christians are called to minister to friends, extended family, and whole communities by seeking opportunities to reconcile and build bridges between the Church and various groups or organizations. When all people recognize their dignity, mission, and ministry as members of the priesthood of the faithful, the Church will be better able to win the world to Christ.

9. Pastoral Concerns

Canon law states that the age of confirmation is the age of discretion or the age stipulated by the conference of bishops. Because confirmation has been considered a sacrament of maturity, it is usually celebrated in early or later teenage years. This exact age of confirmation is a debatable issue, and so the age varies from diocese to diocese.

Confirmation traditionally has concluded one's formal religious education. This tradition has spawned the idea that one needs no further faith formation. Just as commencement marks one's entry into real life, so confirmation marks the beginning of one's deeper involvement with one's faith.

But Catholics need ongoing formation to be conversant in issues facing today's Church. Where the Holy Spirit is alive, parishes provide meaningful liturgies, activities, and enrichment programs for every age and interest group, as well as outreach to the needy and the suffering. Ideal parishes are those in which the love of God is manifested, and the parishioners radiate this in joy and dedication.

10. Essentials

Name: Sacrament of Confirmation.

Sacramental Identification: Sacrament of initiation.

Minimum Age: No minimum age.

Can Be Repeated? No.

Sacramental Character Imparted? Yes.

Matter: The imposition of hands and anointing with chrism.

Form: "Be sealed with the Gift of the Holy Spirit."

Ordinary Minister: Bishop.

Extraordinary Minister: Priest.

III. Eucharist

The holy Eucharist completes Christian initiation. Those who have been raised to the dignity of the royal priesthood by Baptism and are configured more deeply to Christ by Confirmation participate with the whole community in the Lord's own sacrifice by means of the Eucharist (CCC 1322).

1. Jesus and the Eucharist

Jesus evidently shared many meals with his friends and his apostles. We know from the gospels that Jesus shared meals with people from all walks of life, a practice that caused his enemies to comment: "This fellow welcomes sinners and eats with them" (Lk 15:2). We also have other examples from the gospels that clearly illustrate his concern that the people who accompanied him were nourished and taken care of: the wedding feast at Cana (Jn 2:1–10) and the multiplication of the loaves and the fishes are two examples (Mt 14:15–21). Finally, after the Resurrection, we know that Jesus ate at least two times with his disciples: once on the shore of the lake (Jn 21:9–13) and the second time when he appeared to them in the upper room (Lk 24:41–43).

All of these are examples of Jesus' sharing essential nourishment with his friends and his apostles, but none of these occasions, as important and as pleasant as they might have been, compare to the meal that he shared with his apostles on the night before he died. This meal, which we now call the Last Supper, was unique and special. At this meal, Jesus took some bread, blessed it and broke it saying: "This is my body, which is given for you." At the end of the meal, he passed around the cup and said, "This cup that is poured out for you is the new covenant in my blood" (Lk 22:19–20).

Perhaps this simple sharing of the bread and wine, because it took place the night before he died, is the primary reason that it is remembered so clearly by the apostles and understood as so important. Perhaps it was because this meal took place within the context of the remembering associated with the feast of the Passover, a ritual meal and action already understood as important and necessary by those who were in attendance. Or, perhaps, it was because of the fact that Jesus clearly identified his actions of blessing the wine and breaking the bread with a command to his disciples "to do this in memory of me" (Lk 22:7–20; Mt 26:17–29; Mk 14:12–25; 1 Cor 11:23–26). For whatever reason or combination of reasons, the apostles remembered this occasion after the death and resurrection of Jesus and comprehended that this action was to be repeated, again and again, until the Lord had returned as he had promised.

2. The Practice of the Early Church

From the beginning, as recorded in the Acts of the Apostles, the Church was faithful to the Lord's command: "They devoted themselves to the apostles' teaching and fellowship, to the breaking of bread and the prayers" (Acts 2:42). As early as the year 57 A.D., in a letter to the Corinthian community, Saint Paul makes mention of the weekly gathering, always on the first day of the week, in remembrance of the Lord's Resurrection, celebrated in communion with the Body of Christ (1 Cor 10–11). There is no doubt that this early Eucharist (a word taken from the Greek, meaning "to give thanks") was the center of the life of the Church (CCC 1343).

These eucharistic gatherings provided the primitive Church with the opportunity not only to break the bread and to drink from the cup but also to gather and to share stories about Jesus and to listen to those who had directly experienced the Lord in his earthly ministry. Eventually, of course, these stories were collected by the communities of the faithful and written and recorded into the gospels. The early Christian communities also shared the letters that they received from Paul and from the other apostles.

As early as the year 200 A.D., a distinct pattern had taken shape in these eucharistic gatherings. On Sunday, very early in the morning, the people would gather. An opening prayer and greeting was prayed by the presider, a designated member of the community would read a selection from the gospels and occasionally from the Old Testament, and some sort of explanation of what had just been proclaimed was shared with the community. The community would then be led in a prayer of thanksgiving, and the presider would recall the events and words of Jesus at the Last Supper. The bread and the wine were then shared, and the gathering would be dismissed, with the invitation to return on the following Sunday. This basic structure is the outline of the present day celebration of the Eucharist.

There is some disagreement among scholars about exactly what the early Christian community believed that they were celebrating in these eucharistic gatherings. Most would agree that the early community understood it to be a memorial, not only of the Last Supper, but also a commemoration of Christ's death and resurrection. There is also agreement that the early Christians understood the meal as a sacrificial meal, because they believed that Jesus identified his death on the cross as an offering of himself to God, and the Resurrection confirmed that God the Father had accepted this offering. The real disagreement is over the meaning of the words "this is my body" and "this is my blood."

Although the results of studying the nuances of language and custom can shed valuable light on the meaning of these words, a discussion of such results is far beyond the scope of what is essential in this handbook. For our purposes here, perhaps, the Gospel of John might serve as a summary of what the early Christian community believed about the Eucharist, without going into too much detail. "My flesh is true food and my blood is true drink. Those who eat my flesh and drink my blood abide in me, and I in them" (Jn 6:55–56).

3. Before the Council of Trent

By the sixth century, the Eucharist had evolved into a rich ritual of ceremony, prayers of petition and thanksgiving, and a procession of gifts and offerings. The primary reason for this change in the Eucharist from a simple meal of fellowship to a more elaborate ritual was a result of the fact that Christianity moved from being a persecuted sect to being an official religion, and the central act of worship clearly reflected this change in status. A secondary reason, related to the first, was that the Christian eucharistic gatherings moved from the homes of the faithful to the churches and basilicas erected for this purpose. Simple tables gave way to elaborate and permanent altars, presiders were dressed in distinctive vestments, and Sundays, which at one time were just another day for work, had been set aside as the "Lord's day." As a result of these changes, certainly more cultural than theological, as much time as was needed was available for the celebration.

The great saints of the day also contributed to the formation of the eucharistic liturgies of the time. Saint Basil the Great and Saint John Chrysostom composed magnificent eucharistic liturgies that featured prayers, songs, and ceremonies that were intended for the worship of God. In addition to these carefully constructed liturgies, other changes were slowly incorporated. Litanies of prayers were added, some penitential in nature, which petitioned, "Lord have mercy" and "Christ have mercy," and the tradition of praying the Our Father was incorporated as an action of the assembly before the reception of Communion.

But perhaps the greatest change in the Eucharist was the change from a community-centered action that depended on the gathering of the faithful to a clerical-centered action in which the assembled community did not participate but rather attended and watched. This change is very obvious in the description of Mass from around the year 600 A.D., recorded in the Gregorian Sacramentary, one of the earliest Roman liturgical books, attributed to Pope Saint Gregory I (540–604).

In the description of the Mass as recorded in this liturgical book, the pope processes, along with a long line of clergy and monks, from his residence to the door of the basilica where he is met with the singing of a psalm while he is being vested for the liturgy. He processes down the aisle of the basilica, is greeted at the altar with a sign of peace, and he then prostrates himself in prayer. A choir of monks sings "Lord have mercy" and a hymn of praise and glory to God. Then the pope prays an opening prayer. There follows the readings and a sermon, after which the altar is draped in white, and the loaves of bread and the wine are presented to him by a procession of the nobles present at the gathering; other gifts are presented to his assisting ministers by the common people. The pope and his assisting ministers pray a solemn eucharistic prayer, share the sign of peace among themselves, and then the pope distributes Communion first to the clergy, then to the nobles, and finally to the lay people. A prayer of concluding blessing is prayed, and the pope processes out, followed by his clergy, the nobles, and then finally the common people.

In the centuries that followed, in the Eastern remnant of what had been the Roman Empire, the eucharistic liturgy remained stable, with very few changes, while in the West, the liturgy continued to develop until it was standardized by the reforms of the Council of Trent. The greatest developments in the liturgy of the West were the introduction of the private Mass and the use of Latin as the official language of worship.

The private Mass, where the priest celebrates the Mass alone or with only a very small congregation present as opposed to the public worship described in the Gregorian Sacramentary, was the result of at least three distinct developments. The first, seemingly unrelated, was the growing need to duplicate the Sunday Eucharist as a result of the increased Christian population; there were simply too many people who desired to be present for the liturgy and no one place could accommodate them all. The decision to allow for more than one Sunday liturgy paved the way to allow for additional exceptions. The second occurred because in some places the Mass was beginning to be celebrated at other times during the week, and not just on Sunday, in memory of the Christian martyrs and, often, as the result of some need for which the people desired the intervention of God on their behalf. The third development was the rise of monasticism and the desire of the individual monks, often away from their monastery engaged in missionary activity, to celebrate daily Mass, as was their custom while at home. These three developments were the main contributors to the practice of the institution of the private Mass.

Latin, as the official language of worship, was not the result of any particular development in theology or culture, but simply a reaction that might be summed up as "it has always been done this way." Only the clergy understood Latin, and even some of them would have been hard pressed to explain the meaning of what they said. The result was that few people understood what was really going on during the Mass, except for what they were told.

Theologically, during this period of development, the main issues concerned two practical questions: when did the sacrifice take place in the Mass and how did the bread and wine change into the body and blood of Christ?

Theologians, despite their best efforts, were unable to agree on exactly when the sacrifice took place. Some argued that it took place when the host was broken, while others argued that it took place at the moment of Communion. In answer to the second question, the theologians coined the term *transubstantiation*, which basically meant that there was a change in the substance or reality of the bread and wine; however, at that time no theologians had thought out the details of an explanation of how this happened except to state that it occurred because of "the power of the Holy Spirit."

4. The Council of Trent

When the bishops gathered for the opening session of the Council of Trent, they were faced with the challenge of the Protestant reformers who did not doubt the fact that the Eucharist was central to the Christian community but who did vehemently protest some of the customs and practices that surrounded the eucharistic gathering. Martin Luther, in particular, was scandalized by the development of the system of stipends, literally offerings to a minister, which resulted in the practice of the Mass being offered for the specific intentions of a person or group of people. Luther saw this practice, and the potential for misrepresentation and corruption that could result from it, as unacceptable. In his *Confessions Concerning Christ's Supper* he noted, "I regard the preaching and the selling of the Mass as a sacrifice or a good work as the greatest of all abominations." The bishops of the council may have agreed with his perception but certainly disagreed with his proposed remedy.

Because of the challenge of Martin Luther, the writings of the other reformers, and their own experience and conviction, the bishops of the council determined three specific responses and clarifications of Catholic teaching about the Eucharist. In 1551, they promulgated a document on the Blessed Sacrament, in 1562, they proclaimed a document on the reception of holy Communion, and also in 1562 they issued a document on the Mass as a sacrifice.

On October 11, 1551, in eight chapters and eleven canons, the bishops declared that Christ was present in the Eucharist, body, soul, and divinity, by virtue of the words of consecration prayed by the celebrant. In addition, the bishops reaffirmed the doctrine of transubstantiation and the practice of the adoration of the Host outside of Mass.

On July 16, 1562, the bishops declared that Christ was truly and completely present in the consecrated bread and wine, and that people received holy Communion when they received either the bread or the wine. It was not necessary, as some reformers had suggested, that a person receive both the bread and the wine in order to validly receive holy Communion.

On September 17, 1562, the bishops declared that the Mass was to be understood as a true sacrifice, an unbloody representation of Christ's sacrifice on the cross, and that the merits of this sacrifice could be applied to both the living and the dead. In this document, they also dealt with particular superstitions and matters of discipline concerning the Mass.

5. The Tridentine Mass

But perhaps the Council of Trent is remembered not so much because of the individual decrees and clarifications, as important as they are, but rather because its deliberations and pronouncements on the form of the Mass, universally known as the Tridentine Mass. Beginning in 1570 with a new Roman Missal, promulgated by Pope Pius V, and continuing until 1960, every word, every gesture, every tone, every prayer prayed during the Mass was almost identical for a period of four hundred years. Although it took a period of time for the Tridentine Mass to be established, once it was established it did not change without the express permission of the pope.

For most Catholics, the Mass became an opportunity for private prayer and devotion, except at the moment of consecration when the Blessed Sacrament was adored. Music became more prominent, churches became more elaborate, and the tabernacle became the primary focus of attention, before, during, and after the celebration of the Mass. Latin was the only approved language that could be used for the celebration of the Mass.

There was also a separation between the Mass and holy Communion. Communion was often distributed before Mass began or after it had been concluded, so as not to interrupt the sacrifice. At a solemn high Mass, only the priest celebrant would receive Communion. As a result, fewer and fewer people would receive Communion. The practice of the reception of holy Communion was further complicated by a rising sense in the people of their own "unworthiness" to receive the sacrament. This feeling of unworthiness was a result of a heresy called Jansenism (which insisted on the requirement of going to confession before receiving Communion).

In a very real sense, the Eucharist, which at the beginning of the Church was a communal action, had now developed into a private act of worship.

6. Other Consequences of the Council of Trent

It was perhaps not intended, but the fact that the bishops of the council addressed the Eucharist as distinct components made up of the Blessed Sacrament, holy Communion, and the sacrifice of the Mass perpetuated the belief and the practice of the faithful of thinking about each of these manifestations of the Eucharist as special and unique practices of their faith and piety. Catholic people understood each manifestation as distinct from the other. For example, when they spoke about the Blessed Sacrament they were referring to the Eucharist that was instituted by Christ at the Last Supper and which was reserved for adoration and worship in the tabernacle of the church; when they spoke about holy Communion, they understood that they were talking about the reception of the body and blood of Christ; when they spoke about the Mass, they understood it as the "sacrifice of the Mass."

This separation of the Catholic practice of the Eucharist into three distinct manifestations and appreciations strongly influenced the practice of Catholic piety and devotion. It was possible to reflect and pray about the Blessed Sacrament without reference to either holy Communion or the Mass. It was possible to receive holy Communion before or after Mass and at other times during the week, even though the practice of the frequent reception of holy Communion was not common, with a proper genuflection to the reserved sacrament and attendance at the sacrifice of the Mass as part of a communal thanksgiving. And, finally, it was possible to attend the sacrifice of the Mass, and understand that the Blessed Sacrament was reserved in the tabernacle and, without actually receiving holy Communion, still feel fulfilled and satisfied.

This understanding and practice of piety and devotion took deep root with the Catholic faithful and is still manifested today even though contemporary sacramental theology tends to emphasize a unified theology of the Eucharist.

7. Contemporary Practice

The bishops who met during the Second Vatican Council (1962–1965) gathered in a completely different atmosphere and environment than the bishops who had met and deliberated at the Council of Trent. The bishops of Vatican II also had significant advantage over the bishops of Trent because they had available to them historical research and a sense of what had developed in the Church and why—a beginning position, perception, and overview that would prove to be essential and which strongly supported the position of those who believed that change was both necessary and overdue.

The first document issued by the Second Vatican Council was the Constitution on the Sacred Liturgy. This document mandated significant change in the liturgy and called for a return to what many believed were the basics of Catholic eucharistic worship. The central thrust of the document was to again situate the people of God, not as a type of spectator of the "holy sacrifice of the Mass," but rather as an assembly of the faithful, active and integral to the liturgical celebration of Word and Eucharist.

Without changing the belief and the dogmas about the Eucharist that had been defined for previous generations of Catholics, Vatican Council II nevertheless chose to emphasize different truths from the richness of the eucharistic tradition. The emphasis included in this document was that the Eucharist is understood as an opportunity to offer thanks and praise to the Father, as the sacrificial memorial of

Christ and his body, and as the presence of Christ by both the power of his Word and the power of the Holy Spirit.

Thanks and Praise to the Father: The primary meaning of Eucharist is "thanksgiving" and, as such, the Eucharist is humankind's opportunity to thank God the Father for all with which we have been blessed and for all that has been accomplished through creation, redemption, and sanctification. This prayer of thanksgiving is offered to the Father through Christ and with Christ and in Christ (CCC 1359–1361).

A Sacrificial Memorial: The Eucharist is a memorial of Christ's Passover, but not in the sense of a mere recollection of what happened long ago, but rather in a sense that it is both present and real for the people of God today. This memorial is a living sacrifice of the Church, united with the offering and intercession of Christ, not only for the benefit of those here on earth, but also for all of the faithful departed, "who have died in Christ" (CCC 1362–1371).

Christ Is Present in Word and Spirit: As the Scriptures tell us, Christ is present whenever "two or three are gathered in my name" (Mt 18:20) and in the poor, the sick, and the imprisoned (Mt 25:31–46), but Christ is present in the fullest possible way in the Blessed Sacrament of the Eucharist, "the body and blood, together with the soul and divinity, of our Lord Jesus Christ, and, therefore, 'the whole Christ is truly, really and substantially contained'" (Council of Trent DS 1651 and CCC 1374).

In addition to this specific theological emphasis, the Second Vatican Council mandated changes in the liturgical practice of the Mass, a reform that would be mindful of the needs of a church that was active and alive in many different cultures and peoples. A new edition of the Mass was published and, for the first time since the Council of Trent, translated into many different languages. The altar, which had been turned into the back wall of the church, was now turned around, which allowed the priest to face the people. The people were invited, in fact were expected, to fully participate, in song and response, to the prayers and the invocations. The richness of the biblical tradition from both the Old and the New Testament was once again prominent. Finally, people were urged to go to Communion (CCC 1417); and, in many places, Communion was now received not just in the form of the host, but also in the form of the cup, the bread and the wine of the Eucharist (CCC 1390).

8. The Eucharistic Liturgy

The two principal parts of the Mass are the Liturgy of the Word, which focuses on the Scriptures (both the Old Testament and the New Testament) and the preached word, and the Liturgy of the Eucharist, which consists of prayers of praise and thanksgiving and the distribution of holy Communion.

The eucharistic liturgy begins with an entrance rite, during which the gathered assembly sings a hymn and the priest and the ministers (deacon, acolytes, lectors, and extraordinary eucharistic ministers) process to the altar. When all have gathered, the priest begins with the Sign of the Cross and welcomes everyone to the assembly. A brief penitential rite follows in which all present take a moment to reflect on their lives and to ask the Lord for forgiveness of any sins that they may have committed. The Gloria, an ancient hymn of praise to the Father, Son, and Holy Spirit, is recited or sung on all Sundays and feast days of the Church.

The Liturgy of the Word follows; three selections from Scripture are usually proclaimed: the first is from the Old Testament, the second reading is from one of the epistles or the writings of Saint Paul, and the third reading is from one of the gospels. The homily follows in which the priest (or the deacon) explains the readings and offers a practical application of the teaching of the Scriptures to the daily lives of the assembly. After the homily, there is a brief period of silence so that all can reflect on what they have just heard and then the assembly stands and recites the Creed, a profession of faith which dates back to the fourth century. The Creed expresses the faith and the belief of the assembly in the Trinity, in Scripture (that is, belief in the resurrection and the life of the world to come), and in selected dogma and doctrine of the Church (that is, the forgiveness of sins and the communion of saints).

The concluding action of the Liturgy of the Word is the prayer of intercessions that follows the praying of the Creed. In this prayer, specific intentions and needs of the universal Church, the local Church, the gathered assembly, and those specific needs that come from the lived experience of the people are prayed. The intention is simply stated: "For all of God's people, that they may be open to the power of the Spirit in their lives, we pray to the Lord." And the people respond, "Lord, hear our prayer," or with some other suitable response.

The Liturgy of the Eucharist follows and opens with the preparation of the altar and the presentation of the gifts. Members of the assembly bring forward the bread and the wine (matter) that will be blessed and consecrated (form) and also bring forth the monetary gifts that are offered for the support of the community. The priest offers all of these gifts to the Father through prayers of thanksgiving, and the people respond, "Blessed be God, for ever."

With all in readiness, the priest begins the eucharistic prayer by inviting the people to "Lift up your hearts," to which the people respond, "We lift them up to the Lord." Then one of the eucharistic prayers is prayed, consisting of the preface, epiclesis, institution narrative, anamnesis, and concluding with the intercessions:

Preface: a prayer which gives thanks to God the Father, through Christ, by the power of the Holy Spirit, for all of the works of creation, redemption, and sanctification (CCC 1352).

Epiclesis: The Church asks the Father to send the Holy Spirit on the gifts of bread and wine so that they may become the body and blood of Jesus (CCC 1353).

Institution Narrative: The power of the words prayed and the action of Christ, with the power of the Holy Spirit, make the body and blood of Christ sacramentally present (CCC 1353).

Anamnesis: The passion, resurrection, and the glorious return of Jesus is recalled and offered to the Father, which is a reconciling action, reconciling the people of God with God the Father (CCC 1354).

Intercessions: The Eucharist is celebrated in union with the pope, the bishops and their clergy and people, not only for and with the Church on earth, but also for and with the Church in heaven (CCC 1354).

The entire eucharistic prayer is concluded and summarized by the doxology that follows:

Through him,
with him,
in him,
in the unity of the Holy Spirit,
all glory and honor is yours,
almighty Father,
for ever and ever.

To which the assembly responds, "Amen."

All is now in readiness for the distribution of holy Communion, but before Communion is distributed, all join in praying the Our Father (a tradition in place from the fourth century on) and in exchanging with one another some sign of God's peace in their lives. Both of these actions signify the hope and desire of the Christian community to be joined together in peace, as brothers and sisters, waiting in anticipation of the kingdom of God which is to come, but which is experienced in the Eucharist that has been celebrated and in the communion that follows.

Communion is received standing rather than kneeling as it once was before the reforms of the Second Vatican Council. The consecrated host is offered to the communicant with the words, "Body of Christ," and the response is made, "Amen." It is the option of the communicant to receive the host on their outstretched hand or tongue; the vast majority of Catholics choose to receive Communion in their hand.

Some time is reserved after Communion for the singing of a hymn of thanksgiving and a period of silent reflection. When this period is finished, the priest prays a concluding prayer and then blesses the people, again in the form of the same Sign of the Cross under which the community had originally gathered. The people are then dismissed with the words, "The Mass is ended, go in peace to love and serve the Lord," to which the assembly responds, "Thanks be to God."

A concluding hymn is sung as the priest and the ministers process out of the sanctuary and back to the doors of the church, where they often gather to greet the people.

9. The Effects of the Eucharist

The principal effect of the Eucharist is a more intimate union with Jesus (CCC 1391). In the words of the gospel, the believers who "eat my flesh and drink my blood abide in me, and I in them" (Jn 6:56). Catholics believe that this intimate union is necessary for the spiritual journey and for growth in the Christian life and that the nourishment of the Eucharist is the "spiritual food" that preserves, increases, and renews the life of grace within those who receive it (CCC 1392).

The Eucharist separates the Christian from a life of sin; in a very real sense, it wipes out those daily weaknesses and choices that could lead us away from the kingdom (the traditional concept of venial sin) and strengthens us in the struggle against more serious sin (mortal sin) that could destroy our relationships with the Lord. The concept is a simple one; the more a person enters into this intimate relationship with the Lord, the less and less inclined they will be to choose anything that could jeopardize this relationship (CCC 1394–1395).

Since the Eucharist is the core sacrament of the Church, the Catholic understanding of Eucharist also includes the concept that it is formative of not only the individual person, but also of the entire community of believers. The sharing of the one bread and the one cup shapes and forms the assembly into the one Body of Christ (CCC 1396): "Because there is one bread, we who are many are one body, for we all partake of the one bread" (1 Cor 10:17). This is the formation of one community, united in Christ, and committed to the poor (CCC 1397) and to the unity of all Christians (CCC 1398).

Finally, although the Eucharist celebrates the presence of Christ, it is also a sacrament that reminds the gathered assembly that it still waits for the fullness of the coming kingdom of God. In the words of one of the eucharistic prayers, the Church waits "to share in your glory when every tear will be wiped away. On that day we shall see you, our God, as you are. We shall become like you and praise you for ever through Christ our Lord" (Eucharistic Prayer III and CCC 1404).

10. Pastoral Concerns

The Eucharist celebrates complete membership in the Catholic Church and is a sign of perfect unity in faith. Only those who fully share in the Catholic faith of Eastern or Western rites may celebrate Communion in Catholic churches. Roman Catholics may celebrate Communion in Eastern rite Catholic churches, but not in churches that are not united with Rome. Communion in the Orthodox Church is recognized as valid, but a Catholic may celebrate Communion in an Orthodox Church only in exceptional cases. This applies when no Roman rite is available or when a person is in danger of death (Canon 844 of the Code of Canon Law).

11. Essentials

Name: Sacrament of the Holy Eucharist.

Sacramental Identification: Sacrament of initiation.

Minimum Age: Age of Reason, traditionally at least seven years old, however, at any age if the person is able to distinguish the body of Christ from ordinary food and receive holy Communion reverently (Canon 913 of the Code of Canon Law).

Can Be Repeated? Yes.

Sacramental Character Imparted? No.

Matter: Wheat bread and natural grape wine.

Form: For the bread: "Take this, all of you, and eat it: this is my body which will be given up for you." And, for the wine: "Take this, all of you, and drink from it: this is the cup of my blood, the blood of the new and everlasting covenant. It will be shed for you and for all so that sins may be forgiven. Do this in memory of me."

Ordinary Minister: Priest.

Extraordinary Minister: None.

PART THREE

The Sacraments of Healing

The sacraments of initiation incorporate a person into the life of the Church and into the fullness of life with Christ. However, the encounter with both Christ and his Church does not stop with the initiation process but rather continues throughout the life of faithful. Human beings are earthen vessels, "clay jars" (2 Cor 4:7), and, as such, they will experience in their lives moments where they will be in special need of the healing power of God, made present through the working of the Holy Spirit. This healing is manifested in the sacrament of penance and reconciliation and in the sacrament of the anointing of the sick. In both of these sacraments, Jesus is the "Divine Physician," restoring health to our souls and bodies just as he did in his earthly ministry (CCC 1420–1421).

I. Penance and Reconciliation

Those who approach the sacrament of Penance obtain pardon from God's mercy for the offense committed against him, and are, at the same time, reconciled with the Church which they have wounded by their sins and which by charity, by example, and by prayer labors for their conversion (Dogmatic Constitution on the Church as quoted in CCC 1422).

1. Jesus and Sinners

Even people who do not believe that Jesus is the Son of God are nevertheless left with the impression that he was a person with an unusual capacity for forgiveness. Not only was he able to forgive sinners, he was also able to forgive those who had sinned against him (Lk 23:34). The gospels are filled with illustrations of his forgiveness in action; the parable of the Prodigal Son (Lk 15:11–32), the parable of the Lost Sheep (Lk 15:3–7), and the story of the woman caught in adultery (Jn 8:3–11) are some obvious examples.

The message that Jesus preached, a message preached by John the Baptist (repent and believe) but completed by Jesus (because the kingdom of God is among you), was a message that called people to *metanoia*, a Greek word that means "to change one's life and one's heart." Jesus' message was more than one of calling people to repentance, which means to be sorry for what you have done; Jesus wanted people to be sorry but he also desired that they be fundamentally changed by their sorrow and their personal experience of forgiveness. This fundamental change, the reordering of their life and their decisions, was to be understood as *gospel* (good news) because it would usher in a new way of life and a new way of living, which Jesus called the "kingdom of God."

Jesus was so insistent on *metanoia* and on the ramifications of this life-changing decision that when the apostle Peter asked him for further clarification, saying: "How often should I forgive," Jesus answered Peter: "Not seven times, but…seventy-seven times" (Mt 18:22). In other words, in the kingdom of God there was no limit to what could be forgiven and no limit to what needed to be forgiven. "Forgive us our sins, for we ourselves forgive everyone indebted to us," says Luke (11:4).

After his Resurrection, Jesus appeared to his disciples and spoke to them in the words that have traditionally been understood as the words that instituted the sacrament of penance and reconciliation: "If you forgive the sins of any, they are forgiven them; if you retain the sins of any, they are retained" (Jn 20:23). Within the context of his life and ministry, it can be understood that although the power to "bind someone" is certainly a prerogative, the intention of Jesus was to not bind but rather to loose, to free people from that which held them fast and set them firmly on the path to the kingdom of God.

2. The Practice of the Early Church

The primary sacrament of forgiveness in the early Church was baptism. The apostles preached the gospel as it had been given to them by Jesus and invited people to turn away from their lives of sin and to embrace the good news. It was understood by all that baptism reconciled a person to God and forgave all their sins, but it was also understood that it could be received only once. There was a problem with those people who had already been baptized and who did not live up to their baptismal promises; what could be done on their behalf?

The early Christian community looked first, as might well be expected, to their Jewish roots and heritage for an answer. Jewish rabbis had a practice that was known as "binding and loosing." If a member of the community somehow offended the community, the rabbis would bar them from the community, and if they later repented of their offense, the rabbis would welcome them back. This procedure was a practical application of the admonition of Jesus, if all else fails between you and a brother and a sister, "[take] it to the church" (Mt 18:15–18) for judgment. Saint Paul may well have been referring to this practice when he instructed the community in Corinth that they should have taken this kind of action when a certain member of the community had violated the marriage laws by "living with his father's wife" (Lev 18:8; 1 Cor 5:1–13). Paul expected that the community would expel the man, and then later accept him back into the community if he reformed his life (2 Cor 2:5–11).

The practice of binding and loosing was useful, but by the second century the Church had developed a practice by which a person who had fallen into serious sin (that is, murder, adultery, idolatry) could become a penitent (from the Latin *paenitentia* which means "repentance"). Penitents formed a special group within the community who would spend an extended period of time in fasting, prayer, and giving alms, all the while asking for the strength to be faithful to their baptismal promises. The Christian community would join them in prayer during their period of penitence. When the bishop of the community determined that they had indeed reformed their lives, he would welcome them back in the name of the community, lay his hands on their head as a sign of reconciliation and forgiveness, and invite them once again to join the community in the celebration of the Eucharist. A person was permitted to become a penitent only once in his or her lifetime; to be admitted more than once, in the words of Clement of Alexandria, "would make a mockery of God's mercy."

The group of penitents was very small, because most people did not commit the kind of sins that were considered serious enough for this type of public penance. Others, aware of the fact that they could seek public forgiveness and reconciliation only once in their lives, postponed entrance into the group of penitents for as long as possible. For most people, however, forgiveness was something that they routinely asked for and received from their brothers and sisters in the community or something they asked God for at the beginning of the eucharistic liturgy. As long as the Christian community was small, this form of public penance and reconciliation worked well, but as the community grew larger and larger, the practice became more and more strained and seemed not to fit the needs of the growing body of Christians.

A further strain was put on this particular form of the practice of sacramental reconciliation by the persecutions suffered by the Christian community in the third century. Some members of the community went to their death as martyrs while others chose not to accept martyrdom. Those who did not become martyrs performed the required sacrifices to the gods and renounced Jesus, and then later, when the furor of persecution had settled down, asked to be readmitted to the Christian community. Some bishops freely accepted these returning apostates but other bishops and communities were not so inclined. Apostasy, according to one bishop of the time, was the "unforgivable sin" (Mt 12:31) and could not be forgiven. A consistent and pastoral approach to this situation was never agreed upon.

Eventually, the practice of public penance and reconciliation slowly died out. It was replaced by a different practice, a practice with roots in the burgeoning monasteries. Monasticism was beginning to flourish throughout the Mediterranean and across much of Europe, into England and Ireland.

3. Before the Council of Trent

Monastic training often included the concept of what today might be called a "mentor." A new recruit in the monastery would be assigned to an older monk who was entrusted with the task of teaching him all about being a monk. The younger man would visit the older man once a week and, in their conversations, the younger monk would often confess his faults and failings to the older monk, and ask for the direction and the advice that might be helpful in overcoming the younger monk's faults. At the end of their session, the older and younger monks would pray together and ask for the forgiveness of any sins that they may have committed.

In the fifth century, at the direct request of the papacy, the monks, who up until this moment were centered in their monastic compounds, were entrusted with the task of converting to the Christian faith the Germanic tribes that were migrating into former territory of the Roman Empire. These monks, particularly the monks from Ireland, brought with them the practice of confessing their sins to another and they urged their new converts to do the same. The monks understood the practice as a way of keeping the new Christian faith alive and vibrant in the lives of their new converts. The practice seemed to be well accepted and popular among the people because it spread very quickly.

When this new penitential practice reached parts of the former Roman Empire in Southern Europe, the first reaction of the bishops in that area was to condemn it, but eventually the practice took root, even in those places where it was vigorously opposed. People wanted some assurance that they were loved and forgiven by God, and the traditional practice of public penance did not fulfill their needs. They also preferred to confess their sins directly to a priest, which this new practice permitted, and not to a bishop, which was required in the more traditional practice. By the seventh century, private confession of sins had taken root in most places and within a few centuries it was accepted throughout the Church.

During the period of the Middle Ages, the practice of private confession of sins continued to be both practiced and developed. For example, the penance assigned for the remission of sins at first needed to be completed before a person was accepted back into Communion, perhaps a concept adopted from the old practice of public penance. Eventually, however, it was understood that the penance could be performed and the person could return to Communion at the same time. The penances themselves also changed. Originally the assigned penance would be closely related to the sin; if a person stole one goat, they would have to return two goats to the aggrieved party, but eventually the recitation of certain prayers were all that was normally required, as long as proper restitution was made.

The other development was that the role of the priest evolved more and more into the role of a judge and the keeper of God's mercy. This was a distinct development because it seemed that in the original format popularized by the monks that the priest would simply assure penitents that their sins had been forgiven by God, but eventually this evolved into the practice where the priest would absolve penitents from their sins. The absolution was given in the name of God but it could be surmised and, at least for some people, it was assumed that the forgiveness was dependent on the priest and not on God. This became the primary "fuel" that powered the Protestant Reformation's insistence that people seek forgiveness directly from God and not from a priest.

Other developments during this period of time impacted on the Church's understanding of the sacrament of penance and reconciliation even more profoundly. These developments included the distinction between mortal sin and venial sin, perfect and imperfect contrition, and the punishment of sins.

Mortal Sin and Venial Sin: There had been a long tradition in the Church that distinguished between serious sins (which required public penance) and less serious sins (which were forgiven in the Eucharist). Serious sin was understood as sin that was so grievous (murder, adultery, idolatry) that it was "deadly" to the soul and to the life of grace within a person. It was understood that if a person died in this state that they would be denied heaven. Other sins were considered less serious and very pardonable. In the Middle Ages, a listing of mortal (serious) sins and venial (pardonable) sins was never detailed, but there was agreement among theologians of the time that it was possible for a person to deliberately reject God through his or her choices and actions. It was understood that such a rejection of God and the law of God would bring a person to the everlasting fires of hell for all eternity.

Perfect and Imperfect Contrition: Sorrow for sin that is motivated by fear of punishment is understood as imperfect contrition; it is considered imperfect because even the most hardened criminals might regret that they will be punished but might not regret their choices and actions. Perfect contrition, on the other hand, is contrition that is based on the recognition within a person that the pursuit of sin has no place in their lives if they are trying to live their baptismal promises; this kind of contrition is necessary for a life of conversion and repentance.

Punishment of Sin: Sin, because it was understood as an offense against God, needed to be punished. People understood the consequences of breaking the civil law, for example, and recognized that even if forgiven, there were still consequences as a result of their actions. Sin was understood in much the same way; God would forgive sin, if the sins were confessed and absolution was received and the penance was performed, but there was still the consequence of sin. Theologians of the time differentiated between the *temporal* punishment due (punishment for sin after death, but for a set period of time) and the *eternal* punishment due (forgiven in the sacrament, but if not forgiven, punishment that would last for all eternity). The place where temporal punishment was experienced was *purgatory* and the place where eternal punishment was experienced was *hell*.

4. The Council of Trent

The Council of Trent, in direct response to the Protestant reformers who saw little need for the confession of sins to anyone except directly to God, issued strong directives and teachings about the sacrament of penance and reconciliation. The complaints and challenges issued by Martin Luther were particularly singled out for discussion, and in his excommunication by Pope Leo X in 1520, twelve of his ideas concerning penance were condemned.

The council reaffirmed that it was the will of the Lord and the constant tradition of the Church that the "integral confession of sins" was necessary after baptism for the forgiveness of sins. The council understood that this integral confession would include the specifics and the particulars of all mortal sins committed; venial sins could be confessed but it was not necessary to do so since they were forgiven in the sacrament of the Eucharist. This integral confession of sins was necessary so that the priest could judge the severity of the sins committed and assign the necessary penance.

The end result of the teaching of the Council of Trent was that most Catholics continued their practice of going to confession once a year in preparation for their annual reception of holy Communion. This remained the common practice in the Church until early in the twentieth century when Pope Pius X encouraged the frequent reception of holy Communion. Catholics responded to his request, but because of their training and understanding, also assumed that it was necessary to go to confession before the reception of Communion. As a result of this assumption, practically unchallenged and perhaps even encouraged by the clergy, Catholics would go to confession once a month or once a week, depending on how often they went to holy Communion.

5. Contemporary Practice

By the time of the Second Vatican Council, it could be argued that there was general agreement and understanding that the sacrament of penance and reconciliation needed reform. Although for some Catholics the celebration of the sacrament was certainly an opportunity to deepen their relationship with the Lord and experience the Lord's abundant mercy, for many others, confession was an obligation, a rule or requirement that needed to be fulfilled so that they would meet the minimal requirements of the law (see the entry for "Precepts of the Church" in the glossary section). The purpose of the sacrament was an opportunity for conversion, confession, and forgiveness (CCC 1423–1424) and not a test of discipline.

The reforms of the Second Vatican Council reaffirmed two basic principles about sacramental confession and reconciliation, principles that were considered as essential to the *fundamental structure* of the sacrament. The first principle is that contrition, confession, and satisfaction are the graced action of the Holy Spirit, calling the individual person to ongoing conversion of life. The second principle is that the action of God is manifested through the ministry of the bishops and priests, through which the person is healed and restored to ecclesial communion with the Church (CCC 1448). The Church has affirmed that it is only God who can forgive sins but also reaffirmed that the Church itself is a sign and an instrument of the forgiveness and reconciliation of God (CCC 1441–1442).

The contemporary practice of the sacrament begins with the premise that the celebration of the sacrament is primarily a liturgical action that contains the following elements: a greeting and blessing, proclamation of the Word of God, exhortation to repentance, the confession of sins, the imposition and acceptance of penance, and, finally, absolution along with a prayer of thanksgiving and praise (CCC 1480). Understanding of the sacrament reaffirms the necessity for individual and integral confession and absolution (Council of Trent) but also introduces two new forms of the sacrament: communal celebration of the sacrament (with individual confession and absolution as part of the observance) and a communal celebration of the sacrament with general confession and general absolution (in cases of grave necessity) (CCC 1482–1483).

6. The Rite of Individual Reconciliation

Although it is not at all unusual for the individual celebration of the sacrament to begin with the traditional words, "Bless me, Father, for I have sinned," the ritual suggests that the celebration begin with the Sign of the Cross and a greeting from the priest, such as "May God, who has enlightened every heart, help you to know your sins and to trust in his mercy." This change is not a mere change in words for the sake of change but is intended to immediately emphasize that which is to be celebrated is a sacrament of conversion and renewal. The proclamation of the Word of God, which immediately follows the greeting, also reminds both the penitent and the celebrant that what they are doing is meant to be an encounter with the Lord and his abundant mercy, and not just a rote recitation of faults and weaknesses.

The place where the sacrament is celebrated today is also an attempt to encourage an understanding of the sacrament as truly a celebration. In most places, the traditional confessional, where the penitent kneels in anonymous darkness behind a screen (the traditional practice since 1614), has been replaced with a reconciliation room where the priest and the person celebrating the sacrament are seated and face each other. Although the practice of the confession of sins behind a screen is still presented as an option, it is encouraged that the face-to-face encounter take place.

After the greeting and the reading from Scripture, the person celebrating the sacrament enters into a dialogue with the priest about the penitent's Christian journey of faith. In this dialogue, serious sin (mortal sin) would of course be discussed and explained but so also are what may be understood as venial sins (faults and weaknesses). (In the traditional understanding of the sacrament, the confession of sin is understood as the *matter* of the sacrament.) The purpose of this dialogue is to review the circumstances and the conditions of the penitent's life, along with the decisions and choices that have been made, and to receive the direction, encouragement, and, at times, the correction that may be necessary. At the end of this discussion, the priest then offers a penance which is something that should be directly related to what has been discussed and which may be helpful to the person as they live their life. Often the penance offered is a particular prayer, but more and more the practice might be to suggest a particular passage from Scripture for meditation and reflection or a concrete action that will effectively address the struggle or issue. (For example, a penance might be to dedicate a certain amount of time each day to actively listening to your spouse.)

Once the penance is accepted, the person celebrating the sacrament is invited to express contrition, either in the traditional words of the Act of Contrition or in words of his or her own choosing such as, "I am sorry that I have not been open and cooperative with the Holy Spirit in my life. I recognize the fact that I could spend more time and more effort in my Christian life and I ask for the necessary grace to do so. I give thanks and praise to the Lord for his forgiveness and love."

The priest, as he extends his hands over the person in the traditional liturgical gesture of blessing, prays the words of absolution (the *form* of the sacrament):

> God, the Father of mercies,
> through the death and resurrection of his Son,
> has reconciled the world to himself
> and sent the Holy Spirit among us
> for the forgiveness of sins;
> through the ministry of the Church
> may God give you pardon and peace,
> and I absolve you from your sins
> in the name of the Father, and of the Son,
> and of the Holy Spirit.

The person receiving the sacrament responds, "Amen."

The celebration of the sacrament ends with the priest praying, "Give thanks to the Lord, for the he is good." The person receiving the sacrament responds with the words, "His mercy endures for ever." And the priest continues, "The Lord has freed you from your sins. Go in peace." To which the response is often prayed, "Thanks be to God."

Although the sacrament of penance and reconciliation may be celebrated at any time, parish communities usually have a specific time announced when the priest is available for the celebration of the sacrament. Most parishes also encourage members of the parish to make an appointment with the priest at any time outside of the announced periods of reconciliation if they desire to celebrate the sacrament. During the seasons of Advent and Lent, it is very common for parishes to increase the opportunities for the individual celebration of the sacrament and also to sponsor reconciliation services for the entire parish.

7. The Effects of Penance and Reconciliation

The effects of the sacrament include reconciliation with God and the return of the activity of grace in the life of the person and reconciliation with the Church and a return to full participation in the sacramental life of the Church, which is restored (in the case of mortal sin) and repaired (in the case of venial sin). The experience of a sense of peace and serenity of conscience is often a tangible result of the celebration of the sacrament (CCC 1496).

8. Pastoral Concerns

Perhaps the most pressing pastoral concern regarding the sacrament of penance is that many people find confessing to a priest very difficult. People wonder why they cannot just confess their sins to God. They overlook the fact that sin is not a private affair.

The healing power of Christ is made visible through Christ's official representative, the ordained priest. Sin offends against the community, and so the priest represents and forgives in the name of the community.

That Catholics are not making regular use of the sacrament of penance is another pastoral concern. This attitude stems from our culture's seeming loss of a sense of sin. Immorality is condoned and even glorified, as easily seen in portrayals in the media. As a result, a certain moral apathy has greatly diminished the painful reality of sin. We need a renewal of values that sensitizes us to right and wrong, and a deeper appreciation of God's compassionate forgiveness in the sacrament of penance.

9. Essentials

Name: Sacrament of Penance and/or Reconciliation.

Sacramental Identification: Sacrament of healing.

Minimum Age: Age of Reason, traditionally seven years old, the ability to distinguish between that which is morally "right" and that which is morally "wrong."

Can Be Repeated? Yes, as often as necessary. The confession of serious sin is required at least once a year (Canon 989 of the Code of Canon Law).

Sacramental Character Imparted? No.

Matter: Understood as proximate and remote. The remote matter consists of sins committed after baptism, which have not been previously confessed; the proximate matter consists of contrition, confession, and penance.

Form: "God the Father of mercies, through the death and resurrection of his Son, has reconciled the world to himself and sent the Holy Spirit among us for the forgiveness of sins; through the ministry of the Church may God give you pardon and peace. And I absolve you from your sins in the name of the Father, and of the Son, and of the Holy Spirit. Amen."

Ordinary Minister: Priest.

Extraordinary Minister: None.

II. Anointing of the Sick

By the sacred anointing of the sick and the prayer of the priests the whole Church commends those who are ill to the suffering and glorified Lord, that he may raise them up and save them. And indeed she exhorts them to contribute to the good of the People of God by freely uniting themselves to the Passion and death of Christ (Dogmatic Constitution on the Church and CCC 1499).

1. Jesus the Healer

A distinct portrait found in the gospel presentation of Jesus provides the clear impression that Jesus was a healer. There seems to be little doubt that not only the people of that time and place understood that Jesus was a healer but also that this ministry of healing was one of the ways that Jesus identified himself. When the disciples of John the Baptist came to Jesus and asked him: "Are you the one who is to come, or are we to wait for another?" Jesus responded: "Go and tell John what you have seen and heard: the blind receive their sight, the lame walk, lepers are cleansed, the deaf hear, the dead are raised, the poor have good news brought them" (Lk 7:20–22).

The original meaning of the word *salvation* is derived from the Latin word *salus,* which means "health." One understanding of salvation, an interpretation construed from the root meaning of the word and from the experience of those who have been "saved," is that salvation is restoration of health both to the physical being of a person but also restoration of health to the spiritual being of a person. In the life and the ministry of Jesus, this connection between the physical health of a person and the spiritual health of a person was understood by the people of the time. There was little distinction between the physical and the spiritual worlds, and people fully expected that if a person experienced something in one reality there would be a parallel experience in the other reality. In a very real sense, it was a holistic approach to the meaning of life.

In the miracle stories of the gospels, Jesus cures blindness (Mk 10:51; Jn 9:1), deafness (Mk 7:37; Lk 7:22), lameness (Mk 2:9), and other diseases (the physical), but in other instances he cures spiritual illnesses by driving the devil out of people (Mk 9:25) and restoring them to mental health. In some instances, he cures both a physical malady and a spiritual malady at the same time, for example, in the story of the paralyzed man who is brought to Jesus. In this example Jesus states first, "Your sins are forgiven," and secondly, "Stand up and walk" (Mt 9:1–8).

2. The Practice of the Early Church

The apostles and the disciples, after Jesus had risen from the dead and ascended into heaven, continued preaching the Word of God but also continued the ministry of healing. Again and again, the apostles demonstrated the power of the Word that they preached by reaching out to the sick and curing them in the name of Jesus. Perhaps the clearest example of this twofold ministry of preaching and healing can be seen in the words of the apostle Peter: "I have no silver or gold, but what I have I give you; in the name of Jesus Christ of Nazareth, stand up and walk" (Acts 3:6).

There is also some evidence that this ministry of healing was an established ministry. Saint Paul, for example, lists healing as one of the many spiritual gifts that have been given to the community (1 Cor 12:9–10), and the apostle James makes it very clear that the use of oil and prayer was something that was quite commonplace in at least the Jerusalem community: "Are any among you sick? They should call for the elders of the church and have them pray over them, anointing them with oil in the name of the Lord. The prayer of faith will save the sick, and the Lord will raise them up; and anyone who has committed sins will be forgiven" (Jas 5:14–15).

At the same time, however, it is difficult to demonstrate that the practice of prayer and anointing, at least in our understanding of the present day sacrament of the anointing, was a clearly established practice in the early Church. Certainly we can demonstrate that olive oil was routinely used as a remedy for the sick in common everyday life, and we can certainly assume that a prayer for healing might not have been that uncommon, but that is about as far as can be demonstrated. A prayer attributed to Hippolytus of Rome in the year 217 A.D. and prayed during the eucharistic liturgy over oil intended to be used for the sick, "May it strengthen all who use it," is probably an indication of the Christian belief that blessed oil was beneficial for the sick.

The practice of anointing the sick with oil continued as a pastoral practice for centuries, popular in some parts of the Christian world and not as popular in others, until the year 813 A.D. when the Council of Chalon in France urged that the anointing with oil be "taken more seriously." This council urged priests to carry the sacred oil with them when they traveled, in case they might need it, and also emphasized the anointing by the priest and discouraged anointing by lay people. The anointing that this council promoted was understood as an anointing of the sick, in which the Sign of the Cross was signed on the parts of the body in pain, and performed in the hopes that it would lead to some kind of recovery and healing.

A parallel practice and understanding was developing at the same time in which the anointing was understood not so much as an anointing that would lead to healing but rather an anointing that was the "last consolation" of the Church, preparing a person for death. As this practice developed, a person was anointed, not on the places of the body that were in need of healing, but rather on the senses, hands, and feet, all the while praying that God would forgive the sins that had been committed by the person being anointed. It was this anointing, which by the time of the Middle Ages had prevailed, and which came to be known as the last anointing, *extrema unctio*, extreme unction, the ultimate preparation, following reconciliation and Communion, which prepared a person for the everlasting life to come.

3. Before the Council of Trent

By the time the scholastic theologians such as Saint Thomas Aquinas and Saint Bonaventure discussed the sacrament of the anointing in the thirteenth century, it had been firmly established as a sacrament for the dying, and that was their only experience and understanding of the sacrament. As such, the definitions applied to the sacrament by these theologians reflected this understanding and pastoral practice. Saint Thomas Aquinas, for example, understood that the sacrament of extreme unction was the last liturgical rite of the Church by which Christians were forgiven their sins but also were offered grace to overcome sin and prepare themselves for final judgment. He accepted the fact that the sacred oil (matter) and the prayer prayed (form) during the anointing was always effective because of the promise of Scripture: "The prayer of faith will save the sick" (Jas 5:15).

The only significant debate about the sacrament concerned whether extreme unction should be offered to children and adults who may be unconscious as a result of their illnesses. Saint Thomas taught that children should not receive the sacrament unless they were able to fully comprehend what the prayers signified and were thus able to cooperate with the grace given by God. He did not offer an opinion on whether or not the sacrament could be given to those who were unconscious, which was determined later by other theologians who concluded that it could be administered; the effects of the sacrament would be dependent on whether the soul would choose to cooperate with the grace of God.

From a pastoral point of view, since extreme unction was celebrated only with a seriously ill person (Saint Bonaventure felt that celebration with a person who might recover would not be fulfilling the purpose of the sacrament), it was not celebrated with any regularity. Only the very well-off could afford to have a priest in attendance while they were dying; others had to take their chances and often would die before the priest arrived.

Despite the uneven historical development of the sacrament, which was for the most part unknown because of a lack of access to necessary records, extreme unction was listed and accepted as one of the seven ecclesiastical sacraments and declared to have been instituted by Christ. In 1439, the Council of Florence affirmed this teaching, leaving little doubt that the sacrament was a sacrament of the dying, and making no direct reference to it as the sacrament of the sick.

4. The Council of Trent

The Protestant reformers spent very little time discussing the sacrament and dismissed it almost immediately from consideration. Martin Luther, joined by John Calvin, argued that there was no way that the biblical reference from the apostle James could ever be understood in relationship to extreme unction; James was speaking about anointing sick people, not people who were dying. Since the practice of the sacrament was obviously intended for people who were dying, it was "utter nonsense" to believe that this was what James had in mind.

The Council of Trent did not accept the arguments of the reformers and clearly defined the sacrament as a sign of God's mercy and a way that the Lord prepared the soul for eternal life. The bishops did admit that the institution of the sacrament, when Christ sent out his apostles to preach and heal (Mk 6:13), might not be clearly seen, but the matter was firmly established by the apostle James and therefore accepted as coming from the Lord. The council also taught that the sacrament was intended for those who were sick, but especially for those "so dangerously ill that they seem to be at the point of death."

With the publication of the official sacramentary of 1614, the ritual for the celebration of the sacrament as extreme unction was established. There was little or no change to the practice or the understanding of the sacrament until the Second Vatican Council.

5. Contemporary Practice

The Second Vatican Council, in one of its first acts, declared that a better name for extreme unction was the sacrament of the anointing of the sick. The bishops taught that this sacrament "is not a sacrament only for those who are at the point of death. Hence, as soon as anyone of the faithful begins to be in danger of death from sickness or old age, the fitting time for him to receive this sacrament has certainly already arrived" (Constitution on the Sacred Liturgy, §73). In this one action, centuries of pastoral practice and sacramental interpretation were dramatically reversed, not on a whim, but rather because the bishops had available to them the results of modern historical research, which enabled them to direct the Church to restore the sacrament to its original purpose.

The most significant change in the pastoral practice of this sacrament was that it was no longer reserved to the dying but rather was to be administered when a person discovered that he or she had any kind of serious illness. One could celebrate the sacrament before going to the hospital for surgery and, in another significant directive, could also celebrate the sacrament upon reaching an advanced age (CCC 1514–1515).

Even the words prayed during the anointing vividly illustrate the restoration and emphasis: "Through this holy anointing may the Lord in his love and mercy help you with the grace of the Holy Spirit"; and "May the Lord who frees you from sin save you and raise you up" (CCC 1513). Contrasted with the words of extreme unction,

"Through this holy anointing and his tender mercy may the Lord forgive whatever sins you have committed by sight, by hearing...," which suggests a completely different meaning and emphasis.

The restoration of the sacrament not only effected change in the understanding and the rite of the sacrament but also seemed to restore an emphasis on the healing ministry itself. It is not at all unusual for a Catholic parish to encourage prayer for the sick and the infirm during the Prayers of the Faithful in the Mass, to provide an opportunity for home visitation of the sick by specially trained lay people in addition to the clergy, and to offer numerous opportunities throughout the year for community liturgical celebrations of the healing power of the Lord.

6. The Rite of the Anointing of the Sick

The revised rite of the sacrament provides for opportunities for the sacrament to be celebrated individually, in a special group such as a group of residents in a nursing home, and in a larger communal celebration during a special Mass in the parish. Of course, the sacrament is still celebrated at the bedside of a person who is seriously ill and near death. At times, the celebration of the sacrament is preceded by a celebration of the sacrament of penance and reconciliation and followed by the sacrament of the Eucharist (CCC 1517). Regardless of where and with whom the sacrament is celebrated, it consists of the proclamation of the Word of God, an act of repentance, the laying on of hands, and the anointing with the blessed oil (CCC 1519).

The liturgical celebration of the sacrament for an individual person during a home visitation by the priest, for example, begins with the greeting, "Peace to this house and to all who live in it," or with something similar. The priest then reminds everyone present that the sacrament that is to be celebrated is intended for healing, reminding everyone of the words of the apostle James (5:14–15). He then asks all to reflect for a moment on their own need for healing. After a few moments of reflection, a brief penitential prayer is prayed, followed by a reading from the Word of God and a short homily.

In response to the Word of God, a litany is prayed which focuses the attention of everyone on the person who is to be anointed and his or her particular need for an experience of God's healing power. At the conclusion of the litany, the priest then imposes his hands on the head of the person who is to be anointed and all silently pray. The priest then anoints the person on the forehead, praying as follows: "Through this holy anointing / may the Lord in his love and mercy help you / with the grace of the Holy Spirit," and on their hands, while praying "May the Lord who frees you from sin / save you and raise you up."

The ritual of the anointing concludes as the priest prays, "Lord Jesus Christ, our Redeemer, / by the power of the Holy Spirit, / ease the sufferings of our sick sister (brother) / and make her (him) well again in mind and body. / In your loving kindness forgive her (his) sins / and grant her (him) full health / so that she (he) may be restored to your service. You are Lord for ever and ever. Amen."

At this point holy Communion, or in the case of those very near death, Viaticum (a Latin word, meaning "food for the journey") is often distributed. In preparation for the Eucharist, all are invited to pray the Our Father together, and then the priest raises the host and prays, "This is the Lamb of God / who takes away the sins of the world. / Happy are those who are called to his supper," to which all respond, "Lord, I am not worthy to receive you / but only say the word and I shall be healed." Holy Communion is then distributed, followed by some time for reflection and silent prayer. The rite is concluded with a blessing and the traditional prayer of dismissal, "Let us go in peace to love and serve the Lord."

7. The Effects of the Anointing of the Sick

The effects of the sacrament include particular gifts of the Holy Spirit, union with the passion of Christ, ecclesial grace, and preparation for the final journey. The Church understands that the particular gift of the Holy Spirit received in this sacrament may include strength, peace, and courage, helping a person give full trust and faith to God, including the forgiveness of sin, and the restoration of health (CCC 1520). Union with the passion of Christ signifies a belief that the sufferings that are being endured as a result of original sin become, through the power of the Holy Spirit, a kind of participation in the saving work of Jesus (CCC 1521). The ecclesial grace that is experienced is the grace of knowing that the entire Church prays with the person and for them, not only for their particular sufferings but also for all those other people who also suffer throughout the world (CCC 1522). Finally, the sacrament is a preparation for the final journey by completing the anointing first received at baptism, then at confirmation, and now at the final moment, bringing the person to the fullness of life in Christ (CCC 1523).

8. Pastoral Concerns

People today are becoming more accustomed to the fact that the sacrament of the anointing of the sick is not for the dying alone. Even if remnants of that attitude still exist, we should not wait until one is at the point of death to call a priest.

However, we must remember the basic purpose of the anointing of the sick as a sacramental healing grace for the seriously ill, the infirm, and the aged. The sacrament is not meant to be a devotional practice for those who feel a need for healing.

The Church acknowledges that there are other valid ways to heal and that certain persons possess the gift of healing. A service over which a faith healer presides is ordinarily a paraliturgical healing service, unless it is designated as a sacrament. These services are beneficial and sometimes effect cures. However, there must be a clear distinction between a paraliturgical healing service, which can be grace-filled, and the sacrament of anointing of the sick, the official Church sacrament.

9. Essentials

Name: Sacrament of Anointing, Sacrament of the Sick.

Sacramental Identification: Sacrament of healing.

Minimum Age: Age of reason, traditionally understood as age seven.

Can Be Repeated? Yes, as often as needed.

Sacramental Character Imparted? No.

Matter: Anointing with the oil of the sick.

Form: "Through this holy anointing may the Lord in his love and mercy help you with the grace of the Holy Spirit. May the Lord who frees you from sin, save you, and raise you up."

Ordinary Minister: Priest.

Extraordinary Minister: None.

PART FOUR

The Sacraments of Communion and Mission

The Church understands the sacraments of initiation—baptism, confirmation, and Eucharist—as sacraments that confer the necessary grace that individuals need in order to respond to their vocation, and the universal call to holiness. The sacraments of initiation provide the opportunity for the Holy Spirit to work in and through the individual person and, as such, are personal gifts of that same Spirit and are necessary for salvation. However, the kingdom of God is not about just personal salvation alone, but also the salvation of all people, which is the particular mission of the Church, in which all the baptized join their talents and their efforts.

Two sacraments, the sacraments of matrimony and holy orders, are sacraments that are directed toward others, and not sacraments specifically for the person who receives them. They obviously help a person live out his or her call and vocation, and they contribute to a person's growth in holiness, but the grace of the sacrament is also meant to be shared, to build up the Body of Christ.

I. Holy Orders

Holy Orders is the sacrament through which the mission entrusted by Christ to his apostles continues to be exercised in the Church until the end of time: thus it is the sacrament of apostolic ministry. It includes three degrees: episcopate, presbyterate, and diaconate (CCC 1536).

1. Jesus the Priest

In the Jewish experience of Old Testament priesthood, a traditional understanding of priesthood would include the qualities of service, authority, and leadership. Within the Jewish tradition, priesthood was a hereditary function, usually reserved to members of the clan of Aaron and the tribe of Levi (Ex 28–29; 32:25–29). The priests of that time and place offered sacrifice, interpreted the Mosaic Law, took care of the holy places, and staffed the Temple in Jerusalem. Their role was not particularly exclusive, however, because in addition to the priests there were also scribes, rabbis, and elders, all of whom shared in the ministry of service, authority, and leadership.

The contemporaries of Jesus recognized Jesus as a person who served, who taught with authority, and who provided leadership, but they never identified him as a priest. The more common titles usually associated with Jesus included rabbi (Mk 9:5), teacher (Lk 11:45), Lord (Jn 11:39), Messiah (Mk 8:29), and prophet (Lk 7:16). Although it can be asserted that the people recognized in his ministry certain functions and qualities that could be associated with the role of a priest, it can also be stated that they never made the connection. It was only later, years after his death and resurrection, that the writer of the Letter to the Hebrews identified Jesus as the "high priest" (Heb 4:14; 5:10). This identification probably happened as a result of the reflection of the early communities on the meaning of Christ's passion and death, a reflection that led them to the conclusion that his death on the cross was a sacrifice, and as sacrifice, Jesus was both priest (the person who offers the sacrifice on behalf of the people) and victim.

But perhaps it was the witness of his life of service that prompted people to accept the designation of Jesus as priest, for it was from this example of service that the early Christian community determined directives and interpretations about their understanding and practice of ministry. The words of Jesus formed the core principle for this ministerial role: "But it is not so among you; but whoever wishes to be great among you must be your servant, and whoever wishes to be first among you must be slave of all" (Mk 10:43–44).

2. Ministry in the Early Church

The apostles and disciples of Jesus clearly exercised authority and leadership in the early communities. They acted as teachers and preachers, not only within the community but also outside of the community, and they seemed to be formed together as a type of council of elders, making necessary decisions about belief and practice (Acts 4–6, 8, 10). They lived their lives in imitation of the life of service and ministry modeled by the Lord, announcing the coming of the kingdom, proclaiming Jesus as the Messiah, healing the sick, and proclaiming God's forgiveness to all (Acts 2–6). The apostle Peter seemed to act as the designed leader of the group (Acts 1:15 16).

The original twelve were referred to as *apostoloi*, which may be translated as "ambassador" (because they had been called and sent by the Lord to preach the kingdom), and the work that they performed was identified as *diakonia*, which meant "ministry" or "service." Eventually, the original twelve were joined in their ministry of service by other *apostoloi* and by *presbyteros* (elder) and *episkopos* (elder in charge; supervisor). Other ministers named *diakonoi* (deacons) served the internal needs of the community and were also appointed (1 Tim 3:8–13; Titus 1:6–9). It seems in most instances that the people chosen for this ministry and service were selected from among the community, were prayed over, and had hands imposed upon them, designating them for their special work (Acts 6:1–6; 1 Tim 4:14).

This gradual development and identity of ministers who were called to serve the community seemed to be well in place by at least the year 110 A.D. In Antioch, for example, the *episkopos* Ignatius clearly understood that he was in charge of the local community and insisted that he be present for all baptisms and for the celebration of the Eucharist. The same authority and leadership was exercised in other communities by each of their *episkopos* also, who were assisted in ministry by the *presbyters* and *deacons*.

In the year 313 A.D., the Roman Emperor Constantine officially recognized Christianity and began to show favor to the new religion. He permitted *bishops* (from the Greek, Latin, and Anglo-Saxon variations of *episkopos*), since they were perceived leaders in their communities, to expand their authority and to act as magistrates and wear the distinctive garb of the office. *Priests* (from the Greek and the Latin *presbyter*) also began to wear distinctive clothing because the community that was now gathered at the Eucharist was quite large and some sort of distinction seemed to be helpful. But it was not only the clothing that was beginning to change; more and more, again because of the tremendous growth of Christianity, other changes, most notably in the role of the priest were slowly introduced. Traditionally, it was the bishop who would preside at the Eucharist but now it was the priest who presided and performed the baptisms, and the bishop more and more assumed a specific role as the primary teacher and administrator.

A distinctive process of selection and ordination of those called to be bishops, priests, and deacons also seems to have been in place. The entire Christian community, or in some places the priests of that place, elected their bishop. The elected bishop was then ordained for service by neighboring bishops. The bishop ordained those selected to be priests, and the local priests with whom they would minister joined the bishop in the imposition of hands. Only the bishop, on the other hand, since it was understood that deacons were in service to the Church through the bishop, ordained deacons.

By the fifth century, bishops and priests had been firmly established and put in place in most of the Christian communities, and a normal pastoral practice and routine seems to have been followed. However deacons, probably because the priests had by this time assumed most of their functions, slowly began to disappear, at least as a distinct ministry; the diaconate was preserved as a "step" in the progression of "holy orders" on the way to the priesthood.

Another development occurred because of the rise of monasticism and the need for the monks to join in the task of converting and baptizing the Germanic tribes that were migrating into Europe. This development was that of celibacy. The monks, because they lived together in monasteries, lived a celibate life. The people, when they experienced celibate priests, seemed to prefer them because they understood celibacy as a sign of priests's dedication to God. Although the first experience of the celibate priesthood occurred in the fifth century, it was not until later, with the reforms introduced by Pope Gregory the Great, that celibacy became common and still centuries later, after the Council of Trent, when celibacy became both mandatory and enforceable.

With all of these developments, some as a result of cultural influences and some as a result of particular councils of bishops responding to a particular need or challenge, came the establishment of a specific clerical class. The Christian clergy were formed into a hierarchical group with the bishop at the top and the porters (the lowest ecclesial ministry) at the bottom. In an empire that was slowly disintegrating, it was only a matter of time before this distinct clerical class would step into the authority vacuum that resulted from the collapse of the governmental structures. Governance by the decaying Roman Empire was slowly replaced by a system of power and authority, which today we recognize as feudalism.

3. Ministry Before the Council of Trent

The Christian world before the Council of Trent was a world that was neatly divided into two realities—each of which affected the lives of most people. A feudal system of power and authority was in place where the king, who claimed to be chosen and anointed by God, ruled through his vassal lords (who were dependent on him for their power and authority) down to the landed peasantry. In the Church, authority was more and more exercised by the pope, through the bishops, to the priests and the lower clergy, to the people of God. Unfortunately, there was often an intermingling between the two lines of authority because bishops, chosen from the upper classes, possessed not only spiritual authority but were also vassal lords to a secular king. This intermingling of secular power and spiritual power would eventually cause problems that would affect both the secular hierarchy and the spiritual hierarchy.

Although it would be an oversimplification, many of the problems that confronted the Council of Trent were the direct result of the uneasy intermingling that existed between secular power and spiritual power. Because authority and power in the Church was exercised through those who had received holy orders and had been ordained, this spiritual/secular struggle and its ramifications obviously influenced the Church's understanding and practice of ordained ministry.

Although ministry was still understood as service, the emphasis seemed to be more and more on authority and on jurisdiction (the power and the permission to exercise the authority). Holy orders was conferred on a candidate for ordination by the bishop who possessed both the jurisdiction and the authority to do so. The newly ordained priest, for example, was invested with the symbols of his power at the time of ordination, the stole and the chasuble, the chalice and the paten. He was presented with these symbols by the bishop, who at his consecration had also received the symbols of authority, stole, ring, crosier, and miter (after the eleventh century). Other candidates for holy orders, who were progressing through the steps of the sacrament, also received their symbols of authority: for example, the porter received a key; the lector received the book of the epistles; the acolytes a candle; and the transitional deacon received the book of the gospels.

In the eyes of the people, this presentation of the symbols of power and authority was something with which they were very familiar because of its similarities to the feudal system. The king, for example, would be presented with a crown and a scepter as a sign of his power and authority, and so it seemed not at all unusual that those who exercised spiritual power would also receive symbols of their spiritual power and authority.

4. The Council of Trent

The Protestant reformers rejected most of the Catholic understanding and practice of the priesthood that had developed over the centuries and insisted on a return to their interpretation of the biblical understanding of ministry. Martin Luther, for example, argued that the commission to preach, teach, and baptize was given by Christ to the entire Church (1 Pet 2:5), and not just to bishops and priests. He therefore rejected the idea of a specially selected and ordained group of ministers, except as a matter of Church discipline and order. Not surprisingly, the bishops of the Council of Trent did not accept Luther's viewpoint, and they firmly reasserted that holy orders was a sacrament instituted by Christ, and that the development of the sacrament could be traced directly to Jesus and to the writings of the Fathers of the Church.

Most of what the council said about the priesthood was related to the role of the priest in each of the sacraments as they are defined (for example, the role of the priest in the celebration of the sacrifice of the Mass). The council did, however, affirm that Christ at the Last Supper instituted the priesthood and that Christ intended that the memorial of his sacrifice on Calvary be celebrated again and again. As such, Christ had established a new priesthood that replaced the priesthood of the Old Testament. The council argued that holy orders was a sacrament and that it conferred grace on the person who received it (2 Tim 1:6). Although the council did not say anything directly about celibacy as a requirement for priesthood, nevertheless the reforms in the pastoral practice of ministry in the Church and the training of ministers effectively reinforced this requirement.

Perhaps, however, the model of Church that was established and put in place by the council can best illustrate the lasting Tridentine reform and teaching. Within years after the work of the bishops had been completed, a seminary system for the training of priests had been established. Priests were trained in theology and prayer, but also instilled with an understanding of Church order and discipline. The hierarchical structure of the Church, from the pope, to the bishops, to the priests, to the lay people, eventually provided a stable and formidable structure, which for all intents and purposes did not change for almost four hundred years. Everyone understood and accepted their role in this structure, and all seemed to be confident and assured that all was well and intended by God to be this way.

5. Contemporary Ministry

Since the Second Vatican Council, the idea of ministry in the Church, and the role of those who have been ordained for ministry in the Church, has been evolving. Perhaps the most profound changes have occurred in the role and expectations of the ordained priesthood, and the parallel development of a substantial ministry regularly performed by members of the laity, both men and women. Theological and cultural realities have contributed to this sustained development and continue to do so. Tasks that were routinely performed by a priest, such as visiting a person in the hospital or someone who is homebound, more and more are performed by the members of the laity, or in some cases, by a reconstituted and energized permanent diaconate. In addition, traditional roles of administration are now routinely delegated by the resident pastor of a parish to a lay business manager or administrator: the priest has become focused on the sacramental and liturgical life of the community.

As the role of ministry has changed and developed in response to the needs of the Christian community, the theology of ordained ministry and the role and purpose of those who receive the sacrament of holy orders have also changed. The Second Vatican Council emphasized the idea of the "priesthood of the faithful," a return to the biblical teaching of the people of God as "a kingdom of priests and a holy nation" (Ex 19:6; Isa 61:6). At the same time, the council repeated the teaching that even though all share in priesthood and therefore in the mission of the Church by virtue of their baptism (CCC 1546), certain members of the Church are nevertheless designated as ministers of the Word and the sacraments (CCC 1538–1540).

Ordained ministry, which is understood as "ministerial or hierarchical" (CCC 1547), is exercised in the name of Jesus. The priest, by virtue of the sacrament of holy orders, acts in *persona Christi Capitis,* or in other words, acts in the place of the person of Christ himself (CCC 1548). This presence of Christ in the priest does not mean that the priest is somehow preserved from human weakness or sin, but rather that the power of the Holy Spirit guarantees and enables the specific graced encounter with Christ that is intended by the sacramental action (CCC 1550). In addition to acting in the name of Christ, the ministry of the priest is also performed in the name of the Church, since the Church is the Body of Christ (CCC 1552–1553).

Ministerial priesthood consists of three distinct orders (from the Greek *taxeis,* meaning "that which forms a hierarchy"): the order of *episcoporum* (bishop), the order of *presbyterorum* (priest), and the order of *diaconorum* (deacon). Admission into one of these three orders is not a simple matter of election, or delegation, designation, or institution, but rather is understood as a gift of the Holy Spirit, which comes from Christ through his Church. The gift is conferred through ordination *(consecratio),* the laying on of hands by the bishop (the matter) with the prayer of consecration being the form (CCC 1537–1538).

6. The Ministry of Bishops

From the earliest periods in the history of the Church, the ordained ministry has been exercised in different degrees: bishops, priests, and deacons (CCC 1554). It has been understood that although all three degrees are manifestations of the gift of the Holy Spirit in ordination, those who have been called, chosen, and anointed as bishops have the "fullness" of the sacrament. Or in other words, it is the bishops who, through an unbroken succession going back to the beginning, are the transmitters of the teaching and tradition of the apostles (CCC 1555).

The bishop is understood as the visible representative of Christ, *in Eius persona agant*, and it is through episcopal ordination that the person ordained becomes teacher, shepherd, and priest, the same qualities and attributes of Christ himself (CCC 1558). A bishop acts collegially in union with other bishops, and as a further sign of the collegial ministry exercised by the bishop, he is appointed to the ministry by the bishop of Rome (the pope), "the supreme visible bond of the communion of the particular Churches in the one Church and the guarantor of their freedom" (CCC 1559).

The specific ministry of a bishop is the pastoral care of a particular area, a diocese or archdiocese, where he ministers with his coworkers, the priests assigned to the diocese. Although a bishop is viewed as the primary administrator of the diocese and all of the ministerial efforts within the diocese, his primary obligation is not administration but rather sanctification, pastoral care, and teaching.

7. The Ministry of Priests

The priest, although he shares in the ministry of the bishop by virtue of his ordination, ministers by the authority of his bishop. It is the bishop who delegates to the priest particular responsibilities and tasks and, for this reason, a priest is understood as a "co-worker of the episcopal order" (CCC 1562). For priests, the fullness of their ordination is celebrated when they function as the celebrant of the Eucharist, the sacrifice of the Mass (CCC 1566).

For most Catholics, the priest is their primary contact and relationship with the Church. They may well be vaguely aware of the theology of priesthood and understand on some level that only the bishop has the "fullness of holy orders" but, for them, in their everyday experience, it is the priest who celebrates Mass, who teaches and preaches the Word of God, who baptizes, forgives their sins in the name of Jesus, witnesses their marriages, is present to anoint them when they are sick, and bury them when they are dead.

8. The Ministry of Deacons

The restoration of the diaconate as a separate ministry in the Church and not simply a transitional step on the path to priesthood was the result of the work of the Second Vatican Council. The permanent diaconate, which can be conferred on married men, is a sharing in the sacrament of holy orders, but it is an ordination to ministry and not to priesthood (CCC 1569). A deacon assists the bishop and the priest in the celebration of the Eucharist, proclaims the gospel and preaches, presides over funerals, and may witness and bless a marriage. A deacon may also baptize.

9. The Rite of Ordination

Ordination to the priesthood takes place within the context of the Eucharist, usually at the cathedral parish but occasionally at the home parish of the person who is to be ordained. The assembly gathers, and the bishop, along with many other priests of the diocese, and those who are to be ordained to the priesthood, process into the church. The candidates for priesthood (at this point they have been transitional deacons for an extended period of time), process into the church wearing an alb and a stole.

The Mass begins as usual and continues in the normal way through the proclamation of the gospel at which time the bishop puts on his miter and sits in a chair that has been placed in front of the altar specifically for this occasion. After he is seated, the bishop says, "Those to be ordained priest please come forward."

The candidates are then presented to the bishop, usually by someone who has been associated with their training and education, with the words, "Most Reverend Father, holy mother Church asks you to ordain these men, our brothers for service as priests." The bishop asks, "Do you judge them to be worthy?" The person who presents the candidates responds, "After inquiry among the people of Christ and upon recommendation of those concerned with their training, I testify that they have been found worthy." The bishop then indicates that he accepts the recommendation, to which the people may respond, "Thanks be to God," or even more common, the gathered assembly breaks out into applause, indicating that they too accept the recommendation and are willing to have the candidates ordained to the priesthood (election).

The candidates are then seated and the bishop begins his instruction, usually while seated in the chair, in which he explains to the congregation the meaning of ordination and the expectations of the Church of those who are to be ordained. When he completes his instruction, he then asks those who are to be ordained if they are ready to celebrate the sacraments, preach, and lead a holy and prayerful life. The candidates indicate that they are willing to do so. The bishop continues by inquiring if the candidates are willing to respect and obey him as bishop, and his successors, to which the candidates respond by promising, "I do." The bishop concludes this portion of the rite by praying, "May God who has begun the good work in you bring it to fulfillment."

Next, the bishop invites the gathered assembly to kneel, and he invites those who are to be ordained to prostrate themselves on the ground before the altar while the community prays. It is traditional that after a few moments of silent prayer the Litany of the Saints is sung, invoking the names of the apostles, familiar and well-known saints, and often the patron saints of the diocese and of the candidates. At the conclusion of the litany, the candidates present themselves, in silence, to the bishop who imposes his hands on them. After the bishop imposes his hands, all of the priests who are present, as a sign of solidarity and communion, also impose their hands on the heads of the candidates, all the while in silence (CCC 1568).

When the imposition of hands is completed, the bishop, with the priests of the diocese on either side of him, extends his hands in blessing, joined by all the priests, and he prays the solemn prayer of consecration: "Come to our help, / Lord, holy Father, almighty and eternal God; / you are the source of every honor and dignity, / of all progress and stability. / ...Almighty Father, grant to this servant of yours / the dignity of the priesthood. / Renew within him the Spirit of holiness. / As a coworker with the order of bishops / may he be faithful to the ministry / that he receives from you, Lord God, / and be to others a model of right conduct...."

When the prayer of consecration is prayed, other symbolic actions take place. The newly ordained priest is invested in the chasuble, the outer garment worn by the priest at Mass. This investiture is sometimes performed by the bishop, sometimes by the parents of the new priest, or sometimes by a priest mentor. After the investiture, the newly ordained presents himself to the bishop who anoints his hands with sacred chrism while praying, "The Father anointed our Lord Jesus Christ / through the power of the Holy Spirit. / May Jesus preserve you to sanctify the Christian people / and to offer sacrifice to God."

After the anointing with oil, the newly ordained present themselves to the bishop who presents them with the symbols of the Eucharist, the gifts that the priest will offer in sacrifice to the Father, through the power of the Holy Spirit. The priest accepts the chalice (which holds the wine) and the paten (which holds the host) as the bishop says, "Accept from the holy people of God the gifts to be offered to him. Know what you are doing, and imitate the mystery you celebrate: model your life on the mystery of the Lord's cross." Finally, in a sign of the fraternal care that they have for each other, the bishop then embraces the newly ordained with the sign of peace and invites all the other priests present to also share this fraternal symbol. It is customary for the newly ordained to greet relatives and friends with the sign of peace immediately after this ritual and before the Mass continues in the usual way with the presentation of the gifts.

The newly ordained join the bishop and the rest of the priests in concelebrating their "first Mass." Although there will be other "first Mass" celebrations that follow with family and friends, the Mass of ordination is truly the first Mass celebrated by the newly ordained, and it is fitting that it is so, since the Eucharist celebrated with the bishop is "an expression of the Church gathered around the altar, with the one who represents Christ" (CCC 1561).

10. The Effects of Ordination

The effects of the sacrament include an indelible spiritual character (mark) signifying that the person has received a special grace of the Holy Spirit for ministry and service. Holy orders, like baptism and confirmation, cannot be repeated once it has been celebrated; it is also considered a permanent transformation in the relationship with the Lord and for this reason is never considered as a temporary state in life (CCC 1581–1582). The sacrament also confers the necessary grace proper to the order received: for a bishop, the grace of strength and a governing spirit, which impels him to preach the gospel (CCC 1586); for a priest, the grace to proclaim the ministry of the Word and sacrifice (CCC 1587); and for a deacon, the grace to minister in service of the gospel and in works of charity (CCC 1588).

11. Pastoral Concerns

The law of celibacy is perhaps one of the major pastoral concerns of the sacrament of holy orders. Celibacy is being challenged today more than ever before. However, celibacy remains the norm for priests of the Roman rite. The Church looks upon celibacy as a special gift of the Lord and is committed to upholding it. By not attaching oneself to any particular person, the celibate priest is a powerful reminder that all human relationships have their source and root in God.

Perhaps the most widely felt pastoral concern in the Church today regarding holy orders is the shortage of priestly vocations. Although there is increased participation of laity in the ministries of the Church, the priest makes it possible for the liturgical and sacramental life of the Church to continue. The dearth of priests has somewhat been eased by the admission of second-career men to the priesthood and policies concerning a more equable distribution of priests to areas that have a shortage of priests.

Although optional celibacy and women's ordination are debated issues, the Church is determined not to depart from its long-standing law and deepest tradition of a celibate male priesthood.

12. Essentials

Name: Sacrament of Holy Orders (also called Ordination).

Sacramental Identification: Sacrament of communion and mission.

Minimum Age: For a priest, the age is 25; for transitional deacons 23; for permanent deacons who are not married, 25; and for permanent deacons who are married, 35, with the consent of their wife (Canon 1031 of the Code of Canon Law).

Can Be Repeated? No.

Sacramental Character Imparted? Yes.

Matter: Imposition of hands.

Form: Specific prayer of consecration for each order received is found in the sections that follow.

Ordinary Minister: Bishop.

Extraordinary Minister: None.

13. Prayer of Consecration for Deacons

Almighty God,
Be present with us by your power.
You are the source of all honor,
you assign to each his rank,
you give to each his ministry.
You remain unchanged,
but you watch over all creation and make it new
through your Son, Jesus Christ, our Lord:
he is your Word, your power, and your wisdom.
You foresee all things in your eternal providence
And make due provision for every age.
You make the Church, Christ's Body,
grow to its full stature as a new and greater temple.
You enrich it with every kind of grace
And perfect it with a diversity of members
to serve the whole Body in a wonderful pattern of unity.

You established a threefold ministry of worship
    and service
For the glory of your name.
As ministers of your tabernacle you chose the sons of Levi
and gave them your blessing as their everlasting inheritance.

In the first days of your Church
under the inspiration of the Holy Spirit
the apostles of your Son appointed seven men of good repute
to assist them in the daily ministry;
so that they themselves might be more free for prayer
    and preaching.
By prayer and the laying on of hands
the apostles entrusted to those chosen men the ministry
    of serving at tables.
Lord,
Look with favor on this servant of yours,
whom we now dedicate to the office of deacon,
to minister at your holy altar.

Lord,
Send forth upon him the Holy Spirit,
that he may be strengthened
by the gift of your sevenfold grace
to carry out faithfully the work of the ministry.
May he excel in every virtue:
in love that is sincere,
in concern for the sick and the poor,
in unassuming authority,
in self-discipline,
and in holiness of life.
May his conduct exemplify your commandments
and lead your people to imitate his purity of life.
May he remain strong and steadfast in Christ,
giving to the world the witness of a pure conscience.
May he in this life imitate your Son,
who came, not to be served, but to serve,
and one day reign with him in heaven.

We ask this through our Lord Jesus Christ, your Son,
Who lives and reigns with you and the Holy Spirit,
One God, for ever and ever. Amen.

14. Prayer of Consecration for Priests

Come to our help,
Lord, holy Father, almighty and eternal God;
you are the source of every honor and dignity,
of all progress and stability.
You watch over the growing family of man
by your gift of wisdom and your pattern of order.
When you had appointed high priests to rule your people,
you chose other men next to them in rank and dignity
to be with them and help them in their task;
and so there grew up
the ranks of priests and the offices of Levites,
established by sacred rites.

In the desert
you extended the spirit of Moses to seventy wise men
who helped him to rule the great company of his people.
You shared among the sons of Aaron
the fullness of their father's power,
to provide worthy priests in sufficient number
for the increasing rites of sacrifice and worship.
With the same loving care
you gave companions to your Son's apostles
to help in teaching the faith:
they preached the gospel to the whole world.
Lord,
grant also to us such fellow workers,
for we are weak and our need is greater.

Almighty Father,
grant to this servant of yours
the dignity of the priesthood.
Renew within him the Spirit of holiness.
As a coworker with the order of bishops
may he be faithful to the ministry
that he receive from you, Lord God,
and be to others a model of right conduct.

May he be faithful in working with the order of bishops,
so that the words of the gospel may reach the ends of the earth,
and the family of nations,
made one in Christ,
may become God's one, holy people.

We ask this through our Lord Jesus Christ, your Son,
who lives and reigns with you and the Holy Spirit,
one God, for ever and ever.
Amen.

15. Prayer of Consecration for Bishops

God the Father of our Lord Jesus Christ,
Father of mercies and God of all consolation,
you dwell in heaven,
yet look with compassion on all that is humble.
You know all things before they come to be;
by your gracious word
you have established the plan of your Church.

From the beginning
you chose the descendants of Abraham to be your holy nation.
You established rulers and priests,
and did not leave your sanctuary without ministers to serve you.

111

From the creation of the world
you have been pleased to be glorified
by those whom you have chosen.

(All the consecrating bishops recite the following part of the prayer.)

So now pour out upon this chosen one
that power which is from you,
the governing Spirit
whom you gave to your beloved Son, Jesus Christ,
the Spirit given by him to the holy apostles,
who founded the Church in every place to be your temple
for the unceasing glory and praise of your name.

(The principal consecrator bishop continues alone.)

Father, you know all hearts.
You have chosen your servant for the office of bishop.
May he be a shepherd to your holy flock,
and a high priest blameless in your sight,
ministering to you night and day;
may he always gain the blessing of your favor
and offer the gifts of your holy Church.
Through the Spirit who gives the grace of high priesthood
grant him the power
to forgive sins as you have commanded,
to assign ministries you have decreed,
and to loose every bond by the authority
    which you gave to your apostles.
May he be pleasing to you by his gentleness and purity of heart,
presenting a fragrant offering to you,
through Jesus Christ, your Son,

through whom glory and power and honor are yours
with the Holy Spirit
in your holy Church
now, and for ever. Amen.

II. Matrimony

The matrimonial covenant, by which a man and a woman estab-
lish between themselves a partnership of the whole of life, is by its
nature ordered toward the good of the spouses and the procreation
and education of offspring; this covenant between baptized persons
has been raised by Christ the Lord to the dignity of a sacrament
(Canon 1055.1 of the Code of Canon Law and CCC 1601).

1. Jesus and Marriage

In the time of Jesus, marriage was not so much a religious matter as
it was a family matter. This is not to say that marriage did not have
religious meaning or consequence, but is rather an attempt to discuss marriage within its sociological context, or at least within the
context of how Jesus may have experienced marriage and how he
may have understood what he experienced. For example, in the first
century, marriage was a state in life, expected in the normal course
of events for all men and women. Marriage was understood as an
agreement, contract, or covenant that was arranged between two
families; our modern notion of romance rarely influenced the choice
of a spouse. The fathers of the bride and groom mutually agreed
upon the union, determined the gifts that would be exchanged, and
even presided over the ceremony.

In the culture of first century Palestine, as it was in most of the
ancient Near East, marriage was understood as a kind of partnership
and each partner had specific duties and responsibilities that he or

she was expected to fulfill. The husband was expected to provide some kind of living for the family, either through a learned trade or perhaps as a day laborer, and to provide the necessary leadership and make required judgments and decisions. The wife was expected to bear children and to manage the normal tasks of the household. No one assumed that the partnership was one of equality but it was routinely understood and accepted by all that if the man and woman in the marriage performed their tasks and completed their responsibilities the marriage would be a successful partnership, effectively contributing to their eventual happiness and the stability of the society in which they lived. There were no doubt religious concerns, for example, fidelity to the requirements of the covenant and a regular practice of the traditions, but the overriding consideration was the specific roles and functions to be fulfilled.

A core value within this kind of partnership was the assumption that both spouses would be faithful to their appointed tasks and to each other; if this was not the case, the partnership would be weakened and the stability of the family and, by extension, the stability of the society would be threatened. For this reason, a very severe penalty for adultery was imposed—death by stoning. A secondary concern was if, despite the best efforts of the man and the woman, the partnership became intolerable, some remedy would need to be applied. For this reason, divorce was accepted and could be initiated by the man; in such an instance, the woman would be sent back to her family and certain gifts (dowry) would be returned to the woman's family. There was no remedy available to a woman who found herself in an intolerable situation; the best that she could possibly hope for would be to be able to convince her husband to divorce her.

Within this cultural context, Jesus interacted with married men and women and (as someone from a very small and intimate village) no doubt participated in numerous marriage ceremonies. However, the gospels speak of only two occasions in which we can find Jesus directly experiencing a wedding ceremony and commenting on some aspect of marriage. The first is the occasion of the wedding feast at Cana (Jn 2:1–10), where Jesus is portrayed as a wedding guest and where he performs a miracle of changing the water into wine. The second, and perhaps the most important, is the occasion which is reported in the Gospel of Matthew (5:31–32) and the Gospel of Mark (10:6–9), when Jesus is asked by the scribes and the Pharisees his opinion about divorce. Jesus clearly states: "But from the beginning of creation, 'God made them male and female.' 'For this reason a man shall leave his father and mother and be joined to his wife, and the two shall become one flesh.' (…) Therefore what God has joined together, let no one separate." The Gospel of Luke (16:18) makes the teaching of Jesus even clearer: "Anyone who divorces his wife and marries another commits adultery, and whoever marries a woman divorced from her husband commits adultery."

2. Marriage in the Early Church

During the first centuries of the Church, marriage was still very much a family matter and not a religious concern. Certainly the early Christian community prayed for married couples and for strengthening family life but there was no other official involvement of either the Church or the Christian community. Marriage was still a function presided over by the fathers of the bride and groom, the couple exchanged their consent, and the partnership began. On those occasions when a priest might be present he was present as a guest. Perhaps he might be called upon to bless the newly married couple, but no one assumed that this blessing was necessary or required.

The apostles, and still later the early bishops of the Church, continued to repeat the teaching of Jesus concerning divorce, but said little else about marriage. The apostle Paul, clearly aware of the teaching of Jesus, did feel empowered to add one more condition when a divorce would be acceptable: when a Christian was married to a pagan: "In such a case the brother or sister is not bound. It is to peace that God has called you" (1 Cor 7:15). However, it was not until the fourth century with the teaching of Saint Augustine that the expectations and viewpoint of the Church about marriage began to be clarified, and a rudimentary theology of the sacrament of matrimony began to emerge, with a focus on something other than the issue of divorce. Even then, the impetus for the teaching was provided by the question of what was required if a marriage was not successful.

Saint Augustine, building his reasoning upon the apostle Paul's understanding of marriage as a sign of the love that Christ has for his Church (Eph 5:21 and following, also 1 Pet 3:1–7), argued that just as the love of Christ is permanent, the love of a husband and wife should also be permanent. Saint Augustine presented this argument at the Council of Carthage in 407 A.D. and although it certainly influenced the understanding of the theology of marriage, it did not significantly influence the everyday practice and understanding of marriage or of separation and divorce.

Even after the Council of Carthage and the efforts of Saint Augustine and other bishops, there were numerous occasions when the question of divorce and the conditions of divorce were debated, but it was almost always a conversation that took place within the context of the family (and the property rights and concerns of the family) and not within the context of religion. There continued to be occasional examples of married couples seeking a blessing for their marriage, and even some development of a beginning matrimonial ritual.

The impetus for change in the practice of marriage and the resulting development of a ritual that was to be understood as sacramental occurred because of the collapse of the secular state that accompanied the fall of the Roman Empire. When the secular authority crumbled, bishops stepped into the vacuum that was created and began to impose ecclesiastical rules and regulations on those who desired to be married. Ecclesiastical rules became even more pronounced as a result of the clash between two secular systems of laws and the interpretations that occurred as a consequence of these laws. The two clashing systems were the Roman system, in place within the empire, and the Germanic system, in place with the people migrating into the empire.

Roman law emphasized that marriage was by consent. A man and a woman exchanged mutual consent and were legally married by this mutual exchange. Roman law certainly understood the different process by which two people arrived at the point where consent was exchanged (for instance, an arranged marriage by the parents of the spouses), but what was important and essential was the exchange of the consent between the man and the woman. Germanic law, on the other hand, did not emphasize the exchange of consent by the man and the woman but rather the fact that the marriage was arranged by the parents (parental consent) and then consummated on the wedding night. Validity was therefore a very different matter and, as both systems clashed with each other, various questions and difficulties invariably arose.

The Church, formed by people of the Roman Empire and the people of the migrating tribes, became the point of contact. Although both systems worked well most of the time, it was the exceptions rather than the rule that provided the need for clarification, as is often the case. The exceptions were those occasions when the man and the woman, without permission of the parents, nevertheless exchanged consent with each other, often in secret. Under Roman law they were married but under Germanic law they were engaging in premarital sex and most certainly not married.

In order to solve this problem, the Church insisted that only marriages witnessed by a priest were valid marriages. Obviously, the most convenient place for such a ceremony of witnessing was in the local church and eventually the ceremonies, which at first consisted of a simple blessing, eventually evolved into much more elaborate affairs. By the twelfth century, a special wedding Mass had evolved that made the occasion even more solemn and special.

With all of the legal and secular questions, the clash of two established and powerful cultures, and the entire question of divorce, it could be assumed that the details of what constituted the beginning of a marriage and the end of a marriage was more important than the meaning of the union. Was marriage seen as simply a secular function or was there any understanding of marriage as a sacrament during all of these years?

The answer seems to be that there was at least an appreciation of marriage as a gift from God, a graced moment in the lives of two people, and a general appreciation among the people of God for the need to ground their relationship in gospel values and Church teachings. It also needs to be noted that there was general agreement that marriage was a sacrament because it was a sign of the love between Christ and his Church and because it was a sacred pledge of fidelity between a man and a woman. However, there was also some uncomfortableness in identifying marriage as a sacrament because it obviously existed before Christ (therefore how could it be said that it was instituted by Christ), and because marriage impacted and concerned property rights (how did grace affect property rights), and, finally, because it permitted sexual relations (which were generally perceived within the climate of the day as necessary for the procreation of children but sinful).

Although there may well have been only a simple and primitive theology of marriage in place, there was, on the other hand, a growing set of laws and customs that led to a well-developed canonical system. This fact may come as no surprise because wherever the existence of property and property rights becomes so entangled in marriage, including the whole idea of legitimate and illegitimate children that may have resulted from various kinds of unions, there needs to be some sort of tribunal to sort everything out. The ecclesiastical courts of the Church provided just such a venue and the canonical point of view provided some sort of stability in determining whether a marriage was valid or invalid, a process known then as it is known today as the process of annulment.

3. Marriage Before the Council of Trent

In 1439 the Council of Florence listed marriage among the seven sacraments of the Christian Church. The council taught that marriage was a sacrament because it was a visible sign of the union between Christ and his Church, a sign of fidelity and a permanent sign of love. In addition, the council accepted some of the reasoning offered by Saint Augustine almost one thousand years earlier and taught that marriage was useful because it provided an opportunity for the procreation and education in the faith of the children that might result from the union. Finally, the council insisted that although it was possible for a married couple to receive a dispensation from their marriage, under no circumstances could they remarry again.

Although the Council of Florence did contribute to the formation of a theology of matrimony, it did not succeed in ending either separation or remarriage. Secular and ecclesiastical courts, depending on the country in which the remedy was pursued, continued the practice of granting annulments to people who were able to prove that their marriage was invalid according to existing canonical standards. However, there was little uniformity in the application of standards: a marriage declared valid in one country might just as easily be declared annulled in another country.

4. The Council of Trent

The Protestant reformers, reacting perhaps not only to their conviction that marriage as a sacrament could not be biblically based but also reacting to the uneven application of annulment laws, did not accept marriage as a sacrament. Martin Luther, in his *Babylonian Captivity of the Church*, argued that marriage could not be a sacrament because it existed from the beginning of time and existed even among "non-Christian peoples." He also argued that the text from Ephesians (5:32–33), in which Saint Paul described marriage as a sign of the love between Christ and his Church, should not be understood literally but rather metaphorically. Luther, and most of the other reformers, agreed that God instituted matrimony, but did so as a natural and a social arrangement, most certainly not as a sacrament, at least in the sense proposed by the Roman Church.

Not surprisingly, the bishops of the Council of Trent did not agree with the reformers. Although they waited until the last session of the council in 1563 to make any pronouncements, when they did so they proceeded in a deliberate and thorough manner. The bishops affirmed that God had intended the bonds of matrimony to be unbreakable, that Christ had raised the natural love between two people to perfect love through the power of the Holy Spirit and the grace of the sacrament received, and, finally, they issued a series of canons that clearly defined the rights and obligations of the Church in relationship to the celebration and the practice of the sacrament.

The Council of Trent also went one step further than might have been expected. The bishops taught that in order for a marriage to be valid it must be celebrated in the presence of a priest and two witnesses. In addition, all marriages had to be publicly announced at least three weeks in advance and recorded in the parish records. This new regulation effectively put an end to the old Roman practice of the sole requirement for a marriage being the exchange of consent between the two people involved.

Two points, however, remained unclear about the sacrament of matrimony at the conclusion of the council. The first point concerned the question of who was the minister of the sacrament and the second point concerned the matter and form of the sacrament.

It took a few more years before both of these matters were completely clarified. In reference to the minister of the sacrament, it was determined that the couple were the ministers and the priest was the official Church witness (some had argued that the blessing of the priest was necessary for validity). In reference to the second question, it was determined that the matter and form of the sacrament could be found in the exchange of the consent, the "I do," if you will. The "I do" was the necessary "matter," and the "I do" was also the necessary "form" of the sacrament.

5. Contemporary Understanding

The Second Vatican Council dramatically refocused the sacrament of matrimony, effectively moving the understanding of marriage as some sort of legal contract to an understanding of marriage as a sacrament solidly rooted in Scripture. In the Pastoral Constitution on the Church in the Modern World, the council presented marriage as "an intimate partnership of life and love," a covenant relationship, similar to the covenant relationship between God and the people of Israel as portrayed in the Old Testament (CCC 1612). The council tried to emphasize that marriage is more about relationship than it is about property, rights, and responsibilities.

Still later, the *Catechism of the Catholic Church* expanded on this theme by teaching that the same God who created humanity out of love also calls the people of God to lovingly respond and demonstrate their love for each other. Marriage is one example of the way that love can become an image of "the absolute and unfailing love" that God has for his people (CCC 1604). Since marriage is a sign of the love of God, it is also a relationship that signifies and communicates grace, not only to the spouses, but also to the entire Church (CCC 1617).

The *Catechism* does not ignore the difficulties expressed first by the Protestant reformers and other people of good faith, but rather explicitly addresses their concerns. Although marriage is definitely present in all societies both Christian and non-Christian, and although there is no doubt that the health and well-being of society is dependent in a large part on the health and well-being of family life, marriage is more than a human institution (CCC 1603). It is only through the help (sacramental grace) provided by the Holy Spirit that man and woman will be able to achieve the union of their lives for which they have been created (CCC 1608). It is for this reason that marriage is a "true sacrament of the New Covenant" (CCC 1617).

Finally, the contemporary theology of the sacrament reaffirms the teaching that it has been consistently the will of God that marriage is to be understood and accepted as a sacrament of unity and indissolubility. Rooting sacramental theology in the words of Scripture, specifically in the books of Ruth, Tobit, and the Song of Songs, the faithful are reminded that marriage is a reflection of God's love—a love "strong as death" that "many waters cannot quench" (CCC 1611 and Song 8:6–7).

One contemporary nuance of the sacramental theology of marriage, a fundamental reason for the sacramental union of a man and a woman but not really an issue or a concern until recently, is the procreation of children. It has not been until modern times that the emphasis on procreativity has become a concern because it is only recently that the whole issue of family planning has entered center stage, at least in certain regions and countries. Needless to say, the teaching of the Church is clear and unambiguous. Marriage must be open to procreation and the education of children: "the fundamental task of marriage and family is to be at the service of life" (CCC 1653).

6. The Rite of Matrimony

The rite of matrimony, even though it is often surrounded by a very elaborate preparation and investment of both time and money, is in fact a very simple rite. It can be celebrated either with the celebration of the Eucharist, which is the preferred method (CCC 1621), or within the context of the celebration of the Liturgy of the Word. In either instance, the sacrament is witnessed by a priest or deacon who receives the consent of the spouses in the name of the Church and gives the blessing of the Church (CCC 1630).

In the Latin Church, it is the exchange of consent between the spouses (the ministers of the sacrament) that is considered essential for the celebration of the sacrament of matrimony. However, in the Eastern churches, it is the priest or bishop who is considered the minister of the sacrament (CCC 1623) because, after receiving the mutual consent of the spouses, he crowns the bridegroom and the bride as a sign of the marriage covenant. This ceremony is called the "Crowning."

The rite of matrimony in the Latin Church, celebrated within the context of the Eucharist, begins with the priest, the altar servers, and the groom, walking out into the sanctuary of the church and turning to face the assembly gathered. With musical accompaniment, the rest of the bridal party, including the two official witnesses that are required by canon law, process into the church and into the sanctuary. The bride, accompanied by her father, are the last two people to enter the sanctuary and the father of the bride, reflecting the long-since forgotten Germanic custom, presents the bride to the bridegroom. Both the bride and the groom then enter the sanctuary where the priest is waiting and the nuptial Mass begins.

After the opening rite of the Mass is celebrated and the priest prays the opening prayer, selected readings from both the Old Testament and New Testament are read. Often these readings have been preselected by the bride and groom and are reflective of their hopes and beliefs as they begin their new life together as a married couple. The priest then proclaims the gospel and preaches a homily, drawing the lessons from the Scripture and applying it to the couple and to the gathered assembly. After the homily is preached, the rite of matrimony begins.

The priest addresses the couple with these words: "Have you come here freely and without reservation to give yourself in marriage? Will you love and honor each other as man and wife for the rest of your lives?" and the priest adds, if the couple is not advanced in years, "Will you accept children lovingly from God, and bring them up according to the law of Christ and his Church?" After each question the couple answers in the affirmative, usually in their own words but often with a simple, "We will," which suffices.

After receiving the couple's answers to the questions posed, the priest continues. "Since it is your intention to enter into marriage, join your right hands and declare your consent before God and his Church." Then, following the lead of the priest, and often simply in their own words, the couple declares separately and to each other, "I take you to be my wife (husband). I promise to serve you in good times and in bad, in sickness and in health. I will love you and honor you all the days of my life." After each spouse has declared his or her consent, the priest says, "You have declared your consent before God and the Church. May the Lord in his goodness strengthen your consent and fill you both with his blessing. What God has joined, men must not divide." Although the rite continues, at this point the couple is now man and wife, and nothing more is required sacramentally, even though tradition and custom has more to contribute to the ritual being celebrated.

The priest then takes the wedding rings from the best man and blesses them. The groom takes one of the rings and places it on his wife's finger and prays, "Take this ring as a sign of my love and fidelity. In the name of the Father, and of the Son, and of the Holy Spirit." The bride takes the other ring, places it on her husband's finger, and prays the same prayer.

At this point in the celebration, different customs and traditions dictate what happens next. In some traditions, the Eucharist proceeds with the praying of the prayers of the faithful, prayers usually composed the by the newly married couple, praying for the Church, their family and friends, and their new lives in Christ. In still other traditions, the newly married greet their parents and then present the gifts of bread and wine to the priest, gifts which will be used in the celebration of the Eucharist. In still other traditions, the newly married couple light a special candle called a "Unity Candle" by using the two candles previously lit to light one central candle that now represents their union. Regardless of local custom and tradition, at some point the Mass continues as usual through the prayers of the offertory, the Preface of the Mass (a special preface suitable for the celebration of matrimony and filled with biblical references to marriage), and then the praying of the eucharistic prayer.

The assembly is then invited to pray together the Lord's Prayer, and at the conclusion of the prayer the priest faces the bride and groom and prays, "My dear friends, let us turn to the Lord and pray that he will bless with his grace this woman now married in Christ to this man and through the sacrament of the body and blood of Christ, he will unite in love the couple he has joined together in this holy bond." After the entire assembly has taken a few moments to pray, the special nuptial blessing is prayed, asking the Lord to bless the new couple, to fill them with love and trust for each other and for the Word of God, and praying in a special way that they remain faithful to the promises that they have made to each other. The traditional prayer ends with these words: "May they live to see their children's children. And, after a happy old age, grant them fullness of life with the saints in the kingdom of heaven. We ask this through Christ our Lord."

The exchange of the sign of peace and the distribution of holy Communion follow. Traditionally, the bride and groom, and at least the members of the wedding party, receive Communion under both species of bread and wine. At the conclusion of the Communion rite, a time of silence is usually maintained and, in some places, another custom and tradition is expressed at this time.

After the period of silence is observed, the newly married couple takes a specially prepared bouquet to the shrine of our Blessed Mother in the church and spends a few moments in prayer, asking for the intercession of the Blessed Mother on their new lives. In some places, a special song to our Blessed Mother is often sung at this point.

The couple then returns to their place at the altar to receive the final blessing of the priest, which often is a longer blessing than usual, again asking for special graces and help for the couple in their new lives together. The words of the blessing include the following: "May the peace of Christ live always in your hearts and in your home. May you have true friends to stand by you, both in joy and in sorrow. May you be ready and willing to help and comfort all who come to you in need. And may the blessings promised to the compassionate be yours in abundance."

Traditionally, in many places, the priest then presents the couple to the gathered assembly, after which they process out of the sanctuary, through the church, to greet family and friends who offer their congratulations and support.

The rite of matrimony may also be celebrated within a Liturgy of the Word, which follows the same pattern outlined about, but which eliminates any part of the ritual that is reserved to the Eucharist. In addition, on those occasions when the couple who are to be married are not both Catholics, the rite permits the presence of a minister or a rabbi. This is certainly the result of a greater ecumenical sensibility than existed in prior times in the Church but is also reflective of the fact that it is the couple themselves who are ministers of the sacrament and that the priest is the official witness of the Church. Because of this fact, certainly a minister or a rabbi can be an official witness of his or her own religious tradition.

7. The Effects of Matrimony

The primary effect of matrimony, which occurs as a result of the exchange of consent between the man and the woman, is the marriage bond, a bond that can never be broken. The marriage bond, which has been established by God, is the covenantal guarantee of fidelity: just as God's promised covenantal guarantee cannot be broken or severed so also the bond between a man and a woman is understood as irrevocable (CCC 1640). However, this bond is not a burden or something that is imposed by God, the couple then being left alone and on their own. The grace of the sacrament, with Christ himself as the source of this grace, provides the spouses with the assistance to follow him, to endure sufferings and hardship, to forgive one another, to reverence and love each other, and to nourish their mutual love in tenderness, which is a foretaste of heaven (CCC 1641–1642).

8. Pastoral Concerns

There are a number of pastoral problems relating to marriage that the Church is aware of and attempts to meet with compassion and understanding.

Annulments: The Church upholds the indissolubility of the marriage bond and does not condone divorce. Yet the Church recognizes that some relationships lack certain essential elements vital to a sacramental marriage: freedom, maturity, and responsible decision. The Church also realizes the complications and harm that many innocent people often endure; in response, the Church is understanding and compassionate and may grant an annulment. The decree of nullity is granted only if, in the eyes of the Church, there has not been a valid marriage. This annulment is the official statement by the Church that, after thorough investigation, no sacramental marriage ever existed. When a decree of nullity is officially granted, the couple is free to remarry.

Interfaith and Interracial Marriage: The Church recognizes interfaith and interracial marriages provided the ceremonies take place in a Catholic church, or in the place of worship of the party who is not Catholic, and provided a Catholic priest or deacon is present as the Church's witness. Interfaith marriages face the issue of raising any children of the union in the Catholic tradition. The Church asks that Catholic spouses promise to do everything possible to raise the children in the faith. Non-Catholic spouses are no longer required to make any promise at all about raising the children Catholic, but they must be informed of the promise made by the Catholic party. The Church's main concern is that family unity, love, and religious values are upheld.

Divorce and Separation: The Church recognizes that many Catholics are affected by divorce. One of the growing and much needed services the Church can offer today is ministry to the divorced and separated. Persons suffering the pain of loss and the fear of an uncertain future as a result of divorce can find support and healing through sharing with others. Parishes need to consider this compassionate outreach to the divorced and separated as a vital and necessary pastoral concern.

9. Essentials

Name: Sacrament of Matrimony.

Sacramental Identification: Sacrament of mission and service.

Minimum Age: For a male, age 16, for a female, age 14, although the National Conference of Catholic Bishops may also set a higher minimum age (Canon 1083 of the Code of Canon Law).

Can Be Repeated? No, unless a spouse dies and then the surviving spouse may remarry.

Sacramental Character Imparted? No, but an indissoluble bond is created.

Matter: The free exchange of consent.

Form: The free exchange of consent.

Ordinary Minister: The man and the woman celebrating the sacrament.

Extraordinary Minister: None.

PART FIVE

Traditional Prayers and Meditations

S ome of the sacraments, in particular the sacraments of Eucharist and penance, have been the object of prayerful reflection over the centuries. Saints, theologians, and everyday people have recorded some of their thoughts in the form of prayers, which are reflective of their particular understanding and appreciation of the sacraments. Some of the most popular prayers and some of the more traditional prayers are collected here.

The prayers particular to each sacrament are introduced by a reflection/meditation on the sacraments from the writings of Bernard Häring, C.Ss.R. (1912–1998). Father Häring was the author of more than eighty books and one thousand articles. He was a professor of moral theology at the Accademia Alfonsiana in Rome for forty years. A theologian, popular teacher, retreat director, and confessor, he was truly a man of God. The introductory reflection for each of the following sections ends with a prayer also composed by Father Häring.

I. Prayers for the Sacrament of Baptism

1. Bernard Häring's Meditation on Baptism

When Jesus was baptized in the Jordan, his meeting with all the others who were baptized at the same time was very important. He joined them in a wonderful solidarity—the person for all others, the person for all people.

To those who know that they are sinners—who are baptized in the hope of and readiness for conversion—the coming of Christ becomes an epiphany: a revelation of the Holy Spirit, and of the love of the Father for his Son who is ready to bear the burden of all humankind.

When he comes into our life, the Father's love for him, and for us, becomes visible. On the cross, when Jesus is baptized again in his own blood, the blood of the covenant, he is near to all of us, praying for those who have crucified him and welcoming into his reign the thief at his side.

By our baptism, we partake in the baptism of Christ. He himself baptizes us, through the Spirit, calling us into the covenant sealed with his blood. Christ meets the baptized, wanting to abide with us, and to transform us into mirror images of his own solidarity and all-embracing love. When we have learned to make our decisions and to orient our lives around prayer—"What can I give to the Lord for what he has given me?"—the happy awareness that Christ is with us in our daily lives becomes more and more intense.

But it is not just at the moment of the reception of the sacrament that we meet Christ. He comes into our life to be with us and in us; and to awaken our consciousness to the wonder of his abiding presence and to gratitude for it.

Lord, you have given us parents to reveal to us your kindness and your tender love. Each day you send us friends, who by their gentleness draw our attention to you. You send us people who are so generous that only you can be the source and fulfillment of their good will. You allow us to meet people who receive us and encourage us, and so help us to experience your love, which gives us our greatest hope. You send us people who listen to us and understand us. Then we know again that you always listen to us and understand us. You are always with us, Lord. You call us and wait for us. Make us grateful; make us alert.

2. The Apostles' Creed

The Apostles' Creed is a summary of Christian faith expressed in twelve articles. Its name came from a popular belief that it was actually written by the twelve apostles; its substance clearly stems from the New Testament. Historians, however, date the actual text anywhere from 150 A.D. to 400 A.D. It is clear that at a very early date the Western Church required catechumens (new members) to learn the Apostles' Creed before baptism. It is still considered an excellent summary of the Christian faith. The "Profession of Faith," in the *Catechism of the Catholic Church*, follows the Apostles' Creed (CCC 194, 196).

I believe in God, the Father almighty, creator of heaven and earth. I believe in Jesus Christ, his only Son, our Lord. He was conceived by the power of the Holy Spirit and born of the Virgin Mary. He suffered under Pontius Pilate, was crucified, died, and was buried. He descended into hell. On the third day he rose again. He ascended into heaven, and is seated at the right hand of the Father. He will come again to judge the living and the dead. I believe in the Holy Spirit, the holy catholic Church, the communion of saints, the forgiveness of sins, the resurrection of the body, and life everlasting. Amen.

3. Your Baptism in Christ

Today you enter into the waters
as Jesus did on Jordan's shore.
And at the water, God will claim you:
"This is my beloved child,
with whom I am well pleased."

May the promises you make today
be strengthened by the faith of all
who welcome you and cheer your way.
May a thousand prayers surround you as,
cleansed in the fountain of true faith,
you join the family of our Lord.

When, may our loving God of faith,
set your feet upon the journey
that leads us all to Emmaus,

135

to the breaking of the bread,
to the knowing of the Lord,
and to everlasting life.

4. A Prayer for Our Catechumens

Lord Jesus, we ask your blessings on these men and women who aspire to join your Church through our parish community.

As they ponder your Word and share their stories, may the fabric of their lives become interwoven just as our lives are—into the very Body of Christ, your Church.

As they grow in knowledge and understanding of the faith, so too may they continue to plumb the depths of their hearts and find the awesome goodness of you, God of all, in the hearts of others. As they hunger for you, may they also proclaim you, boldly and joyfully. Give to us, Spirit of Love, the grace to walk their journeys with them in faith. And, Creator God, may we all be one in you, as you are One—a Trinity of being in a continuously revolving circle, never-changing yet ever-changing, that cannot be comprehended but only adored. Amen.

5. A Catechumen's Prayer

Eternal God,
as I reflect upon your Word,
I can but marvel at your eternal
presence in the lives of your people;
a presence that I am
becoming more and more
aware of in my own life.
I bow before you and ask your blessing
upon my heart and mind, that I may be drawn
ever closer to your infinite love.

My heart is restless, O God,
for you are my heart's one true desire.
My appetite will not be sated, for you have
put a hunger within me that can only be
filled by your Word of everlasting life.
You, who are all things to all people,
speak to me out of my need.
Give me the ears to hear so
that my own words can speak to others
in their need. And hear me, O God,
as I profess my faith in you—
Father, Son, and Spirit.
Instill in me a steadfast faith that
will allow me to stay the course.
Amen.

6. Baptismal Prayer

In awareness of the reality of our baptism and in gratitude for it, we praise you Father, Lord of heaven and earth. We praise you because your servant, Jesus Christ, wanted to be baptized with the crowd of humble people who knew that they were sinners. We thank you that, through baptism, you gather your people, to make them one and holy.

We beg you, Father, to grant to your Church a deeper knowledge of what you mean by baptism: that infants should be baptized not only with water and words, but that they should be truly inserted into the community of believers, thus to experience the joy and strength of faith. Help us to build up that reign in which we can more fully understand what baptism in the Holy Spirit means for us. Send us your Spirit, that our lives may bear the fruits of the Spirit in kindness, gentleness, generosity, spontaneity, and creativity. Assist our efforts in prayer. Let our prayer, and our lives, bring to the whole Church the message that the Spirit is truly our life and our guide. Amen.

7. A Meditation on Baptism and Faith

Love is something real. We can experience it. But it's not a physical object that we can hand to someone else. So we give gifts—flowers or candy perhaps; we say the words; we embrace. That's the way it has to be. We are physical beings, living in a physical world, and we communicate in a physical way. These physical expressions of love are not the same as love itself, but they are all we have.

Jesus used physical signs to convey love too. He especially used touch and words; he laughed, and he wept. And he is still using physical signs today—the signs of the sacraments. Sacraments bring about what they symbolize. Thus the ritual of baptism symbolizes the soul being cleansed of original sin at the same time that God is making that cleansing happen. But, just as our own limited signs of love cannot keep a relationship going without reciprocation on the part of the gifted one(s), a sacrament's great potential can only be turned into actuality if we do our part. And that's the hard part. It means taking a risk. It means trusting. It means not only having faith, but also being willing to "keep the faith," no matter what.

The word *baptism* means "a plunging." When we are baptized, we plunge into the life, death, and resurrection of Jesus. Jesus even called his passion and death a baptism: "I have a baptism with which to be baptized, and what stress I am under until it is completed!" (Lk 12:50).

Baptism confers the very character of Christ. It is permanent and irrevocable, a once-and-for-always sacrament. It is the sign of salvation given to us by Christ to bring us into the kingdom of God (Jn 3:5). It gives the baptized a share in Christ's priesthood, and the power, therefore, to worship. That is why baptism is the first sacrament, before which no other sacraments can be celebrated.

Saint Paul emphasized that baptism was the beginning of a deep and vital union with the risen Lord (Rom 6:4–11). The baptized person lives "in Christ," and since all the roads Jesus traveled led to Jerusalem and the cross, so too it must be for the Christian. There are no shortcuts to resurrection.

One who is plunged into the baptismal waters emerges a new creature with a new life. This new life is the Holy Spirit, who makes a home in us and gives us the power not only to know God but also to do all that God requires. Christ's invitation to baptism is one of universal and limitless love, therefore open to all, infants and children as well as adults. But being baptized is only the beginning of faith.

8. **Life-Giving Water**

"I have a baptism with which to be baptized, and what stress I am under until it is completed!" (Lk 12:50).

Christian baptism is our initiation into the priesthood of believers. This primary sacrament of the Church is the plunging of the baptized into the life, death, and resurrection of Christ. We are gifted with both the right and the obligation to offer the very sacrifice that Christ offered—our prayers, our works, our very lives. Baptism is not an event in life but a process of life. It is the process of being ordered and conformed to the will of our High Priest.

We are responsible for each other by virtue of our baptism. At baptism, the entire community enters into a relationship with the one being baptized, and all are responsible for that person's spiritual well-being. That is why we speak of baptism's indelible spiritual mark.

Scientists believe that all life can be traced to the waters of the sea. They tell us, too, that water is the main element that makes up living tissue—as much as ninety-nine percent. No wonder our Lord chose water to represent the beginning of the new, Christian life.

139

But water reminds us of death as well: tragedies at sea, floods, drowning. This is another reason why our Lord chose water to represent the end of the old life and the beginning of the new, Christian life.

God has often used signs of water throughout the Bible. God's Spirit breathed on the waters at the beginning of creation. God parted the waters to lead the Israelites out of slavery and into the Promised Land. Naaman was cleansed of leprosy by washing in the waters of the Jordan. Water and blood flowed from the side of Christ on the cross. And Jesus was, himself, baptized with water. It was after his baptism that Jesus began his public ministry. We are called to be imitators of him. If a sacrament's great potential is to be turned into actuality, we must do our part.

One of the effects of baptism is grace. Grace has been defined as God sharing the divine life with us. When we receive grace, we experience real change; we move toward oneness with God. Such radical change is accompanied by forgiveness of actual sins. The Christian call is rooted in a foundation that is the direct work of grace. One of its effects is an insertion into the mystery of hope. By virtue of our baptism, we are ordered into a life of eternal hope. Our call is to change the world, and the theological virtues of faith, hope, and love provide a key to our job description.

The theological virtues are difficult to pursue today. The stakes are high, the need is great, and the critics are quick. But when we use them, we are a people of faith; and when we act in faith, we do inspire hope; and wherever the two work together, there is love.

"And now faith, hope, and love abide, these three; and the greatest of these is love" (1 Cor 13:13).

II. Prayers for the Sacrament of Confirmation

1. Bernard Häring's Meditation on Confirmation

At confirmation the bishop anoints the baptized Christian on the brow with chrism—in the form of a cross—and says: "I sign you with the sign of the cross and confirm you with the chrism of salvation, in the name of the Father and of the Son and of the Holy Spirit." In "the Spirit of strength" we can stand up to the spirit of evil in the world around us, and firmly and joyfully confess our faith in the gospel, even when to do this means sacrifice and the cross for us. The chrism of the love of God means that in the face of opposition and persecution we can win the victory of the cross, the victory of self-sacrificing love. The grace and calling of confirmation is that we can "bear witness without fear and without weakness" (The Synod of Elvira). "Do not forget the Spirit! He will stamp on you the mark of heaven and of God which strikes fear into demons. He arms you for the battle, he gives you power. He will be your guardian and defender. He will watch over you as over his solders" (Cyril of Jerusalem, PG 33, 996).

It is now clear that the life of a baptized and confirmed Christian is directed essentially to making a *public witness of his faith*. This is as much an essential part of his life as it was the essential meaning of Christ's baptism in the Jordan that he should testify to the purpose of his Father's love, and that the Father should bear witness in an audible voice to his Son, or that the "baptism" of Christ in the blood shed o n Good Friday, and the glory of Easter Sunday, is essentially the decisive act of witness in the eyes of the world.

A baptized and confirmed Christian must be an apostle, a witness of Christ, otherwise he does not really become what God has engraved on his soul.

And yet the grace of confirmation teaches us that the vital thing is not the public, external apostolate, but self-surrender, our willingness to be taught by the inward guidance of grace. For in Christ it was revealed—both at the baptism in the Jordan and in the mystery of the passion and resurrection—that the power to bear witness lies entirely in the love, the mutual self-giving, of the Father and the Son. The Holy Spirit given to Christ as the Son of God in fullness, and to us in abundance, as the ratification by God of our acceptance as his children, and to bring us the duty of bearing witness, is the bond of love between the Father and Son.

Send out your Spirit and renew the face of the earth! O God, you teach the hearts of the faithful your law by your Holy Spirit, the Spirit of truth and love. We pray you, let us, through him, take pleasure in all that is good in your sight, and help us to carry out with joy what we have recognized as your will. Through Jesus Christ your Son, who lives and rules with you in the unity of the same Holy Spirit, God, world without end. Amen.

2. Prayer to the Holy Spirit

O Holy Spirit let your finger touch me, your finger that drops down wine and oil and the choicest myrrh. Let your finger touch me, most beloved Lord, and when it has rid me of corruption, let it restore my wholeness, so that, when you come to dwell in me, you may find me not a thoroughfare, nor a bag with holes, but a dwelling intact and entire, founded on the truth of faith, erected in the certainty of hope, and completed in the zeal of charity.

Come, most welcome guest, knock, and enter into my soul. Open the door, and let no one shut it. Enter, and close the door behind you. For all the things that you possess are in peace, and there is no peace apart from you. You are indeed rest for those that toil, peace for those that strive, bliss for those who grieve, comfort for the weary, coolness for the fevered, merriment for mourners, light for those in darkness, and courage for those who are afraid. What more is there to say? You are all good. Amen.

3. A Traditional Prayer of Petition to the Holy Spirit

O Holy Spirit, who filled the soul of the most holy Mary with immense graces, and who inflamed the hearts of the apostles with holy zeal, inflame, I beseech you, my heart with your love.

You are the Divine Spirit; give me courage against all evil spirits. You are Fire; enkindle in me your love. You are Light; enlighten my mind with the knowledge of eternal things. You are the Dove; give me innocence of life. You are gentle Breeze; disperse the storms of my passion. You are the Tongue; teach me how to bless you always. You are the Cloud; shelter me under the shadow of your protection.

And lastly, you are the giver of all heavenly gifts, animate me with you grace, sanctify me with your charity, enlighten me with your wisdom, and save me in your infinite mercy. May I ever bless you, praise you, and love you, first during this life on earth and then in heaven for all eternity. Amen.

4. Prayer to the Holy Spirit

(William Browning, C.P.)

O Holy Spirit, give me stillness of soul in you.
Calm the turmoil within, with the gentleness of your peace.
Quiet the anxiety within, with a deep trust in you.
Heal the wounds of sin within, with the joy of your forgiveness.
Strengthen the faith within,
    with the awareness of your presence.
Confirm the hope within, with the knowledge of your strength.

Give fullness to the love within,
  with an outpouring of your love.
O Holy Spirit, be to me a source of light,
Strength, and courage, so that I may
Hear your call ever more clearly and
Follow it more generously. Amen.

5. Come Holy Spirit

Leader: Come Holy Spirit.

Response: Fill the hearts of your faith and make the fire of your love burn within them.

Leader: Send forth your Spirit and there shall be another creation.

Response: And you shall renew the face of the earth.

Leader: Let us pray: O God, you have instructed the hearts of the faithful by the light of the Holy Spirit. Grant that through the same Holy Spirit we may always be truly wise and rejoice in his consolation. Through Christ our Lord. Amen.

PRAYER FOR A NEW PENTECOST

We ask you, Lord, to give to your Church the experience of a new Pentecost. May all the languages, all the temperaments and charisms of all people, unite in a great chorus to your praise. Grant us a community of sisters and brothers who, with their deep faith and prayer, can strengthen our faith where it falls short. Cleanse us, O Lord, and unite us in a joyous faith through which we can comfort the sufferers and support them in their faith.

Come, Holy Spirit, free us from closed minds, from isolation, from anguish and mistrust. Make us free for you, docile to your inspirations, so that all our lives may become one voice, one outcry of joy: "Abba, Father!"

6. The Gift of the Spirit

We believe that only through the undeserved gift of the spirit can we come to truthful adoration of your name, O Lord. When the Spirit dwells in us and we docilely accept that divine presence, we can, in joy and in truth, call you "Our Father." But we know, through your revelation, that your abundant gifts and promises do not allow us to be lazy. You ask, and make possible, our creative cooperation.

Make us grateful, Lord. Make us vigilant, so that each of us, within our families and our communities, may join hands and energies to create the best possible conditions for the synthesis of faith and life, of prayer and service to our sisters and brothers. Amen.

7. A Confirmation Meditation

The work of Christ was never meant to rest solely upon the Holy Spirit, acting in some disembodied fashion, nor solely upon a select group of ordained ministers. Each member of Christ's Body works in harmony with the rest and is as indispensable as the rest.

"The spirit of the Lord shall rest on him, the spirit of wisdom and understanding, the spirit of counsel and might, the spirit of knowledge and the fear of the LORD" (Isa 11:2).

The sacrament of confirmation is conferred by the laying on of hands followed by anointing (marking the forehead with the Sign of the Cross) with oil of chrism. The laying on of hands is an important biblical sign of the coming of the Holy Spirit. Jesus healed with his touch, and his same healing power was passed on to the disciples after Pentecost. When hands are laid upon us in confirmation, we are symbolically healed of any human impediments to our Christian ministry.

Chrism is olive oil mixed with balsam. The oil itself is a symbol of strength, while the perfume is a symbol of the "fragrance of Christ"

145

that Christians must spread. Jesus was called "the Anointed One"—that is the meaning of both "Messiah" and "Christ"—because those who were anointed (priests and kings) were believed to have been chosen by God. Our anointing in confirmation symbolizes the same thing: God has chosen us.

The Holy Spirit is given in both baptism and confirmation, but the function of the Holy Spirit is different in each. Saint Augustine explained that in baptism we are mixed with water so that we might take on the form of bread—the body of Christ. But bread needs to be baked in the fire. This fire is supplied by the chrism, which is "the sacrament of the Holy Spirit," revealed in tongues of fire (see Acts 2:1–4). Thus, in baptism we are made members of the Body of Christ, but in confirmation we are given the power of God to bear fruit in our Christian lives: to speak before the world boldly and so draw others into the Church.

"We boast in our hope of sharing the glory of God...and hope does not disappoint us, because God's love has been poured into our hearts through the Holy Spirit that has been given to us" (Rom 5:2b, 5).

Hope can only be as strong as our reasons for expecting that what we desire will be achieved. Christian hope is rock-solid because it is based on a pledge from God. Hope assures us that complete happiness is attainable; shields us from discouragement and despair; and unites us firmly to Jesus through his gift of the Holy Spirit.

Hope is confidence inspired by love. We become bearers of hope when we stir up in others the confidence that they can draw upon the power of God's love to change their own lives and even the very world around them. It is part and parcel of the gifts of confirmation: gentle strength, compassionate courage, words and works of mercy. Hope, in other words, is a virtue that confirmation brings into our hearts and hands and voices.

III. Prayers for the Sacrament of the Eucharist

1. Bernard Häring's Meditation on the Eucharist

The summit of the presence of the risen Lord and the Holy Spirit is the eucharistic celebration. The Eucharist is the great mystery of faith in which Christ speaks to us by giving himself to us as the bread of eternal life. Christ is present to us in his Word as well: he himself is the Good News for us. Whenever we are open to the grace of the Holy Spirit in a community of believers, united in Christ who is our hope, and ready to receive his Word and to act on it, we discover anew that Christ's Word is, for us, "spirit and life" (Jn 6:63).

The whole eucharistic celebration is a Word and a gift of life that aims at our total conversion, our complete transformation in the Lord. The Eucharist is infinitely more than a memorial of past events; it is the Word Incarnate who reminds us of those past events, which then become a present reality for all believers.

Christ's presence in the Eucharist, through his living Word, and under the species of bread and wine, is not separated into two entities. We distinguish two different aspects, but they are one reality: Christ meeting us, speaking to us here and now, revealing to us the final meaning of all the events of the history of salvation. "The bread of life" gives life to the world, so that the world may live in him, with him, and through him.

The eucharistic presence of Christ is the strongest, the most miraculous, and the most effective presence in the world. When Christ meets us in the power of the Spirit, whom he bestows on us, we can receive this wonderful gift with thanks and praise, and respond by entrusting ourselves wholeheartedly to him, to become his witnesses to the ends of the earth.

Only through the power of the Spirit does the eucharistic celebration become a peak experience in which we reach full reciprocity of consciousness. Through the Spirit, who is the self-giving love between the Father and the Son, we receive—in the Eucharist—a share in the love of the Son for the Father and Father for the Son. Thus we receive the greatest gift: Christ himself. And we too can give ourselves totally to him and to his mission.

Lord, you have promised us wonderful things: that we shall always be with you. All that you have done and entrusted to us is a part of your promise, a sign of your faithfulness. You have promised the beatitude of a life where you are, with all our sisters and brothers, all your children. Now, in this in-between time, you are our Way. You are on the road with us, the road that leads to you and the final joy of your presence. Lord, you are always near to us; you call us and wait for us. Make us grateful; make us ready.

2. A Traditional Prayer Said by Those Who Instruct Children for First Holy Communion

O Jesus, who has loved us with such exceedingly great love as to give us the ineffable gift of the holy Eucharist, inflame us with a burning zeal to promote your glory by worthily preparing the little children who are to approach your holy table for the first time. Protect, O Eucharistic Heart of Jesus, these young souls from the assaults of evil, strengthen their faith, increase their love, and endow them with all the virtues that will make them worthy to receive you. Amen.

Saint John the Baptist, forerunner of the Messiah, prepare the way for Jesus in the hearts of these children. Saint Tarcisius, keep safe the children who are making their first Communion. Amen.

3. A Traditional Prayer Before the Reception of Holy Communion

Let the reception of your body, O Lord Jesus Christ, which I, though unworthily, do presume to receive, not result for me in judgment and condemnation, but, according to your mercy, let it be profitable for the reception of healing and protection, both of my soul and my body, you who live and reign for ever and ever. Amen.

4. Prayer of Thanksgiving After the Reception of Holy Communion

I give you thanks, holy Lord, Father Almighty, everlasting God, who has determined to feed me, a sinner, your unworthy servant, for no merits of my own, but only out of the goodness of your great mercy, with the precious body and blood of your Son, our Lord Jesus Christ. I pray that this holy Communion may be to me, not guilt for punishment, but a saving intercession for pardon. Let it be to me an armor of faith and a shield of good will. Let it be to me a casting out of vices, a driving away of all evil desires and fleshly lusts, an increase of charity, of patience, humility, obedience, and all virtues, and a firm defense against the plots of all my enemies, both seen and unseen. Let this Communion be a perfect quieting of all motions of sin, both in my flesh and in my spirit, a firm cleaving to you, the only and true God, and a happy ending of my life. And I pray that you at last bring me, a sinner, to the ineffable Feast, where with your Son and the Holy Spirit, are to your holy ones, true light, full satisfaction, everlasting joy, and consummate pleasure and perfect happiness. Amen.

5. *Anima Christi*

Anima Christi, listed in the Missal of Pope Paul IV as the "Prayer to Our Redeemer," is a prayer appropriate for a person's thanksgiving after the reception of holy Communion. It was known in the fourteenth century but the exact date and the author of the prayer is unknown. Tradition ascribes it to Saint Ignatius of Loyola who certainly recommended that it be prayed. The translation that follows is from John Henry Newman.

> Soul of Christ, sanctify me.
> Body of Christ, save me.
> Blood of Christ, inebriate me.
> Water from the side of Christ, wash me.
> Passion of Christ, strengthen me.
> Good Jesus, hear me.
> Within thy wounds, hide me.
> Let me not be separated from thee.
> Guard me should the foe assail me.
> Call me when my life shall fail me.
> Bid me come to thee above
> With all thy saints to sing thy love forever.
> Amen.

6. Prayer of Saint Bonaventure

Saint Bonaventure (1217–1274) was a philosopher and theologian, and is a Doctor of the Church. His insistence on the role of grace and the absolute necessity of total dependence on God are the cornerstones of his spiritual writings.

My Lord, who are you, and who am I, that I should dare to take you into my body and soul? A thousand years of penance and tears would not be sufficient to make me worthy to receive so royal a sacrament even once; how much more am I unworthy of it, who fall into sin daily; I the incorrigible, who approach you so often without due preparation. Nevertheless, your mercy infinitely surpasses my unworthiness. Therefore, I am bold to receive this sacrament, trusting in your love. Amen.

7. Prayer of Saint John Vianney

Saint John Marie Vianney (1786–1859) is also known as the Curé of Ars. A parish priest known for his simple wisdom and his devotion to the sacrament of penance, he was a much sought after confessor.

My Jesus, from eternity it has been your plan to give yourself to us in the sacrament of your love. Therefore, you have implanted in us such longing as you alone can satisfy.

I may go from here to the other end of the world, from riches to greater riches, from pleasure to pleasure, and still I shall not be content. The entire world cannot satisfy the immortal soul.

Sweet it is when we set our hearts on loving you, my God. It sometimes happens that the more we know our neighbors, the less we love them; but with you, O God, it is never so. The more we know you, the more we love you.

My Jesus, how sweet it is to love you. Let me be like the disciples on Mount Tabor, seeing nothing else but you, my Savior. Let us be as two friends, neither of whom can ever offend the other. Amen.

8. Prayer of Blessed Padre Pio

Blessed Padre Pio (1887–1968) is the only priest to ever bear the stigmata (the wounds of Christ's passion and death); he was a monk and a much sought after spiritual director.

Stay with me Lord, for it is necessary to have you present so that I do not forget you. You know how easily I abandon you.

Stay with me Lord, for you are my light and without you I am in darkness. Stay with me Lord, to show me your will. Stay with me Lord, so that I hear your voice and follow you. Stay with me Lord, for I desire to love you very much and always be in your company. Stay with me Lord, if you wish me to be faithful to you. Stay with me Lord, as poor as my soul is I want it to be a place of consolation for you, a nest of love. Stay with me Jesus, for it is getting late and the day is coming to close and as life passes, death, judgment, and eternity approach. It is necessary to renew my strength, so that I will not stop along the way and for that, I need you. It is getting late and death approaches, I fear the darkness, the cross, the sorrows. How I need you, my Jesus, in this night of exile!

Let me recognize you as your disciples did at the breaking of the bread, so that the eucharistic Communion be the light which disperses the darkness, the force that sustains me, the unique joy of my heart.

Stay with me Lord, because at the hour of my death, I want to remain united to you, if not by Communion, at least by grace and love.

Stay with me Lord, for it is you alone I look for, your love, your grace, your will, your heart, your spirit, because I love you and ask no other reward but to love you more and more.

With a firm love, I will love you with all my heart while on earth and continue to love you perfectly during all eternity. Amen.

9. Prayer of Saint Thomas Aquinas

Saint Thomas Aquinas (1225–1274) is acclaimed as the universal teacher of the Church, primarily because of his *Summa Theologica*; he is also a Doctor of the Church and patron of all scholars and theologians.

Lord, Father all powerful and ever-living God,
I thank you, for even though I am a sinner,
Your unprofitable and unworthy servant,
In the kindness of your mercy,
You have fed me with the precious body and blood of your Son,
Our Lord Jesus Christ.

I pray that this holy Communion
May not bring me condemnation and punishment,
But forgiveness and salvation.
May it be a helmet of faith
And a shield of good will.
May it purify me from evil ways
And put an end to my wayward passions.
May it bring me charity and patience,
Humility and obedience,
And growth in the power to do good.

May it be my strong defense
Against all my enemies, visible and invisible,
And the perfect calming of all my evil impulses,
Bodily and spiritual.
May it unite me more closely to you,
The one true God,

And lead me safely through death
To everlasting happiness with you.

And I pray that you will lead me, a sinner
To the banquet where you,
With your Son and Holy Spirit
Are true and perfect light,
Total fulfillment, everlasting joy,
Gladness without end,
And perfect happiness to your saints.
Grant this through Christ our Lord. Amen.

10. The Divine Praises

The Divine Praises are a traditional representation of ejaculatory prayers, usually prayed at the conclusion of Benediction. Louis Felici probably compiled them in 1779, in part to intone for blasphemy and profanity. Additions to the original listings include the Immaculate Conception in 1856, the Sacred Heart in 1897, Saint Joseph in 1921, the Assumption of the Blessed Virgin Mary in 1950, the Precious Blood of Jesus in 1960, and the Holy Spirit in 1964 during the Second Vatican Council.

Blessed be God.
Blessed be His Holy Name.
Blessed be Jesus Christ, true God and true man.
Blessed be the name of Jesus.
Blessed be his Most Sacred Heart.
Blessed be his Most Precious Blood.
Blessed be Jesus in the Most Holy Sacrament of the Altar.
Blessed be the Holy Spirit, the Paraclete.
Blessed be the great Mother of God, Mary most holy.
Blessed be her holy and Immaculate Conception.

Blessed be her glorious Assumption.

Blessed be the name of Mary, virgin and mother.

Blessed be Saint Joseph, her most chaste spouse.

Blessed be God in his angels and in his saints.

11. Eucharistic Prayer

Thank you, Lord, because the memory of your Incarnation, your passion and death, your Resurrection and Ascension, is not just an account that comes to us from past history. You yourself come, graciously, to remind us that you were born for us, you have suffered for us, and you are alive for us. You want to live in us and with us in order to continue, through us, your saving love for all people in all time. Lord we believe you are the life of our life, the strength of our strength, and the road of our salvation.

Thank you, Lord, that our thanksgiving is not ours alone, but that it is united with the thanks and praise you have offered to our heavenly Father. Grant, by the Holy Spirit, that we may always celebrate the memory of your Incarnation, passion, death, Resurrection, and Ascension with such great faith, joy, and gratitude; that all our life becomes, in union with you, praise and thanksgiving to the Father. Help us to honor the name of God by being one with your redemptive love for all the world. Amen.

12. Service for Bringing Communion to the Homebound

What follows is a short and simple way to reverently serve as eucharistic minister to the homebound. Set the stage for this experience of shared prayer by a minute or two of greeting. Sharing some news from the parish or the neighborhood allows a connection, a window out of the lonely isolation of being homebound. Bringing a Bible with you, and reading the Sunday gospel after the Lord's Prayer, allows for a sense of participation in the Church's communal liturgy. If you feel comfortable doing so, you can even share a few thoughts from the homily with the homebound. Be sure to leave a parish bulletin—and the promise of a return visit—before you go.

Minister: "Strengthen your hearts, for the coming of the Lord is near" (Jas 5:8).

Response: I wait for the Lord, my soul waits, and in his Word I hope; my soul waits for the Lord more than those who watch for the morning. For with the Lord there is steadfast love, and with him is great power to redeem. It is he who will redeem Israel from all its iniquities.

The Word of God

Minister: Jesus said to them, "I am the bread of life. Whoever comes to me will never be hungry, and whoever believes in me will never be thirsty."

Silence

Minister: Let us pray as Jesus taught us to pray: Our Father....

Invitation to Communion

Minister: This is the Lamb of God who takes away the sins of the world. Happy are those who are called to his supper.

Response: Lord, I am not worthy to receive you, but only say the word and I shall be healed.

Allow Some Time for Quiet Prayer

Minister: Let us pray. Lord, you feed us with the gift of the Eucharist. May we experience the joy of your healing power in us. May this Eucharist be a pledge of future glory for us who receive it.

Response: Amen.

Blessing

Minister: May God bless us: the Father, Son, and Holy Spirit. Amen.

Response: Amen.

13. Saint Alphonsus Liguori's Meditations on the Eucharist

What is true love? Is true love something that permeates all, that commands all attention, that influences every decision and colors every thought? Can an experience of true love be found or is it the stuff of fantasy and fairy tale, something that a person might read about but that is not really possible? Is true love something to hope for, only to become disappointed and frustrated in the pursuit?

When you read the meditations, prayers, and affections that are collected here, written by Saint Alphonsus Liguori over two hundred and fifty years ago, you will know that true love is possible. You will recognize, in these meditations, a love for Jesus present in the Most Holy Sacrament. You will recognize a love, a devotion, that is all consuming, that is never doubted, and that explodes in every thought, affection, and prayer. Saint Alphonsus is possessed by the true love of Jesus in the Blessed Sacrament!

MEDITATION 1:

THE LOVE OF JESUS IN THE MOST HOLY SACRAMENT

Our loving Redeemer, knowing that he must leave this earth and return to his Father as soon as he had accomplished the work of our redemption by his death, and seeing that the hour of his death had come—"Jesus knew that his hour had come to depart from this world and go to the Father" (Jn 13:1)—would not leave us alone in this valley of tears. What did he do? He instituted the Most Holy Sacrament of the Eucharist, in which he left us his whole self. "No tongue," said Saint Peter of Alcantara, "is able to declare the greatness of the love that Jesus bears for every soul." Therefore this Spouse, as he left this earth, in order that his absence might not cause us to forget him, gave us as a memorial this Blessed Sacrament, in which he himself remained. He would not have any other pledge than himself, to keep alive our remembrance of him.

Jesus would not be separated from us by his death; he instituted this sacrament of love in order to be with us to the end of the world: "I am with you always, to the end of the age" (Mt 28:20). Behold him, as faith teaches us, on so many altars as in so many prisons of love. Behold him in order that every one that seeks him may find him. "But, O Lord," says Saint Bernard, "this does not demonstrate your majesty." Jesus Christ answers, "It is enough that it demonstrates my love."

People feel great tenderness and devotion when they go to Jerusalem and visit the cave where the Incarnate Word was born, the hall where he was scourged, the hill of Calvary on which he died, and the tomb where he was buried. How much greater should our tenderness be when we visit an altar on which Jesus remains in the Most Holy Sacrament! The Venerable Father John Avila used to say that of all sanctuaries there is not one to be found more excellent and devout than a church where Jesus is sacramentally present.

Affections and Prayers: O my beloved Jesus, O God, who has loved me with love exceeding! What more can you do to make yourself loved by ungrateful people? If people loved you, all the churches would be continually filled with people prostrate on the ground adoring and thanking you, burning with love for you and seeing you with the eyes of faith, hidden in a tabernacle. But no, we are forgetful of you and your love. We are ready enough to try to win the favor of a person from whom we hope for some miserable advantage, while we leave you Lord abandoned and alone. If only by my devotion I could make reparation for such ingratitude! I am sorry that I also have been careless and ungrateful. In the future I will change my ways, I will devote myself to your service as much as possible. Inflame me with your holy love, so that from this day forward I may live only to love and to please you. You deserve the love of all hearts. If at one time I have despised you, I now desire nothing but to love you. O my Jesus, you are my love and my only good, "my God and my all."

Most Holy Virgin Mary, obtain for me, I pray, a great love for the Most Holy Sacrament.

MEDITATION 2:
JESUS REMAINS ON THE ALTAR SO ALL MAY FIND HIM

Saint Teresa of Ávila said that in this world it is impossible for all subjects to speak to their king. For the poor the most that they can hope for is to speak to him with the help of a third party. But to speak to you, O King of Heaven, there is no need of a third person; every one who wishes can find you in the Most Holy Sacrament, and can speak to you at their convenience and without conditions. For this reason, the same saint states, Jesus Christ has concealed his majesty in the Blessed Sacrament, under the appearance of bread, in order to give us more confidence, and to take away our fear of approaching him.

Jesus seems continually to exclaim from the altar: "Come to me, all you that are weary and are carrying heavy burdens, and I will give you rest" (Mt 11:28). Come, he says, come you who are poor; come, you who are infirm; come, you who are afflicted; come you who are just and you who are sinners, and you shall find in me a remedy for all your losses and afflictions. This is the desire of Jesus Christ; to console every person who calls upon him.

Jesus remains day and night on our altars, that all may find him, and that he may grant favors to all. The saints experienced in this world such pleasure in remaining in the presence of Jesus in the Blessed Sacrament. For this reason days and nights appeared to them as moments. The Countess of Feria, having become a nun of the Order of Saint Clare, never tired of remaining in chapel in sight of the tabernacle. One day she was asked what she was doing for so long before the Most Holy Sacrament. She answered with surprise, "What do I do before the Blessed Sacrament? What do I do? I return thanks, I love, and I pray!" Saint Philip Neri, while in the presence of the Blessed Sacrament, exclaimed: "Behold my love, behold all of my love." If Jesus were for us, as he is for the saints, days and nights in his presence would appear to us as moments.

Affections and Prayers: O my Jesus, from this day forward I also hope to say always to you, when I come to visit you on your altar: "Behold my love, behold all of my love!" Yes, my beloved Redeemer, I will love no one but you and I desire that you should be the only love of my soul. I seem to die of sorrow when I think that until this moment I have loved creatures and my own pleasures more than you. I have turned my back on you, the ultimate good. But you would not permit me to be lost, and therefore you have been patient with me. Instead of chastising me, you have pierced my heart with darts of love, so that I could no longer resist your kindness. But now that I have freely given myself to you, I see that you desire me to be entirely yours. For this desire to be fulfilled you must make it possible. You must detach my heart from all earthly affections and from my self. You must enable me to seek no other but you, that I may think only of you, and that I may only desire to burn with love for you, and to live and die for you alone. O love of my Jesus, come and occupy my whole heart, and expel from it all other love but that of God! I love you, Jesus in the Blessed Sacrament; I love you, my treasure, my love, and my all.

O Mary, my hope. Pray for me and make me belong entirely to Jesus.

MEDITATION 3:
THE GREAT GIFT OF JESUS' PRESENCE IN THE BLESSED SACRAMENT

The love of Jesus Christ was not satisfied with sacrificing his divine life for us. He sacrificed himself in the midst of a sea of humiliations and torments. He sacrificed himself in order to prove to us his affection. He sacrificed himself in order to oblige us to love him even more. He sacrificed himself so that on the night before his death he left us his whole self as our food in the holy Eucharist. God is omnipotent; but after he has given himself to a soul in this sacrament of love, he has nothing more to give. The Council of Trent teaches that Jesus, in giving himself to us in holy Communion, pours forth all the riches of his infinite love in this gift: "He has, as it were, poured forth the treasures of his love toward us."

How would the servant react, writes Saint Frances de Sales, if his master, while he was eating, would send him a portion of his own plate? Would he not consider himself blessed and esteemed? Jesus in this holy Communion, gives us for our food, not only a portion of his own meal, but all of his body: "Take, eat; this is my body" (Mt 26:26). And together with his body he gives us also his soul and divinity. Saint John Chrysostom says, our Lord, in giving himself to us in the Blessed Sacrament, gives us all that he has and nothing more remains: "He gave all to you, and left nothing for himself." O wonderful prodigy of divine love, that God, who is Lord of all, makes himself entirely ours!

Affections and Prayers: O my dear Jesus, what can you do to make me love you? Make me understand what an excess of love you have shown me by reducing yourself to food, in order to unite yourself to poor sinners! You, my dear Redeemer, have so much affection for me that you have not refused to give yourself again and again entirely to me in holy Communion. And yet I have had the courage to drive you away from my soul on so many occasions! You do not despise a humble and contrite heart. You became human for my sake. You died for me. You even went so far as to become my food. What more can there remain for you to do in order to gain my love? Oh, that I could die with grief every time that I remember that I have despised your grace. I repent, O my love, with my whole heart for having offended you. I love you, O infinite goodness! I love you, O infinite love! I desire nothing but to love you, and I fear nothing but to live without your love. My beloved Jesus, do not refuse to come to me. Come, because I would rather die a thousand times than drive you away again. I will do all that I can to please you. Come and inflame my whole soul with your love. Grant that I may forget everything, to think only of you, and to desire you alone, my sovereign and my only good.

O Mary, my Mother, pray for me; and by your prayers make me grateful for all the love that Jesus has for me.

MEDITATION 4:
THE GREAT LOVE JESUS SHOWS US IN THE BLESSED SACRAMENT

"Jesus knew that his hour had come to depart from this world and go to the Father. Having loved his own who were in the world, he loved them to the end" (Jn 13:1). Jesus, knowing that his hour had come, desired to leave us, before he died, the greatest pledge of his affection that he could give us—the gift of the Most Holy Sacrament. "He would love them with perfect love," which Saint John Chrysostom explains, "He loved them with extreme love." Jesus loved us with the greatest love with which he could love us, by giving us his entire self.

When did Jesus institute this great sacrament, the sacrament in which he has left us himself? On the night before he died! The Lord Jesus, on the night that he was delivered up, took bread and, after giving thanks, broke it saying, "This is my body that is for you. Do this in remembrance of me" (1 Cor 11:24). At the precise moment that his enemies were plotting to put him to death, he gave us this last proof of his love.

The words of affection, which we receive from our friends at the time of their death, remain deeply impressed on our hearts. For this reason Jesus gave us this gift of the Blessed Sacrament just before his death. With reason did Saint Thomas call this gift, "a sacrament and pledge of love." Saint Bernard describes it as "the love of loves." Saint Mary Magdalene of Pazzi called the day on which Jesus instituted this sacrament "the day of love." In this sacrament Jesus united and accomplished all the other acts of love which he had shown us.

Affections and Prayers: O infinite love of Jesus, worthy of being loved with infinite love. My Lord, you love me so much; how is it that I can love you so little in return? O my Jesus, you are so amiable and so loving. Make yourself known; make yourself loved. When shall I love you as you have loved me? Help me to discover more and more the greatness of your mercy in order that I may burn more and more with your love and always seek to please you. Beloved of my soul, I wish that I had always loved you. Regretfully, there was a time when I not only did not love you, but when I also despised your grace and your love! I am consoled by the sorrow that I now feel and I hope to be reconciled because of your promise to forgive those who repent of their sins. To you, my savior, do I give all my affections. Help me, through the merits of your passion, to love you with my whole strength. If only I could die for you, as you died for me!

O Mary, my Mother. Obtain for me the grace to love God alone.

MEDITATION 5:
THE SOUL UNITES WITH JESUS IN HOLY COMMUNION

Saint Dionysius the Areopagite teaches that the principal effect of love is the union of those who are in love. For this purpose Jesus instituted holy Communion, in order that he might unite himself entirely to our souls. He had given himself to us as our teacher, our example, and our victim. All that remained was for him to give himself to us as our food, that he might become one with us, as food becomes one with the person who eats it. Jesus did this by instituting this sacrament of love. Saint Bernardine of Siena says, "the last degree of love is when Jesus gave himself to us to be our food, uniting with us in every way."

Jesus was not satisfied with this unity with our human nature but he would, by this sacrament, find a way to unite himself to each one of us. In this way Jesus makes himself one with the person who receives him in the sacrament. Saint Francis de Sales writes, "In no other action can our Savior be considered more tender or more loving than in this, in which he, as it were, annihilates himself and reduces himself to food, that he may penetrate our souls, and unite himself to the hearts of the faithful."

Because Jesus loves us so much, he desires to unite himself to us in the holy Eucharist, in order that we might become the same thing with him. Saint John Chrysostom writes, "He mingled himself with us, that we might be one, for this belongs to those who love greatly."

Jesus wills, in short, that our hearts and his heart should form one heart. "He wills that we should have one heart with him," prays Saint Laurence Justinian.

Whoever receives holy Communion, has life from Jesus and Jesus lives in them. This union is not mere affection but is a true and real union. "As two candles, when melted," says Saint Cyril of Alexandria, "unite themselves into one, so the person that communicates becomes one with Jesus Christ." Let us, therefore imagine, when we receive holy Communion, that Jesus says to us that which he said one day to his beloved servant, Margaret of Ypres: "Behold, my daughter, the beautiful union between me and you. Come, then, love me, and let us remain constantly united in love, never more to be separated."

Affections and Prayers: O my Jesus. This is what I seek of you, and what I will always seek for you in holy Communion: "Let us be always united, and never more to be separate." I know that you will not separate yourself from me, if I do not first separate myself from you. But this is my fear, that I should in the future separate myself from you by sin, as I have done in the past. O my most Blessed Redeemer, do not permit it. Let me never be separated from you. As long as I am alive, I am in danger of this. Through the merits of your death, I beg you to let me die, rather than be separated from you again.

O God of my soul, I love you. I love you. I will always love you and you alone. I swear before heaven and earth that I desire you alone, and nothing but you. O my Jesus, hear me. I desire you alone and nothing but you.

O Mary, Mother of mercy, pray for me now, and obtain for me the grace never more to separate myself from Jesus, and to love only Jesus.

MEDITATION 6:

JESUS' DESIRE TO UNITE HIMSELF TO US IN HOLY COMMUNION

"Jesus knew that his hour had come" (Jn 13:1). This hour, which Jesus called "his hour," was the hour of the night in which his passion was to begin. Why did he call so sad an hour his hour? Because this was the hour for which he had prepared his whole life. It was in this hour that he determined to leave us the sacrament of the holy Eucharist. It was in this hour and in this sacrament that he desired to unite himself entirely to the souls whom he loved and for whom he was soon to give his blood and his life.

Recall how he spoke on that night to his disciples. "I have eagerly desired to eat this Passover with you" (Lk 22:15). With these words he expresses his desire and anxiousness to unite himself to us in this sacrament of love. Saint Laurence Justinian states that these words were words that came from the heart of Jesus. His heart burned with infinite love: "This is the voice of passionate love."

The same flame that burned in the heart of Jesus on that blessed night, burns in his heart today. Jesus gives the same invitation to all of us today to receive him as he gave to his apostles on that night. "Take, eat; this is my body" (Mt 26:26). In order to entice us to receive him with affection, he promises paradise: "Those who eat my flesh and drink my blood abide in me, and I in them" (Jn 6:56). If we refuse to receive him, he threatens us with death: "Unless you eat the flesh of the Son of Man and drink his blood, you have no life in you" (Jn 6:53).

These invitations, promises, and threats all find their source in the desire of Jesus Christ to unite himself to us in holy Communion, through the love that he bears us. "There is not a bee," said our Lord to Saint Mechtilde, "which seeks the honey out of the flowers with such eagerness of delight, as I have to enter into the souls that desire me." Jesus, because he loves us, desires to be loved by us. Because he desires us he wishes that we desire him in return. "God thirsts to be thirsted after," writes Saint Gregory. Blessed is that soul that approaches holy Communion with a great desire to be united to Jesus.

Affections and Prayers: My adorable Jesus, you cannot give me a greater proof of your love, to show me how much you love me. You have given your life for me. You have willed yourself to me in the holy Sacrament, in order that I may nourish myself with your body and blood. You are anxious that I receive you. How, then, can I become aware of all these proofs of your love and not burn with love for you? All earthly affections leave my heart; you hinder me from burning with love for Jesus as he burns with love for me. What other pledges of love can I expect, my beloved Redeemer, than those which you have already given me? You have sacrificed your whole life for my love. You have embraced for my sake a bitter and infamous death. You have reduced yourself almost to annihilation, by becoming food in the holy Eucharist in order to give yourself entirely to us. O Lord, let me no longer live ungrateful for such great goodness.

I thank you for having given me time to repent of the offenses I have committed against you and to love you during these days that remain to me in this life. I repent for having despised your love. I love you, O infinite goodness! I love you, O infinite treasure! I love you, O infinite love who are worthy of infinite love! O, help me, my Jesus, to discard from my heart all affections that are not directed to you so that from this day forward I may not desire, nor seek, nor love any other but you.

My beloved Lord, grant that I may always find you and grant that I may always love you. Take possession of my whole will, in order that I may never desire anything except that which is pleasing to you. My God, my God, whom shall I love, if I do not love you, who are the supreme good? I do indeed desire you, and nothing more.

O Mary, my Mother, take my heart into your keeping, and fill it with pure love for Jesus Christ.

MEDITATION 7: HOLY COMMUNION OBTAINS FOR US PERSEVERANCE IN DIVINE GRACE

When Jesus comes to the soul in holy Communion, he brings to the soul every grace, and specifically the grace of holy perseverance. This is the principal effect of the Most Holy Sacrament of the Altar, to nourish the soul that receives it with this food of life, and to give it great strength to advance in perfection, and to resist those enemies who desire our death. For this reason, Jesus identifies himself in this sacrament: "I am the living bread that came down from heaven. Whoever eats of this bread will live forever" (Jn 6:51). Even as earthly bread sustains the life of the body, so this heavenly bread sustains the life of the soul, by making it persevere in the grace of God.

The Council of Trent teaches that holy Communion is that remedy which delivers us from daily faults and preserves us from mortal sins. Pope Innocent III writes that Jesus Christ by his passion delivers us from sins committed, and by the holy Eucharist from sins that we might commit. Saint Bonaventure says that sinners must not keep away from Communion because they have been sinners; on the contrary, for this very reason that should receive Communion more frequently. "The more infirm a person feels, the more that person is in need of a doctor."

Affections and Prayers: Miserable sinner that I am, O Lord, how do I lament my weakness when I consider my many falls from grace? How was it possible for me to resist the assaults of the devil while I stayed away from you, who are my strength? If I had more often approached you in holy Communion, my enemies would not have overcome me. In the future, I will not repeat this mistake: "In you, O Lord, I seek refuge; do not let me ever be put to shame" (Ps 31:1). I will no longer rely on my own strength. You alone are my hope, O my Jesus. You will give me strength so that I will no longer fall into sin. I am weak, but through holy Communion, you will make me strong against every temptation: "I can do all things through him who strengthens me" (Phil 4:13).

Forgive me, Jesus, of all the offenses that I have committed against you and from which I repent with my whole heart. I resolve to die, rather than to offend you again. I trust, in your passion, that you will give me your help to persevere in your grace to the end of my life: "In you O Lord I have hoped; I shall not be perplexed forever."

With Saint Bonaventure I will say the same to you, O Mary, my Mother: "In you, O Lady I have hoped; I shall not be perplexed forever."

MEDITATION 8: PREPARATION FOR COMMUNION AND THANKSGIVING AFTER COMMUNION

Cardinal Bona asks, "Why is it that so many souls, after so many Communions, make so little progress in the way of God?" He answers his question by stating, "the fault is not in the food, but rather in the disposition of the person who receives it." In other words, there is not sufficient preparation on the part of the communicant. Fire soon burns dry wood, but not wood that is green, because the green wood is not fit to burn. The saints derived great profit from their Communions, because they were very careful in their preparation for the reception of the sacrament.

There are two principal things that we should endeavor to obtain in order to prepare ourselves for holy Communion and to gain the greatest fruit. The first is detachment from creatures, driving from our heart everything that is not of God and for God. Although the soul may be in a state of grace, if the heart is occupied by other things, the more there is of the earth in the soul, so much less room will there be for the fire of divine love. Saint Gertrude once asked our Lord what preparation he required of her for holy Communion. Jesus answered, "I require nothing more from you except that you come to receive me not full of your self."

The second thing that is necessary in order to harvest the greatest fruit from Communion is the desire to receive Jesus Christ with the intention of loving him more. Saint Francis de Sales writes that the principal intention of a soul receiving Communion should be to grow in the love of God. "He should be received for love because it is out of pure love that he gives himself to us." Saint Mechtilde writes that our Lord told her: "When you are going to communicate, desire all the love that any soul ever had for me, and I will receive it according to the desire, as if it were your own."

It is also necessary to make a thanksgiving after Communion. There is no prayer more dear to God than the prayer that is made after Communion. We must occupy this time in acts of love and prayers. The devout acts of love, which we make at this time, have greater merit in the sight of God. Our acts, at this time, are animated by the presence of Jesus Christ, who is united to our souls. Saint Teresa says that Jesus, after Communion, remains in the soul as on a throne of grace, and says to the soul, "What is it that you hope that I do for you?" The Lord invites us to ask for as much as we need, and to be assured that we will be heard. What treasures of grace do people lose who pray a short time to God after holy Communion!

Affections and Prayers: O God of love, You desire to grant favors to me and yet I seem to not be interested to receive them. What sorrow will I feel at the hour of my death, when I think of this negligence, so pernicious to my soul! O my Lord, forget, I implore you, all that is in my past. In the future, with your help, I will better prepare myself. I will try to detach my affections from everything that prevents me from receiving all those graces that you desire to give to me. After

Communion I will lift up my heart to you as much as I can, in order to obtain your help so that I may grow in love for you. Grant me the grace to accomplish this!

O my Jesus, how negligent have I been in loving you. The time that you in your mercy give to me in this life, is the time to prepare myself for death, and to make amends for the offenses I have committed against you. I will spend my time on earth lamenting my sins and in loving you. I love you, Jesus my love; I love you, my only good; have pity on me, and do not forsake me.

Mary, my hope, do not cease to help me by your holy intercession!

14. Saint Alphonsus Liguori's Visits to the Most Blessed Sacrament

At one time, in the not so distant past, the practice of a daily visit to the Blessed Sacrament was not uncommon. The faithful on their way home from the fields would stop in the village church or coming home from work they would stop in the neighborhood church. Priests, monks, and religious women, living in monasteries and convents with chapels, would often stop into the chapel in the midst of their daily routine and make a quick visit to the Blessed Sacrament. Unfortunately this practice, because of a variety of reasons, fell into disfavor. Today, however, the practice is being revived with a renewed interest, because of the establishment of the practice of Perpetual Adoration in many parish churches and because of a renewed emphasis on the doctrine of the True Presence of Christ in the Blessed Sacrament.

Visits to the Most Blessed Sacrament and the Blessed Virgin Mary by Saint Alphonsus Liguori (1696–1787) is a perennial favorite. Each visit (the saint provides the faithful with an appropriate visit for each day of the month) consists of an opening prayer, a meditation on the Eucharist, a spiritual communion prayer, a visit to the Blessed Mother, and finally a closing prayer.

OPENING PRAYER

My Lord Jesus Christ, I believe that you are really here in this sacrament. Night and day you remain here compassionate and loving. You call, you wait for, and you welcome everyone who comes to you. Unimportant though I am, I adore you. I thank you for all the wonderful graces you have given me. But I thank you especially for having given me yourself in this sacrament, for having asked your own Mother to mother me, for having called me here to talk to you.

I am here before you today to do three things: to thank you for these precious gifts, to make up for all the disrespect that you receive in this sacrament from those who offend you, and to adore you everywhere in the world where you are present in this living bread but are left abandoned and unloved.

My Jesus, I love you with all my heart. I know I have displeased you often in the past—I am sorry. With your help I promise never to do it again. I am only a miserable sinner, but I consecrate myself to you completely. I give you my will, my love, my desires, everything I own. From now on do what you please with me. All I ask is that you love me and that you keep me faithful to the end of my life. I ask for the grace to do your will exactly as you want it done.

I pray for the souls in purgatory—especially for those who were close to you in this sacrament and close to your mother Mary. I pray for every soul hardened in sin. My Savior, I unite my love to the love of your divine heart, and I offer them both together to your Father. I beg him to accept this offering in your name. Amen.

VISIT APPROPRIATE FOR ORDINARY TIME

"O foolish ones of the world," says Saint Augustine, "where are you going to satisfy your hearts?" Come to Jesus, for it is only by him alone that you will find the pleasure that you seek. "Unhappy creatures, where are you going? The good that you seek comes only from him." My soul, don't be one of the foolish ones; seek God alone, "seek for the one good in which are all good things." And if you desire to find Jesus, he is close to you. Tell him what you desire, for it is for this reason that he is in the tabernacle, to console you, and to grant your prayer.

Saint Teresa says that most people are not permitted to speak to kings; the most that can be hoped for is to communicate with them through a third person. To converse with you, O King of Glory, no third person is needed; you are always ready in the Blessed Sacrament of the altar to listen to all. All who desire you will always find you there and converse with you face to face. And even if anyone finally does succeed in speaking to a king, how many difficulties must be overcome before they can do so! Kings grant audiences only a few times a year, but you Lord, in this sacrament, grant an audience to all, night and day, and whenever we please.

O Sacrament of Love, whether you give yourself to us in Communion, or dwell upon the altar, you know how to draw so many hearts to yourself, by the tender attractions of your love. Your people who are enamored of you, and filled with amazement at the sight of such love, burn with joy and constantly think of you. Draw my miserable heart to yourself, for my heart desires to love you, and to live enslaved by your love. For my part I now place all of my interests, all of my hopes, all of my desires, my soul, my body—I place all in the hands of your goodness. Accept me Lord and use me as you please. I will never again complain, O my love, of what you ask me to do. I know that all that you ask of me is rooted in your loving heart, full of love for me, and only for my good. It is enough for me to know that you have willed it, now and for all eternity.

I unite my entire self to your will, which is all holy, all good, all beautiful, all perfect, and all loving. O will of my God, how dear you are to me. My will is to live and die united to you and bound up with you. Your pleasure is my pleasure; I will that my desires are also your desires. My God, my God, help me, make me live for you alone, make me desire only what you desire, and make me live to love only your will for me. Grant that I may die for your love, since you have died and have become in this sacrament the nourishment that I need. I curse those days when I followed my own will and my own desires.

I love you, O will of God. I love you with my whole heart and give myself entirely to you.

SPIRITUAL COMMUNION

My Jesus, I believe you are really here in the Blessed Sacrament. I love you more than anything in the world, and I desire to receive you into my heart. Since I cannot receive you sacramentally at this time, come at least spiritually into my heart. I unite myself to you now as I do when I actually receive you. Never let me be parted from you.

VISIT WITH MARY

My gentle Mother, I have disgracefully rebelled against your son. I am sorry for what I have done. I kneel at your feet, hoping that you will obtain pardon for me. I know you can do so because Saint Bernard calls you the "minister of forgiveness." But I am confident that you will supply me with everything I need: courage to ask forgiveness, perseverance, and heaven. I hope to praise your mercy forever, my Queen, for having gained heaven through your ministry.

CONCLUDING PRAYER

Most Holy Immaculate Virgin and my Mother Mary, to you who are the mother of my Lord, the Queen of the world, the Advocate, the Hope, the Refuge of sinners, I have recourse today—I who am the most miserable of all. I render you my most humble homage, O great Queen, and I thank you for all the graces you have conferred on me until now, particularly for having delivered me from hell, which I have so often deserved. I love you, O most amiable Lady; and for the love that I bear you, I promise to serve you always and to do all in my power to make others also love you. I place in you all my hopes; I confide my salvation to your care. Accept me for your servant and receive me under your mantle, O Mother of Mercy. And since you are so powerful with God, deliver me from all temptations; or rather obtain for me the strength to triumph over them until death. Of you I ask a perfect love for Jesus Christ. From you I hope to die a good death. O my Mother, by the love which you bear to God, I beseech you to help me at all times, but especially at the last moment of my life. Leave me not, I beseech you, until you see me safe in heaven, blessing you and singing your mercies for all eternity. Amen. So I hope. So may it be.

IV. Prayers for the Sacrament of Penance

1. Bernard Haring's Meditation on the Sacrament of Penance

By faith and grace, we recognize the gratuitousness of redemption and the power of the Spirit, and our gratitude moves us to help one another, to strengthen one another, and to bear one another's burdens. Up to the time of Albert the Great and Thomas Aquinas, familial correction, offered in a spirit of gentleness and in awareness that we all depend on God's patience and graciousness, and followed by humble avowal of the fault and by prayer, was considered a kind of sacrament, a particular expression of the sacrament of divine forgiveness. This vision did not at all diminish the special role of the priest as a minister of reconciliation. If we experience Christ's gracious presence in our daily lives, helping one another to overcome limitations and faults, we also come to better understanding of the celebration of the Church's sacrament of penance.

It is always Christ who comes and assures us of forgiveness, but he has chosen to do it in a very visible and effective way through the ministry of the Church. In the sacrament of penance we meet the priest who, through his charism and mission, is truly a sign of the presence of the Good Shepherd, of the Divine Physician. We see then the essence of this sacrament: that it is not so much our own endeavor, but rather Christ's. Through grace, the mercy of the Father, and his own gentle presence and healing power, Christ calls us to the humble avowal of our sins and the redirection of our life toward his goodness. Through the healing kindness of our neighbor and the consoling message of the commissioned messenger of reconciliation, Christ kindles in us a new courage, and the desire to respond to his call to follow him and to carry out our share in the redemptive mission of the Church.

> *O Lord, you lead us to those who are in sorrow and in need of comfort. You come in the guise of the poor and allow us to make them rich with your goodness. You bring to us those who are disillusioned and discouraged, so that we may be a sign of your consolation and encouragement. You send us, Lord, at the same time, so many gifts of your goodness, and those who are in need of your love, so that we may transform your love into love for our sisters and brothers; so that, all together, we can experience that you are always with us, that you call us and wait for us. Lord, make us vigilant and generous. All our lives wait for your final coming.*

2. Saint Alphonsus Liguori's Prayer Before Confession

Saint Alphonsus Liguori (1696–1787), founder of the Congregation of the Most Holy Redeemer (Redemptorists), bishop, and Doctor of the Church composed the following traditional prayers. The first prayer is to be prayed before confession, followed by a prayer to be prayed after reception of the sacrament. Saint Alphonsus Liguori recommended that all people (but especially the members of his congregation) pray them.

O God of infinite majesty, I am at your feet, again guilty of offending you, but now asking in all humility for your pardon. O Lord, do not reject me. You cannot despise a heart that is humble. I thank you for having waited for me up to the present moment, and for not allowing me to die when I was in sin, to be sent to hell, as I had deserved. The patience that you have demonstrated toward me, O God, makes me hope that through the merits of Jesus Christ you will pardon me in this confession. I repent of all of my sins. I am grieved because I have deserved hell and have often lost heaven because I have displeased you, who are infinite goodness.

I love you, O sovereign good, and because I love you, I repent of all of my offenses against you. I have turned my back on you and I have despised your grace and your friendship. In a word, O Lord, I have willfully lost you. For the love of Jesus Christ, forgive all of my sins. I repent of them with all of my heart, I hate them, and I detest them. I promise, with the help of your grace, to never offend you again. I would rather die than sin again.

3. Saint Alphonsus Liguori's Prayer After Confession

My dear Jesus, how much do I owe you! By the merits of your blood I trust that I have been pardoned. I thank you exceedingly. I hope to praise your mercy forever in heaven. My God, I am resolved to really change my life. You deserve all of my love; I wish to love you completely. My will is to never again be separated from you. I have already promised you, and I promise you again at this moment, not to offend you again. I promise to flee the occasion of sin, and to use this means (*mention it here*) so that I will not fail again. But you, Jesus, know my weakness. Give me the grace to be faithful to you until death, and to call upon you in my temptations.

Most Holy Virgin Mary, assist me. You are the Mother of perseverance; all of my hope is in you.

4. Saint John of the Cross's Prayer Before Confession

Saint John of the Cross (1542–1591) was a Carmelite friar who was selected by Saint Teresa of Ávila as the first friar in her reformed congregation. Known for his mysticism, he is a Doctor of the Church and the author of universally acknowledged spiritual classics including *The Dark Night of the Soul* and *The Ascent of Mount Carmel*.

Lord God, my beloved, if you are still mindful of my sins and will not grant my petitions, let your will be done, for that is my chief desire. Show your goodness and mercy, and you shall be known for them. If you are waiting for me to do good works, and upon their performance you will grant my petitions, cause them to be accomplished in me. Send also the punishment for my sins that is acceptable to you. For how will I raise myself to you, born and bred as I am in misery, unless you, Lord, will lift me up with the hand that made me? Amen.

5. Saint Catherine of Siena's Prayer Before Confession

Saint Catherine of Siena (1347–1380) was a mystical theologian and Doctor of the Church. Her legendary powers of persuasion were instrumental in convincing the pope to move back to Rome from Avignon, France.

Merciful Lord, it does not surprise me that you completely forget the sins of those who repent. I am not surprised that you remain faithful to those who revile you. The mercy, which pours forth from you, fills the whole world. It was by your mercy that we were created, and by your mercy that you redeemed us by sending your Son. Your mercy is the light in which sinners find you, and good people come back to you. Your mercy is everywhere. Your justice is constantly tempered with mercy, so you refuse to punish us as we deserve. O my lover! It was not enough that you took on our humanity; you had to die for us as well. Amen.

6. Saint Francis de Sales's Prayer After Confession

Saint Francis de Sales (1567–1622) was a bishop and Doctor of the Church. He is well known for his spiritual works including *Treatise on the Love of God* and *Introduction to the Devout Life*.

Do not look forward to the changes and chances of this life with fear. Rather, look to them with full confidence that, as they arise, God to whom you belong will in his love enable you to profit by them. God has guided you thus far in life. Hold fast to his dear hand, and he will lead you safely through all trials. Whenever you cannot stand, he will carry you lovingly in his arms.

Do not look forward to what may happen tomorrow. The same Eternal Father who takes care of you today will take care of you tomorrow, and every day of your life. Either he will shield you from suffering or he will give you the unfailing strength to bear it.

Be at peace then, and put aside all useless thoughts, all vain dreads, and all anxious imaginations.

7. Traditional Act of Contrition

My God, I am sorry for my sins with all my heart. In choosing to do wrong and failing to do good, I have sinned against you whom I should love above all things. I firmly intend, with your help, to do penance, to sin no more, and to avoid whatever leads me to sin. Our Savior Jesus Christ suffered and died for us. In his name, my God, have mercy. Amen.

8. *Confiteor*

I confess to Almighty God, to blessed Mary ever Virgin, to blessed Michael the Archangel, to blessed John the Baptist, to the holy apostles Peter and Paul, to all the saints, and to you Father, that I have sinned exceedingly in thought, word, and deed, through my fault, through my fault, through my most grievous fault (*here strike your breast three times*), therefore I beseech the blessed Mary ever Virgin, the blessed Michael the Archangel, the blessed John the Baptist, the holy apostles Peter and Paul, all the saints, and you Father, to pray to the Lord our God for me. May God have mercy on me, forgive me my sins, and lead me on to eternal life. Amen.

9. Prayer to Celebrate God's Forgiveness

It is right and fitting, a sign of your gracious presence and a way of salvation, to render thanks always and everywhere to you, all-merciful God. When first we fell into sinfulness and alienation, you did not abandon us. As a sign of salvation, you gave to Adam and Eve sons like Abel and Seth, who knew how to invoke your name and to praise your goodness. When Cain slaughtered his brother, you yourself made a sign on his face that slaughter should not go on. And when the earth was flooded with sin, you saved Noah, his family, and all the species of animals out of the chaos of waters.

You made Joseph, whom his brothers had sold into slavery, a wonderful sign of forgiveness and reconciliation. And when your people in slavery called to you for liberation, you led them out of Egypt, through the Red Sea, through the desert, and over the Jordan, into the Promised Land.

You taught the prostitute, Rahab, to show mercy to the ambassadors of your people, and in turn you taught your people to show mercy to her.

When the anointed king, David, offended you gravely by taking another man's wife and killing her husband, you sent Nathan to shake his conscience and make him aware of his crime. And when he showed repentance, you made known to David your mercy and reconciled him.

At the appointed time you sent Jesus Christ, your Son, and made him the great sacrament of penance, the Good Shepherd who seeks the lost sheep, the Divine Physician who heals the sick, the source of living water who, by the power of the Holy Spirit, can raise to life those who were dead in their sins.

Therefore with angels and saints, with all those who throughout history have been messengers of your peace and ministers of reconciliation, we commit ourselves to the same mission: to be signs of your merciful presence, and thus to praise your name. Amen.

10. Examinations of Conscience

The two examples of examinations of conscience that follow are used in the preparation of an individual person to celebrate the sacrament of penance. The thorough examination of a person's conscience has been a traditional recommendation for those who are preparing for the confession of their sins. Within the spiritual tradition of the Church there are occasions when the examination should be very detailed in preparation for the celebration of the sacrament, and examinations of conscience provide details that are both necessary and useful.

TRADITIONAL EXAMINATION OF CONSCIENCE

The detailed examination of conscience in the traditional model that follows begins with a prayer and a series of preparatory questions and then examines the person in relation to the Ten Commandments and the Precepts of the Church. The detailed examination ends with particular questions for people in different "states in life," such as married, single, or religious and finally, particular questions for people who are doctors, lawyers, pharmacists, and so on. The examination that follows is from *The Mission Book of the Redemptorist Fathers*, a devotional manual routinely used by many Catholics until the Second Vatican Council. The examination will include edited questions pertaining to the Ten Commandments and the Precepts of the Church but will not include the questions for people in different states in life.

Preparatory Prayer

O God, Father of light, who enlightens everyone who comes into this world, give me light, love, and sorrow, that I may discover, detest, and confess all the sins that I have committed.

O Most Holy Virgin Mary, Mother of the Redeemer, so compassionate toward those who desire to repent, help me to make a good confession. My dear Guardian Angel, help me to call to mind all my offenses. All the saints and angels, pray for me that I may now bring forth worthy fruits of penance.

Preparatory Questions

How long ago did you make your last confession? Did you receive absolution? Have you performed your penance? Did you willfully conceal a mortal sin or confess without true sorrow, without the purpose of amendment, or without intending to perform your penance?

First Commandment: *I am the Lord your God, you shall have no gods before me.*

Have you disbelieved or willfully indulged in doubts against any article of faith or suggested or encouraged such doubts in others? Have you attended or joined in false worship? Have you exposed your faith to danger by evil associations? Have you remained a long time, a whole month, or longer, without reciting any prayer, or performing any act of devotion toward God? Have you consulted fortune-tellers or made use of superstitious practices, love potions, or charms?

Second Commandment: *You shall not take the name of the Lord your God in vain.*

Have you been guilty of blasphemy by angry, injurious, or insulting words against God? Have you pronounced in a blasphemous or irreverent manner, or in anger, the holy name of God, the name of Jesus Christ, or that of any of the saints? Have you sworn a false oath? Have you cursed yourself or cursed a neighbor?

Third Commandment: *Remember to keep holy the Sabbath day.*

How often have you on Sundays and holy days of obligation willfully chosen not to attend Mass, or come too late, or left before Mass was over? How often have you performed unnecessary servile work on Sundays and on holy days or caused others to do the same? How often did you desecrate these days by frequenting ungodly company, by sinful amusements, gambling, immodest dancing, or drinking to excess?

Fourth Commandment: *Honor your father and your mother.*

Have you insulted, mocked, ridiculed, or cursed your parents? Have you threatened them, or even lifted your hand to strike them? Have you sorely grieved your parents by your ingratitude or misconduct? Have you neglected or refused to aid them in their wants? Have you neglected to pray for them? Have you neglected to pray for the repose of their souls?

Fifth Commandment: *You shall not kill.*

Have you by act, participation, instigation, counsel, or consent been guilty of anyone's death or bodily injury? Have you intended or attempted to take another's life? Have you injured your health by excess in eating or drinking? Have you been drunk or been the cause of drunkenness in another? Have you by act, advice, or consent done anything to hinder or destroy life? Have you harmed the soul of another person by giving scandal? Have you by wicked words, deeds, or bad example, ruined innocent persons, taught them bad habits or things they should not know?

Sixth and Ninth Commandments: *You shall not commit adultery* and *You shall not covet your neighbor's wife.*

These commandments forbid everything that is contrary to purity. How often have you made use of impure language, allusions, or words of double meaning? How have you made use of impure language, allusions, or words of double meaning? How often have you voluntarily exposed yourself to the occasion of sin by sinful curiosity, by frequenting dangerous company, places, or sinful amusements? How often have you been guilty of improper liberties with others? How far have you carried your sinful conduct? You must mention those circumstances that change the nature of your sin—the sex, the relationship, and the condition—whether married, single, or bound by vow. Were you married or single at the time?

Seventh and Tenth Commandments: *You shall not steal* and *You shall not covet your neighbor's goods.*

Have you stolen money or anything of value? Is it still in your possession? What was its value? How much did you take each time and how often? Have you stolen anything belonging to God or to a sacred place? Have you charged exorbitant prices, or made out false bills, or cheated in the weight, measure, quantity, or quality of your goods? Have you cheated in games? Have you been guilty of forgery? Have you kept things you found without inquiring for the owner? Have you bought, received, or concealed things you knew to be stolen?

Eighth Commandment: *You shall not bear false witness against your neighbor.*

Have you taken a false oath or advised others to do so? Have you signed false papers or forged writings? Have you been guilty of malicious lying? Have you caused ill feelings between others by tale bearing? Have you attempted to repair the harm you have done by contradicting your false reports? Have you been guilty of unjust suspicions and rash judgments?

Concluding Prayer

O most loving Jesus, dying on the cross for my sake, remember that I am a soul redeemed by your most precious blood. Pardon me, I am sorry for my sins. I beseech you by your sacred wounds, by your loving heart, to receive the traitor who now casts himself in sorrow at your feet. My sins fill me with terror; I know that I deserve the flames of hell. But since you have died for me, I hope that you will have mercy on me now that I implore your forgiveness and am firmly resolved to sin no more. I promise to serve you faithfully all the days of my life, and to love you as much as I have offended you. O my most loving Jesus, you have died to save me, let not your blood be shed for me in vain. Grant me the grace to confess my sins humbly and sincerely. Give me the strength to avoid all of the occasions of sin and never more to offend you again.

Holy Virgin Mary, Mother of mercy, my holy Guardian Angel and all my patron saints, help me to lead from this day forward, a truly Christian life. Amen.

CONTEMPORARY EXAMINATION OF CONSCIENCE

This examination is intended to be prayed within the context of silent prayer. It is recommended that the examination be used after a period of time spent reflecting on the Word of God. (See page 216 for suggested Scripture passages for penance and reconciliation.)

Preparatory Prayer

Lord Jesus, open my mind and heart to your Holy Spirit. Show me where I am failing to love your heavenly Father. Show me where I am failing to love you as my Savior, failing to seek you and yield to you as my Lord. Show me where I am failing to love the Holy Spirit, failing to be open and to be led by Wisdom and Love.

(The petitions should be read slowly, with a pause for reflection between each.)

For the times I have failed to see the poor and oppressed, and my failure to do what I could to feed the hungry: I ask pardon, O Lord.

For the times I have failed to respond to the call of the gospel by not doing what I could for those without clothing or shelter; I ask pardon, O Lord.

For the times I have not respected members of my family, my neighbors, and those who work with me; I ask pardon, O Lord.

For the times I have not been sensitive to another's needs and weaknesses; I ask pardon, O Lord.

For those I have hurt by words of unkindness or untruth; I ask pardon, O Lord.

For those I have discriminated against because of race, religion, nationality, age, profession, or gender; I ask pardon, O Lord.

For the times I have caused pain and suffering in the lives of loved ones and friends through my abuse of alcohol, food, or drugs; I ask pardon, O Lord.

For those who have suffered because of my misuse of money; I ask pardon, O Lord.

For the times I have been selfish with the gifts God has given me; I ask pardon, O Lord.

For the times I have been unforgiving; I ask pardon, O Lord.

For the times I have been angry with others and have caused pain and suffering in their lives; I ask pardon, O Lord

Concluding Prayer

Lord, I come before you asking for mercy and forgiveness of my sins. I confess that I am a sinner. Through the ministry of the Church, grant me pardon from all my sins. I give you thankful praise in the name of Jesus, our Lord and Savior. Amen.

11. A Meditation for Reconciliation

Created in the image and likeness of God, we are good. We are whole and happy—in harmony with all of God's creation. From the beginning, this is God's will for us. "God created humankind in his image, in the image of God he created them; male and female he created them" (Gen 1:27).

When we sin, shame and uneasiness replace openness and confidence. We are broken and unhappy because we act contrary to our true selves. A cloak of defensiveness replaces the nakedness of trust. "Then the eyes of both were opened, and they knew that they were naked; and they sewed fig leaves together and made loincloths for themselves" (Gen 3:7).

Sin is a subversive force in the community because it introduces division and problems. Selfishness alienates us from family, friends, and acquaintances. We shift the blame for our own sinfulness onto others and we wither, refusing to either give or accept love. "The man said, 'The woman whom you gave to be with me, she gave me fruit from the tree, and I ate'" (Gen 3:12).

Feeling the weight of guilt and remorse from our sin, we presume God is angry with us too. We grow fearful, hiding behind self-righteous walls of anger or apathy because we judge ourselves so unworthy of God's love. "[T]he man and his wife hid themselves from the presence of the LORD God among the trees of the garden" (Gen 3:8).

God's love is passionate, joyful, intimate, self-giving, forgiving, faithful, listening, understanding, and affirming. In other words, God's is an accepting and reconciling love. It is ours for the taking—and it is ours for the giving. It brings us back to where we started: whole and happy—in harmony with all of creation. "God saw everything that he had made, and indeed, it was very good" (Gen 1:31).

V. Prayers for the Sacrament of the Anointing of the Sick

1. Bernard Häring's Meditation on the Sacrament of the Anointing of the Sick

It is impressive to see how the sick gained trust and confidence whenever Jesus came. He was totally present to them, with all his loving attention and the healing power of his kindness. Christ is ever present to all, the Divine Physician who heals us in our human weaknesses, but he wants to manifest his presence in a very special way to those who are suffering or sick.

Through kind and good caregivers, the Lord makes the sick alert to his own compassionate and consoling presence with them. The sacrament of the anointing of the sick can have a profound significance for sufferers.

Again, presence includes and awakens reciprocity of consciousness. Not only does Christ want to be present to the sick; he wants them to be present to him, to unite themselves and their suffering with the power of the paschal mystery. Christ comes in the sacrament to meet his suffering friends so that they can become truly aware of him, consciously turn to him, and allow him to insert their suffering into the saving event of his own death and Resurrection.

We all have the mission of helping the sick, especially those who are facing death, making them aware of Christ's redeeming presence with them on their way. When we do this, we are one with Christ, who, in the Viaticum, invites the dying to make ready for his final coming.

Lord, make us vigilant and generous. All our lives wait for your final coming. With complete trust we look forward to the hour of your call. You yourself will come; will call us each by name. Then we shall know that your judgment is salvation and compassion if we but faithfully respond to your coming whenever and wherever you call us through our sisters and brothers, through the poor. Come, Lord Jesus, call whenever you want, under whatever conditions you decide. Abide with us. Make us vigilant and ready for your coming. Maranatha.

2. To Christ Our Healer

The physician our Lord and Savior is all powerful.
He restores those who worship and hope in him.
He heals not by the skill of science but by his word.
Though he dwells in heaven, he is present everywhere.
All praise to him. Amen.

3. A Prayer for Healing

Jesus, you are my deliverer, the true physician who comes all the way from heaven to visit the sick. I put myself into your hands. Help me to resolve to put all my trust in you alone and to patiently undergo any treatment. If you will not heal me, my Savior, my case is beyond hope. But if I am to be healed, it is you, Lord, who will heal me. You alone uproot the sickness and give me lasting health. You are my salvation and life, my comfort and my glory, my hope in this world and my crown in the world to come. Amen.

4. Prayer for the Sick

Let us ask the Lord of all health and salvation on behalf of our brothers and sisters who are suffering from bodily illnesses that he alone who is the Dear Physician will help them all.

O God, who bids our lives to run fast or slow, accept the prayers of your servants who in their sickness implore your pity. Save them and change their fear and apprehension to joy.

We call on you, Lord, who has formed our bodies and souls and who governs, guides, and saves all of humankind; may our prayers move you to relent and heal all who are sick; remove their suffering from them, raise up those who must convalesce in bed, so that they may glorify your holy Name, now and forever. Amen.

5. Saint Teresa of Ávila's Prayer at the Time of Death

Teresa of Ávila (1515–1582), Doctor of the Church, mystic, and author of the primary work on the spiritual life, *The Interior Castle.* The prayer that follows is traditionally identified as her "last prayer," prayed as she waited for her final sickness to run its course.

My Lord, it is time to move on.

Well, then, may your will be done.

O my Lord and my Spouse,

The house that I have longed for has come.

It is time for us to meet one another. Amen.

6. A Traditional Prayer for the Sick, Invoking Saint Camillus

O glorious Saint Camillus, special patron of the sick poor, you who for forty years, with truly heroic charity, devoted yourself to the relief of their temporal and spiritual needs, be pleased to assist them now even more generously, since you are blessed in heaven and they have been committed by the holy Church to your powerful protection. Obtain for them from almighty God the healing of all their maladies, or at least, the spirit of Christian patience and resignation that may sanctify them and comfort them in the hour of their passing to eternity. At the same time get us the precious grace of living and dying after your example in the practice of divine love. Amen.

7. A Traditional Prayer for Those Near Death

Eternal Father, by the love you bear toward Saint Joseph, who was chosen by you from among all humanity to exercise your divine Fatherhood over your Son made man, have mercy on us and upon all poor souls who are in their agony.

(Pray an Our Father, a Hail Mary, and a Glory Be to the Father.)

Eternal Son of God, by the love you bear toward Saint Joseph who was your most faithful guardian on earth, have mercy on us and upon all poor souls who are in their agony.

(Pray an Our Father, a Hail Mary, and a Glory Be to the Father.)

Eternal Spirit of God, by the love you bear toward Saint Joseph, who guarded with such tender care your most holy Mary, the beloved Spouse, have mercy on us and upon all poor souls who are in their agony.

(Pray an Our Father, a Hail Mary, and a Glory Be to the Father.)

8. A Prayer for Letting Go of a Loved One Near Death

My Lord and my God,
You have created me in your divine image and likeness.
In you I find the fulfillment of all of my hopes and dreams.
In your great mercy and love you have also gifted me with love,
And have permitted me to love another as I have loved you.

Today, as I stand before you,
Filled with a deep sorrow and an impending feeling of loss,
I know that you are calling one of your loved ones home,
But I still love them too, Lord, and I need to hold on to them,
Not forever, as you one day will,
But just for a few more moments,
A few precious minutes.

You know how difficult it is for me to let go
So be patient with me Lord.
My tears,
The heaviness in my heart,
And the sorrow in my voice
Are not signs of my unbelief
But rather signs of my love.
They are not meant to deny,
But rather to ultimately celebrate,
That I will rejoice,
I will be strengthened,

And I will eventually accept,
That your will must be accomplished,
On earth this day, as it is in heaven.
Amen.

9. Prayer to the Divine Physician

We pray to you, Divine Physician, to illumine and strengthen all of us, and especially those in the healthcare profession, and the friends and relatives of our sick brothers and sisters, so that we may be able to communicate to them the experience of your loving and healing care.

O Christ, let us experience in the crucial moments of our lives that you are near to us and that we can entrust ourselves to you. Strengthen our faith in your paschal mystery, so that those moments which are meaningless without you can receive, through your presence and our response to you, final meaning for us and for the salvation of the world. Amen.

10. A Healing and Anointing Service

Welcome everyone to our celebration of Jesus' healing power!

Leader: The grace of our Lord Jesus Christ and the love of God the Father and the healing light of the Holy Spirit be with you all.

Response: And also with you.

Leader: We gather in the name of the Lord Jesus Christ who is present among us. Jesus is deeply moved with compassion in seeing the suffering of the sick, the wounded soul of the sinner, and the affliction of the poor. Jesus healed all who came to him and cured those troubled by evil spirits. After his ascension into heaven, he sent the Holy

Spirit for the forgiveness of sins and to continue his healing ministry within the Church. Now we stand before the Lord Jesus in the healing light of his Holy Spirit to seek physical and inner healing for our loved ones and ourselves.

PENITENTIAL RITE

Leader: As we prepare ourselves for the celebration of the healing love of our God, let us acknowledge our sins and, with trust in God's love and mercy, ask for God's forgiveness.

(Brief moment of silence)

Leader: Lord Jesus, you came to seek the lost. Lord, have mercy.

Response: Lord, have mercy.

Leader: Lord Jesus, you heal the sick, give sight to the blind, and enable the lame to walk. Christ, have mercy.

Response: Christ, have mercy.

Leader: Lord Jesus, you call us to pray for each other so that we may experience your healing. Lord, have mercy.

Response: Lord, have mercy.

Leader: May almighty God have mercy on us, forgive us our sins, and bring us to everlasting life.

Response: Amen!

Leader: Let us pray: God our loving Father, you sent your Son Jesus as the Sun of Justice who comes to us with his healing rays. Through your Holy Spirit allow these healing rays to bathe us and heal us in mind, body, and spirit. Grant this through Christ our Lord.

Response: Amen!

Scripture Readings: Acts of the Apostles 5:12–16; Responsorial Psalm 103:1–5, 11–14

Leader: Lord, lay your healing hand upon me.

Response: Lord, lay your healing hand upon me.

Leader: Bless the Lord, O my soul; and all my being, bless his holy Name. Bless the Lord, O my soul, and forget not all his benefits.

Response: Lord, lay your healing hand upon me.

Leader: He pardons all your iniquities, he heals all your ills, he redeems your life from destruction, he crowns you with kindness and compassion, he fills your lifetime with good; your youth is renewed like the eagle's.

Response: Lord, lay your healing hand upon me.

Leader: For as the heavens are high above the earth, so surpassing is his kindness toward those who fear him. As far as the east is from the west, so far has he put our transgressions from us.

Response: Lord, lay your healing hand upon me.

Leader: As a father has compassion on his children, so the Lord has compassion on those who fear him. For he knows how we are formed; he remembers that we are dust.

Response: Lord, lay your healing hand upon me.

Scripture Reading: Gospel of Mark 6:7–13
Homily
Blessing of the Oil

Leader: Let us pray: God of mercy and love, you sent your Son to heal our wounded human nature. Breathe your Holy Spirit upon this oil and bless + it. Through its use may we experience the warmth of your healing love flowing into the depths of our wounded hearts. We ask this through our Lord Jesus Christ, your Son, who lives and reigns with you and the Holy Spirit, one God, forever and ever.

Response: Amen!

THE LAYING ON OF HANDS AND
THE ANOINTING WITH BLESSED OIL

Leader: The laying on of hands and the anointing are not the sacrament of the anointing of the sick. This is a simple anointing service asking for the Lord's healing. All Christians are welcome to receive this anointing. As you come forward, we will impose our hands on your head, pause for a moment of silence, and then anoint you with the blessed oil. (*The ministers will now anoint the people.*)

PRAYER AFTER ANOINTING

Leader: Let us pray: Father in heaven, through the laying on of hands and this anointing give us the healing that we need and deliver us from every affliction. Fill us with the joy and the peace of your Holy Spirit so that we may be filled with gratitude for all that you are doing within us. We ask this through Christ our Lord.

Response: Amen!

THE LORD'S PRAYER

Leader: United together in the healing light of the Lord, we pray: Our Father....

BLESSING AND DISMISSAL

Leader: May God our loving Father bless you in every way and strengthen you in God's grace.

Response: Amen!

Leader: May God fill you with God's peace and transform your hearts in God's love.

Response: Amen!

Leader: May God heal you and those for whom you prayed and lead you all to eternal life.

Response: Amen!

Leader: May almighty God bless you, the Father and the Son and the Holy Spirit.

Response: Amen!

Leader: Let us go in the peace and healing of Jesus our Christ.

Response: Thanks be to God!

VI. Prayers for the Sacrament of Matrimony

1. Bernard Häring's Meditation on the Sacrament of Matrimony

The heart of sacramentality is always love that comes from God and leads to God. Everywhere and at all times, marriage has had the great sacramental value of keeping men and women from loneliness and self-centeredness, of involving them in the long human history of a growing love, and the growing discernment that encompasses this noble sacrament. Without this human experience of love in marriage and family, we should probably have no psychological understanding of what a sacrament is.

Marriage is a sacrament not only for the lovers but also for their children, and for their world. The family is the indispensable living and life-giving cell of the Church. Wherever Christians fully live this great covenant of faithful, creative, life-giving, and generous love, they radiate joy and faith, and they help others to become more fully aware of how God wonderfully enters into our lives.

In marriage, human love achieves a unique reciprocity of consciousness through the mutual awareness and mutual appreciation of husband and wife. As they grow increasingly conscious that their own love is a gift of God's love, a new dimension of reciprocity opens to them. They find that the more they love each other, the more they become conscious of and grateful for God's love for them. Christ's healing presence helps couples to accept and integrate their human failures and limitations, and to trust in God's patient work with them.

Christ loves us as we are. He seeks us where we are in order to transform us into masterpieces of his love, in his own image and likeness. The awareness of gradual transformation, becoming ever more a sacrament, a visible sign of God's love, leads couples to turn to the Holy Spirit, who alone can transform and renew their hearts and increase their capacity to love.

Each day is a new revelation of your love, O Lord. You multiply the signs of your kindness and goodness. Each day you give us the strength to listen to you, to become more aware of your presence and to respond to you. You have given us ears to hear when you call us through your Word, and through our sisters and brothers. Each day you open our eyes to see and to admire your works. Each day you allow us to discover signs of your coming, where others hear only noise and see only disaster. Lord, you are always near to us; you come each day to call us. You always wait for us. Make us grateful, make us vigilant.

2. A Traditional Prayer to the Sacred Heart of Jesus

(To Be Said by Spouses on Their Own Behalf)

O Most Sacred Heart of Jesus, King and center of all hearts, dwell in our hearts and be our King. Grant us by your grace to love each other truly and chastely, even as you have loved your immaculate bride, the Church, and have delivered yourself up for her. Bestow upon us the mutual love and Christian forbearance that are so acceptable in your sight, and a mutual patience in bearing each other's defects; for we are certain that no living creature is free from them. Permit not the slightest misunderstanding to mar that harmony of spirit which is the foundation of the mutual assistance in the many and varied hardships of life.

Grant O Lord God, that there be between us a constant and holy rivalry in striving to lead a perfect Christian life, by virtue of which the divine image of your mystic union with the Church, imprinted upon us on the happy day of our marriage, may shine forth more and more clearly. Grant, we beg you, that our good example of Christian living may be a source of inspiration to our children and spur them on to conform their lives also to your holy law; and finally, after this exile, may we be found worthy, by the help of your grace, for which we earnestly pray, to ascend into heaven, and there to be joined with our children forever, and to praise and bless you through everlasting ages. Amen.

3. A Prayer of Letting Go

I behold the Christ in you.
I place you lovingly in the care of the Father.
I release you from my anxiety and concern.
I let go of my possessive hold on you.
I am willing to free you to follow the dictates
    of your indwelling Lord.
I am willing to free you to live your life
    according to your best light and understanding.
Husband, wife, child, friend—
I no longer try to force my ideas on you,
    my ways on you.
I lift my thoughts above you, above the personal level.
I see you as God sees you, a spiritual being,
Created in God's image,
Endowed with qualities and abilities that make you
    needed and important
Not only to me, but to God and to his larger plan.
I do not bind you.
I no longer believe that you do not have the understanding
    you need in order to meet life.
I bless you.
I have faith in you.
I behold Jesus in you.

4. Psalm 100

(Adapted for Married Couples)

We sing with joyful hearts; in our love for each other we serve the Lord with gladness. The two of us come before God with joy. We know that the Lord is God, and God made both of us; we are God's children, the gentle love that God tends. We enter the days and years of our marriage with thanksgiving. We give thanks to God and bless God's name, for God is good. He is the Lord, whose kindness endures forever, and God's faithfulness endures through all the years of our shared life.

5. A Prayer for Couples

Creator God, through the power of your Holy Spirit and the power of your Word, we have pledged to each other that we will be a sign and a witness of your love. We have pledged that our love will symbolize to the whole world the love that you have for your Church, the love that you have for your people. Help us this day to become the sign that we hope to be. Help us to love each other, to forgive each other, to be patient with our weakness and, in this way, to be filled this day by the power of your abundant grace. Let us not concentrate on what we may not have, or what we think we might need to be complete and whole, but rather to be fully aware and present to that with which we have already been blessed. We pray this prayer in the name and in the power of Jesus who is our Lord and our Savior. Amen.

6. Our Humanity

Help each of us, Lord,
To feel good about ourselves.
Teach us to recognize and appreciate
Our assets and talents

201

And to avoid letting ourselves
Become discouraged by our
Weakness and limitations.
Let us realize that
Because we are human
We are not perfect
We all have faults
We all make mistakes
We do foolish and embarrassing things.
Let us learn how to forgive ourselves
For our mistakes
And our weaknesses.
Let us learn to spend more time
Doing the best we can
With what we have
And less time worrying about
What we can't do or don't have.
When we find it hard to have faith in ourselves, Lord,
Let us know and feel that you have faith in us.
We ask you Lord, not only to love us
When we find it difficult to love ourselves,
But teach us how to view and value ourselves
As the unique, precious individuals we are.
Let us learn to feel secure in your sight.
Let us learn to feel joy
In knowing that you care about
Every one of us
That you love us just as we are. Amen.

7. A Prayer of Thanks

We thank you, Lord, for all the love, kindness, and patience which your presence has structured into families all over the world and in all religions. We praise you for having made known the source and the goal of all this love to those who believe in you and live a sacrament of love and honor.

We beg you Lord, to help those husbands and wives who are experiencing family difficulties. Teach them to love each other, and to love and accept their children and draw them to you. Help them realize that you can, indeed, come into their lives and strengthen them to grow in redeemed and redeeming love.

To all the husbands and wives and parents whose love mirrors your own, grant full consciousness that you alone are the giver of this love, so that they will honor and praise you for it.

Lord, we ask you also to comfort and help those who are unable to build their own marriage and family, and those who are abandoned and live a lonely life. Send them friends, kind and generous people who can become, for them, a sign of your loving presence. Amen.

VII. Prayers for the Sacrament of Holy Orders

1. Bernard Häring's Meditation on the Sacrament of Holy Orders

The priest is called to be, above all, a man of prayer. By his mission, he is a hearer of the Word of God; he treasures it up in his heart and ponders it. He has made the main purpose of his life to be an adorer of God in spirit and in truth, and to help all the priestly people of God to abide in the Word of the Lord, to pray, and to find a synthesis between faith and life, to the honor and glory of God.

Since the priest is sent to speak, not in his own name but in the name of the Lord, to make known the Lord's loving presence, the first condition for his life's fulfillment is that he should live in the deepest possible union with the One who sends him. Only in this way can he live his special charism, to make known to his brothers and sisters that the Lord is near.

The priest must be rich in the qualities of sympathy and human understanding. To the very best of his ability, he has to acquire a wide-ranging and profound knowledge of humankind and of the world in which he lives.

The relationship of the priest with other believers is by no means a one-way street. It is through the Christian community, through his parents and his friends, that he learns how to pray, how to grow in the knowledge and in the joy of faith. To be a sign of God's loving presence, he needs the love, the kindness, the patience, and understanding of those he ministers to.

> *Hear I am, Lord; you have come into my life from the very beginning. You have given me a body and life. You have made me what I am. Here I am, O Lord, to do your will. Send me wherever you want. Make me ready, keep me awake, cleanse my heart even with fire, even by cross and suffering, by difficulties and opposition. Lord, take away from me everything that hinders me from recognizing your coming. Grant everything that leads me closer to you. Lord, here I am, call me; send me.*

2. A Traditional Prayer of Consecration of Priests to the Sacred Heart of Jesus

Lord Jesus, you are our most loving Redeemer and a priest forever; look mercifully on us, your humble suppliants, who you have been pleased to call your friends and partakers of your priesthood. We are yours and we wish to be yours forever: therefore, to your Most Sacred Heart which you have shown to oppressed humanity as their only safe refuge, we dedicate and devote ourselves wholly to this day. You who have promised plenteous fruit in the divine ministry to those priests who are devoted to your Sacred Heart; make us, we plead, fit workers in your vineyard, truly meek and humble, filled with the spirit of devotion and patience, so fired with love for you that we shall never cease to enkindle and quicken the same fire of love in the hearts of the faithful. Renew our hearts in the fire of your love, so that from this moment on we shall desire nothing except to promote your glory and win for you the souls whom you have redeemed by your precious blood. Show your mercy, Good Shepherd, chiefly to those priests, our brethren, if there be any such, who, walking in the vanity of sense, have saddened you and your beloved Spouse, the holy Church, by their lamentable falling away from you. Grant us the grace to bring them back to your embrace, or at least, to atone for their crimes, to repair the harm they have done, and to lessen the sorrow they have caused you, by the consolation of our love. Allow each of us, finally, to pray to you in the words of Saint Augustine: "O sweet Jesus, live you in me, and let the loving coal of your love burn brightly in my spirit, and grow into a perfect conflagration; let it glow in my marrow, let it blaze up in the most secret places of my soul; in the day of my consummation let me be found totally consumed in your presence, who with the Father and the Holy Spirit lives and reigns forever and ever." Amen.

3. A Traditional Prayer to Be Prayed Before the Celebration of Mass

I wish to celebrate Mass and consecrate the body and blood of our Lord Jesus Christ according to the form and purpose of the holy Roman Church, to the praise of almighty God and of all the Court of heaven, to my own benefit and that of all the Church: for all who have commended themselves to my prayers in general and in particular, and for the happy estate of the holy Roman Church. Amen.

4. A Traditional Prayer to Be Prayed by the Confessor Before He Hears the Confessions of the Faithful

Give to me, O Lord, the wisdom of your throne, that I may be enabled to judge your people with justice, and your poor and humble ones with true judgment. Grant me the grace to handle the keys of the kingdom of heaven, that I may open it to none who ought to be shut out, nor shut out any to whom I ought to open. Let my intention be pure, my zeal sincere, my charity long-suffering, and my labor fruitful. Let me be kind without laxity, severe without harshness; let me not look down upon the poor person, nor flatter the rich one. Give me sweetness that I may draw sinners to you; give me prudence in asking questions; give me skill in instruction. Bestow upon me, I beg you, zeal in withdrawing sinners from evil courses, diligence in establishing them in goodness, and earnestness in moving them to a better life: maturity in my answers, rightness in my counsels, light in obscure matters, insight in intricate cases, and victory over all difficulties; let me not be involved in useless talk, nor corrupted by shameful avowals; may I save others, without myself becoming a castaway. Amen.

5. A Prayer for the People of God and Their Priest

Lord, you have called me to a ministry of service,
Which I do not understand,
And I do not always appreciate.
Today, as in most days, I can not begin to comprehend,
why you have chosen me.
I recognize some of my weakness,
I acknowledge some of my petty faults and failings,
But there is still so much more that I ignore,
So much more that I should submit to your loving heart,
But I am unwilling and unable to do so.

Because of my unwillingness to convert and to change,
I realize that I am not always
the instrument of your grace that I promised to be.
And at times, because of my stubbornness,
I tear apart and do not make whole,
I reject and do not accept,
I judge and I refuse to forgive
Those for whom I am called to serve and to love.

Help me this day,
By the power of your abundant grace
To act beyond my natural capacities
To believe more than I may be inclined to believe
To act with compassion and with love
So that in your service this day
To the people whom you have called to be your own
I may recognize your presence and your love
And in your service
Find my own salvation and peace.
Amen.

6. A Prayer of Thanksgiving

We pray to you, Christ, our prophetic high priest, and we thank you, because you inspire men and women to dedicate themselves wholly to your gospel, and to be for us signs of your own total consecration to the gospel of our heavenly Father.

Lord Jesus, we thank you for the priestly ministry that brings us into closer contact with you. Send your Church priests who are also prophets, who have experienced your holiness and your kindness, and are people of faith and hope from whom we can learn what it means to adore God in spirit and in truth. Amen.

PART SIX

Scripture References

The Scripture references that follow are references traditionally accepted as appropriate for the individual celebration of the sacraments, as outlined in the Lectionary of the Church and in the individual rites promulgated for the celebration of the sacraments. Some duplication of references should be expected. Scripture references that are directly related to the specific institution or traditional development of sacramental theology have been noted in the explanatory text of each of the sacraments and are not repeated here.

The references are presented here because they present an opportunity for individual reflection and prayer, either as you prepare for the reception of a particular sacrament, or just on those occasions when you may want to be reminded of a specific sacramental encounter with the Lord. The references are also helpful in coming to an understanding of how the particular theology of the sacrament emerged from the scriptural texts and became incorporated into the practice and liturgy of the people of God.

1. Baptism

Ex 17:3–7—The people thirsted there for water.

Ezek 36:24–28—I will sprinkle clean water on you.

Ezek 47:1–9, 12—Wherever the river goes, every living creature will live.

Rom 6:3–5—All of us who have been baptized into Christ Jesus were baptized into his death.

Rom 8:28–32—Those whom he foreknew he also predestined to be conformed to the image of his Son.

1 Cor 12:12–13—We were all baptized into one body.

Gal 3:26–28—Clothe yourselves with Christ.

Eph 4:1–6—We have one Lord, one faith, one baptism.

Mt 28:18–20—Make disciples of all nations, baptizing them.

Mk 1:9–11— Jesus is baptized in the Jordan River.

Jn 4:5–14—A spring of water is gushing up to eternal life.

2. Rite of Christian Initiation of Adults (RCIA)

Beginning of the Catechumenate

Gen 12:1–4—Go to the land that I will show you.

Ps 33—Happy are the people whom God has chosen as his heritage.

Jn 1:35–42—We have found the Messiah.

The Rite of Election

Gen 2:7–9; 3:1–7—Creation of Adam and Eve and the first sin.

Ps 51—Have mercy on me, O Lord, and cleanse me from my sin.

Rom 5:12–19—The gracious gift of Jesus frees us from sin.

Mt 4:1–11—Jesus fasted for forty days and nights.

First Scrutiny

Ex 17:3–7—The love of God has been poured into your hearts.

Ps 95—Do not harden your hearts when you hear God's voice.

Rom 5:1–2;5–8—The Holy Spirit has been given to us.

Jn 4:5–42—The water that I will give you will become in them a spring of water gushing into eternal life.

Second Scrutiny

1 Sam 16:1, 6–7, 10–13—They anointed David, King of Israel.

Ps 23—The Lord is my shepherd, I shall not want.

Eph 5:8–14—Once you were in darkness...in the Lord you are light.

Jn 9:1–41—A blind man's sight is restored.

Third Scrutiny

Ezek 37:12–14—I will put my spirit within you.

Ps 130—With the Lord there is steadfast love and great power to redeem.

Rom 8:8–11—The Spirit is living within you.

Jn 11:1–45—Jesus is the resurrection and the life.

Presentation of the Creed

Deut 6:1–7—You shall love the Lord your God.

Ps 19—Let the words of my heart be acceptable to you, O Lord.

Rom 10:8–13—If you confess that Jesus is Lord, you will be saved.

Jn 12:44–50—I have come as light into the world.

Presentation of the Lord's Prayer

Hos 11:1, 3–4, 8–9—I have taught you and led you with bands of love.

Ps 103—The Lord is merciful and gracious, slow to anger.

Rom 8:14–17, 26–27—All who are led by the Spirit of God are children of God.

Lk 11:1–2, Mt 6:9–13—Here is the prayer my Father taught.

3. Confirmation

Isa 11:1–4—The spirit of the Lord rests.

Isa 42:1–3—I have my spirit on my chosen one.

Isa 61:1–3, 6, 8–9—The Lord has sent me to bring good news to the oppressed.

Ezek 36:24–28—I will place a new spirit in your midst.

Joel 2:23; 3:1–3—I will pour out my spirit on humankind.

Acts 1:3–8—You will be baptized with the Holy Spirit.

Acts 2:1–6—They were filled with the Holy Spirit.

Acts 8:1–4; 14–17—The two prayed for them that they may receive the Holy Spirit.

Rom 5:1–2, 5–8—God's love has been poured into our hearts.

Rom 8:26–27—The Spirit helps us in our weakness.

1 Cor 12:4–13—To each is given the manifestation of the Spirit.

Eph 1:3, 4:13–19—Speaking the truth in love, we must grow into Christ.

Mt 16:24–27—If any want to become my followers, let them deny themselves.

Mt 25:14–30—Enter into the joy of your master.

Mk 1:9–11—You are my beloved Son.

Lk 4:16–22—The Spirit of the Lord is upon me.

Jn 7:37–39—Out of the believer's heart will flow rivers of living water.

4. Eucharist

Gen 14:18–20—Melchizedek offers bread and wine to God.

Ex 16:2–4, 12–15—The Lord will send bread from heaven.

Ex 24:3–8—See the blood of the covenant the Lord has made with you.

Deut 8:2–3, 14–16—He made water flow for you from flint rock, and fed you with manna.

1 Kgs 19:4–18—He went on the strength of that bread for forty days.

Prov 9:1–6—Eat of my bread and drink of the wine I have mixed.

Acts 2:42–47—They devoted themselves to the breaking of the bread.

Acts 10:34, 37–43—God raised Jesus up and allowed him to eat and drink with us.

1 Cor 10:16–17—Because there is one bread, we are one body.

1 Cor 11:23–26—As often as you eat this bread, you proclaim the death of the Lord.

Heb 9:11–15—The blood of Christ will purify us.

Mk 14:12–16, 22–26—This is my body. This is my blood.

Lk 9:11–17—The people ate until they were filled.

Lk 24:13–35—They recognized the Lord in the breaking of the bread.

Jn 6:1–15—He gave the people all that they needed.

Jn 6:24–35—Whoever comes to me will never be hungry.

Jn 6:41–51—I am the bread of life; whoever eats of this bread will live forever.

Jn 6:51–58—My flesh and my blood are true food and drink.

Jn 21:1–14—Jesus feeds his apostles.

Mass of the Lord's Supper

Ex 12:1–8, 11–14—The first Passover meal is instituted.

Ps 116—What shall I return to the Lord for his bounty?

1 Cor 11:23–26—Eat this bread and drink this cup.

Jn 13:1–5—Jesus washes his disciples' feet.

5. Penance and Reconciliation

Isa 55:6–9—Seek the Lord while he is near.

Ezek 18:21–23, 30–32—Turn away from your sins, do what is lawful, and you shall live.

Joel 2:12–18—Return to me with all your heart.

Jonah 3:1–10—The Lord will hide his face from them because they have acted wickedly.

Rom 6:2–4, 12–14—We are dead to sin but alive to God.

1 Jn 1:5–2:2—The blood of Jesus purifies us from all sin.

Ps 51—Have mercy on me, O God.

Ps 103—Bless the Lord, O my soul.

Ps 130—Out of the depths I cry to you, O Lord. Hear my voice!

Rev 1:5—Jesus Christ is the faithful witness who has freed us from our sins.

Mt 9:1–8—Your sins are forgiven, stand up and walk.

Mk 1:1–8, 14–15—The kingdom of God is near; repent and believe the good news.

Lk 7:36–50—Her many sins are forgiven, hence she has shown great love.

Lk 15:1–3, 11–32—The prodigal son returns and is forgiven.

Lk 24:46–48—Repentance and forgiveness are to be preached in the name of Jesus.

6. Anointing of the Sick

2 Kgs 20:1–6—I have seen your tears.

Isa 53:1–6, 10–11—He shall bear their iniquities.

Acts 28:7–10—Paul cured many people in the name of Jesus.

2 Cor 4:10–18—We carry in our bodies the dying of Jesus.

2 Cor 12:7–10—My grace is sufficient for you.

Jas 5:13–16—The prayer of faith will save the sick.

Ps 102—Hear my prayer, O Lord.

Mt 8:14–17—Jesus heals Peter's mother-in-law.

Mk 16:15–20—They will lay their hands on the sick and they will recover.

Lk 22:39–43—Father, not my will but yours be done.

Jn 15:1–8—The Father prunes every branch that bears no fruit.

7. Matrimony

Gen 1:26–28, 31—God created them male and female.

Gen 2:18–24—A man leaves his father and mother and clings to his wife, and they become one flesh.

Gen 24:48–51, 58–67—Isaac took Rebekah, and she became his wife; and he loved her. So Isaac was comforted after his mother's death.

Tob 7:9–10, 11–15—She is given to you from today and forever. May the Lord of heaven, guide and prosper you both.

Tobit 8:5–7—May God grant that we grow old together.

Song 2:8–10, 14, 16; 8:6–7—My beloved is mine and I am his. Set me as a seal upon your heart, for love is as strong as death.

Sir 26:1–4, 13–16—A good wife is a great blessing.

Jer 31:31–34—I will make a new covenant with them, says the Lord.

Rom 8:31–35, 37–39—Who will bring any charge against God's elect?

Rom 12:1–2, 9–18—You are a living sacrifice, holy and acceptable to God.

1 Cor 6:13–15, 17–20—Do you not know that your body is a temple of the Holy Spirit?

1 Cor 12:31–13:8—If I do not have love, I am nothing.

Eph 5:2, 21–33—Live in love as Christ has loved us.

Col 3:12–17—Above all else, clothe yourself with love.

1 Pet 3:1–9—Wives, let your inner self with a spirit of gentle and quiet beauty be your adornment.

1 Jn 3:18–24—Let us love in truth and action.

1 Jn 4:7–12—God is love.

Mt 19:3–6—What God has joined let no one separate.

Mk 10:6–9—They are no longer two, but one.

Jn 2:1–11—Jesus works his first miracle at the wedding feast at Cana.

Jn 17:20–26—I ask that they may be completely one.

8. Holy Orders

Acts 10:37–43—We are witnesses of all that Jesus did.

Rom 12:4–8—We have gifts that differ, depending on the grace given to us.

2 Cor 4:1–2, 5–7—We proclaim ourselves as your slaves for the sake of Jesus Christ.

2 Cor 5:14–20—All this is from God who has given us the ministry of reconciliation.

Eph 4:1–7, 11–13—You were called to the one hope of your calling.

Heb 5:1–10—Christ did not glorify himself in becoming a high priest.

1 Pet 4:7–11—Be good stewards of the grace of God.

1 Pet 5:1–4—Tend the flock of God that is in your charge.

Mt 9:35–38—Ask the Lord to send laborers into the harvest.

Mt 10:1–7—Proclaim the good news that the kingdom of God is at hand.

Mt 20:25–28—Whoever wishes to be great among you must be your servant.

Lk 10:1–9—The harvest is plentiful but the laborers are few.

Lk 22:14–20—Do this in memory of me.

Jn 12:24–26—Whoever serves me must follow me.

Jn 17:6, 14–19—Sanctify those entrusted to you.

Jn 20:19–23—Receive the Holy Spirit.

Jn 21:15–17—Feed my sheep.

For Deacons

Acts 6:1–7—Select seven men full of spirit and wisdom that we may appoint them.

Acts 8:26–40—Philip proclaimed to him the good news of Jesus Christ.

1 Tim 3:8–13—Deacons must be serious and hold fast to the faith.

For Bishops

Acts 20:17–18, 28–32, 36—Keep watch over the flock that the Holy Spirit has given you.

1 Tim 4:12–16—Do not neglect the gift that is in you which was given by the laying on of hands.

2 Tim 1:6–14—Rekindle the gift of God within you.

PART SEVEN

Sacramentals

S acramentals have long been a part of Catholic life. They are rooted in what may be called the "sacramental principle," which affirms that God comes to us, speaks to us, and touches us through people and through all the good things of creation. Above all, God touched us through the Incarnation. From the moment Jesus Christ was conceived in the womb of Mary, a physical "point of contact" was established between God and the human race, a point of contact that could never be broken. Because God became one of us in Jesus Christ, human beings could look upon the face of God, hear God's voice, and feel God's embrace.

1. What Are Sacramentals?

It is because God has touched us through the good things of creation and because Jesus gave us the sacraments that the Catholic Church has instituted sacramentals. As the Second Vatican Council taught in its Constitution on the Sacred Liturgy, §60, sacramentals are sacred signs, which resemble the seven sacraments. Unlike the sacraments, however, Christ does not institute them, and they do not convey Christ's grace in the same way the sacraments do. Instead, they are instituted by the Church and symbolize spiritual effects which come about primarily through the prayer of the Church. In a special way, sacramentals dispose us to receive the grace of the sacraments and sanctify various occasions in human life.

The special value of sacramentals comes from their connection to the prayer of the Church. When we use the sacramentals of the Church, we are, in a manner that is mysterious yet real, beneficiaries of the graces bestowed upon the Church by Jesus Christ. Our prayerful use of the sacramentals becomes a part of, and is enhanced by, the worship of the whole Church. As a result, sacramentals open us to God's grace in ways that surpass mere personal prayer. Of course, we must approach the sacramentals with faith and devotion in order to be properly disposed to receive God's graces.

There are two main classifications of sacramentals: prayers of blessing and blessed objects. The Sign of the Cross is a sacramental prayer of blessing, and holy water is an example of a blessed object.

2. Sacramental Blessing Prayers

The word *bless* can have many meanings. Bless may mean "to grant some favor or gift," as when God blesses us with life and grace. It may mean "to ask God, through prayer and ritual, to sanctify and show favor to someone or to make something holy," as when we bless someone with the words, "God bless you"; this kind of blessing is also called a benediction. Bless may mean "to honor as holy by praising or glorifying," as when we bless the Lord.

All good things come from God, the source of every favor and gift. Therefore, the blessing prayers of the Church bless people or things by invoking God's grace and sanctification upon them. The prayers bless God with words of praise and thanks.

Both kinds of blessing prayers are found throughout the Bible. The best known of Old Testament prayers asking God's blessing on people has been traditionally called the blessing of Aaron:

> The LORD bless you and keep you;
>> the LORD make his face shine
>>> upon you, and be gracious
>>> to you;
>> the LORD lift up his countenance
>>> upon you, and give you
>>> peace.
>
> NUMBERS 6:24–26

An ancient blessing of people and objects is the blessing of Moses:

> Blessed shall you be in the city,
>> and blessed shall you be in the field.

Blessed shall be the fruit of your womb,
>the fruit of your ground, and the fruit of your livestock,
>both the increase of your cattle and the issue of your flock.

Blessed shall be your basket and your kneading bowl.

Blessed shall you be when you come in,
>and blessed shall you be when you go out.

DEUTERONOMY 28:3–6

There are many Old Testament blessing prayers that praise God. A good example is Psalm 103, whose first verse is an enthusiastic invitation to glorify God:

Bless the LORD, O my soul,
>and all that is within me,
>bless his holy name.

PSALM 103:1

In the New Testament, Jesus blessed both people and things; he blessed the little children (Mk 10:16) and he blessed food (Lk 9:16). There are many New Testament prayers that "bless" God. The Canticle of Zechariah praises God for the gift of salvation:

Blessed be the Lord God of Israel,
>for he has looked favorably on
>>his people and redeemed
>>them.

LUKE 1:68

Saint Paul often "blesses" God in his letters, praising God for favoring us: "Blessed be the God and Father of our Lord Jesus Christ, who has blessed us in Christ with every spiritual blessing in the heavenly places" (Eph 1:3).

BOOK OF BLESSINGS

Most official blessings used in the Church today may be found in the liturgical Book of Blessings, revised by decree of the Second Vatican Council and published in the United States in 1989. This book is a real treasury of prayers and blessings for all Catholics.

The Book of Blessings is a clear expression of Catholic belief in the sacramental principle. The Church, in its prayers of praise and blessing, demonstrates its conviction that "there is hardly any proper use of material things that cannot thus be directed toward human sanctification and the praise of God" (Book of Blessings, General Introduction, §14).

Because the prayers in the Book of Blessings are part of the Church's liturgy, they should ordinarily be used in a communal celebration. Some blessings, such as those used to bless religious articles and those used in connection with a diocesan or parish function, must be celebrated by a bishop, priest, or deacon. But most liturgical blessings given apart from a church setting may be celebrated by any Catholic in virtue of Christ's universal priesthood, shared through the sacraments of baptism and confirmation.

WHAT'S IN THE BOOK OF BLESSINGS?

The Book of Blessings begins with a General Introduction, which offers a fine explanation of blessing prayers in the history of salvation and of the Church. It explains that "blessings are signs that have God's word as their basis and that are celebrated from motives of faith...signs above all of spiritual effects that are achieved through the Church's intercession" (§10). It notes that when there is a blessing of objects or places, this is always done "with a view to the people who use the objects to be blessed and frequent the places to be blessed" (§12). In other words, the purpose of all blessings is to sanctify people, to help them grow in holiness and in their desire and ability to serve and worship God.

The first part of the book contains blessings directly pertaining to persons. Here are found blessings for families, for engaged and married couples, for children, for parents before and after childbirth, for those celebrating a birthday, for the elderly, for the sick, for students and teachers, and for travelers. There are special blessings for particular circumstances, such as blessings for parents after a miscarriage, for parents of an adopted child, for people suffering from addiction or substance abuse, and for victims of crime.

Part Two has blessings related to buildings and to various forms of human activity. There are blessings for homes and many other kinds of structures, blessings for automobiles, boats, tools and equipment, blessings for animals, for fields and flocks, for planting and harvest, and for athletic events. There are several forms of blessings to be used before and after meals.

Part Three includes blessings for objects designed to be used in churches, such as baptismal fonts, lecterns, tabernacles, bells, organs, and Stations of the Cross. There are also blessings of sacred items, such as chalices and patens, and blessings of holy water and of cemeteries.

Part Four offers blessings for religious articles, including such items as rosaries, scapulars, and medals, and Part Five contains blessings related to feasts and seasons of the Church. Some of these, for example, Advent wreaths, nativity scenes, and Christmas trees, are especially suitable for family celebrations. There are blessings of homes at Christmas and Easter, of throats for Saint Blaise Day, of ashes for Ash Wednesday, of food for special occasions, of mothers for Mother's Day, and of fathers for Father's Day. There is also a rite of blessing for visiting cemeteries on All Souls' Day, Memorial Day, and on anniversaries.

Part Six contains blessings for pastoral ministers, readers, altar servers, sacristans, musicians, ushers, parish-council members, lay ministers, and officers of parish societies. It offers blessings to welcome new parishioners and to say good-bye to those who are leaving, blessings for those receiving ecclesiastical honors and for inaugurating public officials. There are general blessings for giving thanks and for asking God to bless people, things, and events not specifically designated elsewhere in the book.

Finally, there are Appendices, which contain blessing prayers for the installation of a new pastor, and the solemn blessings and prayers found in the Roman Missal. These may be used to conclude any of the other blessings, or on any occasion when a priest or deacon is asked to give a blessing.

There are two English editions of the Book of Blessings approved for use in the United States. The first contains all the liturgical blessings of the Church. The second is a shorter edition which omits the blessings to be celebrated at church.

FORMAT OF BLESSINGS

Liturgical blessings follow a typical pattern. After a brief introduction and opening prayer, there is a reading from sacred Scripture followed by a responsorial psalm. Next come General Intercessions, to which may be added special intentions of the participants. The prayer of blessing is then said, accompanied by some outward sign such as the raising of hands, the laying on of hands, the Sign of the Cross, sprinkling with holy water, or the use of incense. The liturgy closes with a brief concluding rite.

3. Sacramental Objects

Jesus gave his Church the sacraments, outward signs of inward grace. The water of baptism, the oil of confirmation and anointing of the sick, the bread and wine of the Eucharist, and all the other signs of the sacraments inspired the Church to appreciate the goodness of material things and their ability to signify spiritual realities. As a consequence, the Church has designated many other signs as sacramentals, blessed objects that bear some resemblance to the sacraments.

Most sacramentals are related to the sacraments. Thus, holy water is water that is blessed to remind us of our baptism. When we dip our fingers in holy water and make the Sign of the Cross, blessing ourselves, we are reminded of our baptism in the name of the Father, Son, and Holy Spirit. As the water of baptism sanctifies those who receive it, so holy water is sprinkled on people and objects to call God's blessing upon them.

At the Easter Vigil, a large candle is lit to symbolize the Resurrection of Christ from the darkness of the grave. This paschal candle is used in the blessing of the water for baptisms at the Easter Vigil. At every baptism, a blessed candle is lit from the paschal candle to symbolize that Christ's life and light are granted to the baptized.

At baptism, a white garment is placed on those baptized. This garment is an important symbol to all Christians that we are clothed with Christ. But the rituals of baptism and the white garment have a particular significance for men and women who join religious communities. The blessings and ceremonies associated with consecration to religious life flow from the rituals of baptism. The habits and special garb worn by many religious are outward expressions of how they "put on the Lord Jesus Christ" (Rom 13:14) through the vows of religious life.

Lay people who have some affiliation with religious communities may express this form of consecration through the use of scapulars. These are small squares of cloth worn around the neck to symbolize one's association with a religious community or membership in a spiritual organization. Blessed medals sometimes substitute for scapulars, and they may be seen as a special sign of baptismal commitment to Jesus Christ, or of devotion to Mary or one of the saints.

Blessed oils are related to our baptismal identification with Christ. The word *Christ* means "anointed one," and the anointings at baptism symbolize the fact that we are members of the Body of Christ.

The bishop of a diocese on Holy Thursday usually blesses the oils used in celebrations of the sacraments. The oil of catechumens is used at baptism and in the Rite of Christian Initiation of Adults. Sacred chrism (perfumed oil) is used at baptism, confirmation, holy orders, and for some blessings. The oil of the sick draws its symbolism of healing from oil-based medicines and is used for the anointing of the sick. The Book of Blessings offers a blessing of oil to be used apart from the sacraments as a symbol of God's grace and healing power.

Church buildings are blessed for the celebration of the Eucharist and the other sacraments. At Mass, candles symbolize the light of Christ, and a sanctuary light reminds us that Christ is present in the Blessed Sacrament. Blessed candles and votive (prayer) lights are related to the Eucharist, as well as to baptism, reminding Catholics that Christ is the "light of the world" (Jn 8:12). Incense, which is blessed with a silent Sign of the Cross, may express our adoration at the Eucharist and at some other liturgical services. Church bells, which are blessed to call people to worship, are thereby related to the Eucharist. Crosses, crucifixes, and the Stations of the Cross call to mind the saving death of Christ made present in the Eucharist. On Passion Sunday, palms are blessed at a celebration of the Eucharist; they remind us of Christ's willingness to accept death on the cross to save us.

On Ash Wednesday, palms from the previous year are burned; the ashes are then blessed and used to sign the faithful in the form of a cross as a call to repentance. This signing with blessed ashes is related to the sacrament of penance.

Wedding rings, which are blessed and exchanged at celebrations of the sacrament of matrimony, are sacramentals, beautiful signs of love and commitment. Being made of precious metal, they are reminders of the pricelessness of God's love. Being circular in form, they remind us that human love originates in the love of God, which has existed from all eternity and will endure forever.

Many of the sacramentals already mentioned are used again at funerals. For example, the paschal candle is placed in a prominent location, expressing our belief that Christ rose from the dead to bring us to eternal life. A white pall, recalling the baptismal garment, is placed on the casket in recognition of the deceased person's efforts to put on Christ. The Eucharist, with its ceremonies and sacramentals, makes present the death and Resurrection of Christ. It reminds the faithful that Christ is the bread of life and that those who believe in him will live forever (Jn 6:48–51). Other sacramentals, such as rosaries, statues, and sacred images, are at least implicitly connected to the sacraments, for they remind us of the supernatural life given us by Christ. All sacramental objects dispose us to "receive the chief effect of the sacraments, and various occasions in life are rendered holy" (Constitution on the Sacred Liturgy, §60).

4. Making Use of the Sacramentals

Blessings and the use of material things as signs of God's presence and power are elements of Catholicism that have their foundation in Scripture. Jesus blessed people and things. He instructed his apostles to anoint the sick with oil, and he used mud and saliva to cure a blind man. The Acts of the Apostles describes how the first Christians used sacramental signs to bring Christ's grace and healing to people: "God did extraordinary miracles through Paul, so that when the handkerchiefs or aprons that had touched his skin were brought to the sick, their diseases left them, and the evil spirits came out of them" (Acts 19:11–12).

Inspired by Jesus and by the testimony of Scripture, the Catholic Church has recommended the use of sacramentals as additional signs of God's care for us. Catholics have embraced sacramentals with enthusiasm because they fit into our natural human inclination to use material things as symbols of profound realities. A gift of flowers is a sign that conveys love and can help love grow. A work of art can express powerful emotions and can elicit them from people who experience it. So, too, sacramentals express God's mighty power and convey God's grace to us through the intercession of the Church. For these and many other reasons, sacramentals are as important and as "up to date" in our modern world as they have ever been.

Sacramentals declare the importance of spiritual realities. A cross or medal worn around the neck can prompt us to pray more often. Crucifixes and statues in the home tell of the presence of Christ and the communion of saints; they also proclaim to the world that this is a Catholic home. The use of holy water, blessed candles, and other sacramentals call to mind the sacraments we have received and the protection only God can give.

Obviously, sacramentals differ from magic incantations and superstitious good-luck charms. Incantations and charms are presumed to have a power of their own. Sacramentals derive their special value from the prayer of the Church, which ultimately is a participation in the prayer of Jesus Christ, the Son of God.

While certain objects, chiefly those we have mentioned above, are sacramentals, not every blessed object can be considered a sacramental. Only those objects, which are in some way identified with the worship of the Church, are true sacramentals. Thus, holy water is clearly a sacramental, as are all the other articles described as related to the sacraments and to worship.

Blessed objects not identified with worship do not become sacramentals. When a pet is blessed, for example, it does not thereby become a sacramental. But the blessing shows pets are gifts that in some way reflect the goodness and creative power of God. In similar ways, all blessed objects, places, and events proclaim that the proper use of material things directs them to our eternal salvation and to God's glory. They call to mind the advice given by Saint Paul: "So, whether you eat or drink, or whatever you do, do everything for the glory of God" (1 Cor 10:31).

Most sacramental blessings may be bestowed on anyone who desires them. Most sacramental objects may be used by anyone, Catholic or not, if the person has the proper dispositions of faith and openness to God's grace.

5. A Listing of Sacramental Objects

Holy water
Paschal (Easter) candle
Religious habit (distinctive garb worn by men and women religious)
Scapulars
Blessed oil
Sanctuary lamp
Candles
Votive lights
Crosses
Crucifixes
Medals of the saints
Stations of the Cross
Palms, used on Palm Sunday
Ashes, used on Ash Wednesday
Wedding rings
Funeral pall
Rosary
Sacred images
Statues
Vestments used at Mass
Advent wreath

6. A Listing of Sacramental Blessings

Blessing of a family
Blessing of a married couple on the anniversary of their marriage
Blessing of an engaged couple
Blessing of a mother before childbirth
Blessing of the parents of an adopted child
Blessing on the occasion of a birthday
Blessing of the sick
Blessing of a victim of crime or oppression
Blessing of missionaries sent to proclaim the gospel
Blessing of catechumens
Blessing of a new home
Blessing of animals
Blessing of seeds at planting time
Blessing of the harvest
Blessing before and after meals
Blessing of articles for liturgical use
Blessing of a cemetery plot
Blessing of religious articles
Blessing of throats on the feast of Saint Blaise (February 3)
Blessing of ashes on Ash Wednesday

PART EIGHT

Glossary of Terms

A

absolution   In the sacrament of penance, absolution is the form (words) spoken by the priest for the forgiveness of sins. The Church teaches that "through the sign of absolution God grants pardon to sinners who in sacramental confession manifest their change of heart to the Church's minister; this completes the sacrament of penance." (Rite of Reconciliation, 6d, and CCC 1449)

acolyte   This word denotes the office or ministry of those who assist at the altar during Mass and at other liturgical functions. Since Vatican II, the term designates the ministry into which men are instituted in a permanent or transitory manner to assist the celebrant at the Mass and to distribute holy Communion when called upon to do so. The term is also commonly used to designate any person who serves Mass or who assists at other liturgical services. (CCC 903)

adoration   A conscious act of an intelligent creature by which God alone—infinitely perfect and having supreme domination over nature—is recognized as worthy of supreme worship. Adoration is essentially an act of the mind and will, but is commonly expressed in external acts of sacrifice, prayer, and reverence. Adoration in the strictest sense is due to God alone. (CCC 2096–2097)

agape meals   In the early centuries of the Church, the separation of the Eucharist to a specific time and place, distinct from the normal and everyday meals of the Christian community, led to the development of "love feasts." The word *agape*, from the Greek, means "love." These special meals did not survive in the everyday practice of the Christian community except as an occasional meal for the poor or the widowed.

age of reason   The time of life at which a person is believed to be morally responsible and able to distinguish between right and wrong, normally at about the age of seven years old. (CCC 1244)

In sacramental practice, the age of reason in the Latin Church is the age when a person first celebrates the sacrament of penance and receives his or her first holy Communion. It is also the required age for the celebration of the sacrament of the anointing of the sick.

Agnus Dei The title of a Latin hymn that is usually translated as "Lamb of God." The hymn, sung in either English or Latin, is often intoned during the fraction rite of the Eucharist in which the bread is broken, immediately before the congregation shares in holy Communion.

Agnus Dei also refers to a sacramental that consists of a small disc of wax with an imprinted figure of a lamb representing Christ on one side and the coat of arms of the pope on the reverse side. These discs are solemnly blessed by the pope on Wednesday of Holy Week during the first and seventh year of his pontificate and are worn by recipients as a protection against Satan, temptations, sickness, fires, tempests, and sudden death, and/or by pregnant women to experience safe deliveries.

alleluia An ancient Hebrew word which means "praise the Lord." The words *amen*, meaning "so be it" or "let it be done," and *hosanna*, meaning "please save us," are other examples of ritual words that also can be understood as sacramentals.

altar A table on which the eucharistic sacrifice is celebrated. According to the Code of Canon Law, an altar may be fixed or movable; it is "*fixed* if it is so constructed that it adheres to the floor and thus cannot be moved; it is called *movable* if it can be removed" (Canon 1235.1). According to Catholic custom, the table of a fixed altar is to be of stone; however, any other material, worthy and solid, in the judgment of the conference of bishops also can be used. A movable altar can be constructed from any solid material appropriate for liturgical use. There is an ancient tradition that the relics of martyrs and other saints can be incorporated into the design and manufacture of a fixed altar.

altar cloth   The fabric, usually of linen or other suitable material, that covers the entire altar during the celebration of the Eucharist. Since the liturgical reforms of the Second Vatican Council, only one cloth is required.

anathema   This solemn formula of excommunication or exclusion from the ecclesial community is used by the Church to assert that some position or teaching contradicts Catholic faith and doctrine. Saint Paul used this expression against anyone who preached a false gospel (Gal 1:8–9) or rejected the love of Christ (1 Cor 5:4–5). Anathema was used repeatedly at the Council of Trent in the pronouncements against the Protestant reformers in such examples as "If anyone states that there are not seven sacraments of the Holy Church instituted by Christ, let him be anathema." The Second Vatican Council abolished anathema.

annulment   A term for what is known in the Code of Canon Law as a decree of nullity—namely, a declaration by a competent authority of the Church that a marriage was invalid from the beginning because of the presence of a diriment (invalidating) impediment, a basic defect in consent to marriage, an inability to fulfill the responsibilities of marriage, or a condition placed by one or both of the partners on the very nature of marriage as understood by the Church. The annulment procedure may be started at the parish level; the investigation of the facts is usually carried out by a marriage tribunal (ecclesiastical court) under the leadership of a bishop. (CCC 1628–1629)

anointing   Holy oil is placed or poured on persons, places, or things in a religious ceremony in order to make the "anointed" sacred and consecrated to God. Anointing is used in the sacraments of baptism, confirmation, anointing of the sick, and holy orders. Churches and altars are anointed when they are consecrated. Oil is used in the blessing of bells and sacred vessels. Bishops are anointed during the rites of their episcopal consecration.

anointing of the sick   A sacrament celebrated by the Church to offer the healing power of Christ to the sick and to the infirm. The scriptural roots of this sacrament can be found in Mark 6:13, "They cast out many demons, and anointed with oil many that were sick and cured them," and also in James 5:14–15, "Are any among you sick? They should call the elders of the church and have them pray over them, anointing them with oil in the name of the Lord." Only a bishop or a priest can administer the sacrament. It is properly administered to "a member of the faithful who, having reached the use of reason, begins to be in danger [of death] due to sickness or old age (Canon 1004.1). (CCC 1511–1513)

asperges   A popular ritual in pre-Vatican II times, replaced by the Rite of Sprinkling. In the Asperges, the water was blessed in the sacristy and then the priest came to the altar and intoned the opening words of Psalm 51, to which the people and the choir responded, "Cleanse me of sin with hyssop, Lord, that I may be purified; wash me, and I shall be whiter than snow," as the priest sprinkled the people with the holy water. When both the singing and the sprinkling had been completed, the priest would recite a few more verses of the psalm and conclude with a prayer. During the Easter season, the *Vidi Aquam,* "I saw water" (Ezek 47:2), was sung in place of Psalm 51.

aspergillum   A word from the Latin, meaning "sprinkler." An aspergillum is an instrument used to sprinkle people with holy water, most often during the Rite of Sprinkling during Mass. The Rite of Sprinkling, in which words of Psalm 51 are often prayed, "sprinkle me with hyssop and I shall be clean. Wash me, and I shall be whiter the snow," is performed, routinely in the Easter season but also at other times in the liturgical year, in order to recall the celebration of baptism.

aumbry   A small boxlike recess, set into the wall of the sanctuary of a church, which is used for the reservation of the holy oils that are used in the celebration of the sacraments of baptism, confirmation, holy orders, and the anointing of the sick. In common liturgical practice today, the oils are often prominently displayed in the sanctuary and so the aumbry is not used as often as it once was.

B

banns of marriage   A public announcement of the promise of marriage. Publication is usually accomplished either through an announcement at the Sunday Masses or written in the parish bulletin. The purpose of the announcement is to discover if any impediments to a marriage exist or if there is any reason why a marriage should be prohibited or postponed. Canon 1067 empowers the bishops' conferences of each country "to issue norms about…the marriage banns or other opportune means to accomplish the investigations necessary before marriage."

baptism of blood   A substitute for the sacrament of baptism in the case of unbaptized adults who suffer martyrdom for the faith. Although technically not a sacrament, theologians since at least the time of Saint Thomas Aquinas have held martyrdom produces the same effect as the sacrament of baptism, insofar that it remits sin and opens the gate to eternal life. Baptism of blood is also called baptism of martyrdom; this term refers to the case of a person who freely and patiently suffered death for the Christian faith before he or she could actually receive the sacrament of baptism—not an uncommon occurrence in the first three centuries of Christianity and in other times and places of persecution. (CCC 1258)

baptism of desire   This term, in the words of Vatican II, refers to those who "through no fault of their own, do not know the Gospel of Christ or his Church, but who nevertheless seek God with a sincere heart, and, moved by grace, try in their actions to do his will as they know it through the dictates of their conscience…" (Dogmatic Constitution on the Church, §16). (CCC 1258)

Baptism of desire is baptism of adults who through "no fault of their own" were not able to receive the sacrament. The clearest example of baptism of desire is of a catechumen, a person preparing for the reception of the sacrament, who dies before he or she is able to celebrate the sacrament in the usual way.

baptismal font   A receptacle used for holding water, where the sacrament of baptism is celebrated. The baptismal font should allow for at least the possible immersion of infants and the pouring of water over the heads of adults. The Code of Canon Law, Canon 858, decrees that every parish is to have a baptismal font.

baptismal name   The name given to the person at baptism; according to a long Christian tradition, this name should be that of a saint, so that the baptized will have a special heavenly patron and will be encouraged to imitate the life and holiness of that saint. The present law of the Church, from the Code of Canon Law, expresses it in this way: "Parents, sponsors and the pastor are to see that a name foreign to a Christian sensibility is not given" (Canon 855).

baptismal preparation   A period of preparation before baptism. An adult who wishes to be baptized must first be "instructed sufficiently about the truths of the faith and Christian obligations, and have been tested in Christian life through the catechumenate" (Canon 865.1). Before the baptism of an infant, the parents, or at least one of the parents, must give consent to the baptism and must give assurance that the infant will be brought up in the Catholic Church. If such assurance is not given, the baptism is to be delayed with the hope that the parents will become more aware of their religious responsibilities. (CCC 1229–1233)

This requirement is not always understood and appreciated in an increasingly secularized society in which there is still some attraction to the customs of the Church but not always a commitment to the fullness of life and service within the Church.

baptismal register A record of a baptism is completed by the minister who administers the sacrament; it is kept in the archives of the parish. A copy of this record is usually given to the baptized at the time of the baptism and is available on request. The celebration of confirmation, matrimony (and annulment, if it occurs), holy orders, and religious profession are also reported to the parish of the baptism, and these events are recorded in the same register.

baptismal sponsors Popularly known as godparents, sponsors play an important role in baptism. Canons 872–874 give the following norms in reference to baptismal sponsors: they help the baptized to lead a Christian life; there must be one male and one female; they are designated by the one who is baptized or by the parents of the baptized; they must be at least seventeen years old; they must be Catholic and have received the sacraments of confirmation and the Eucharist; and they must lead a life in harmony with the Catholic faith. A sponsor cannot be the parent of the one who is baptized. A non-Catholic may not be a sponsor but may serve as a Christian witness, together with a Catholic sponsor.

baptismal vows Promises to renounce Satan and all his works and the profession of faith by the one to be baptized or, in the case of an infant, by the parents and sponsor. The solemn renewal of the baptismal vows is part of the Easter Vigil. The private renewal of these vows is a commendable act of piety. (CCC 1237)

baptismal water During the Easter Vigil, water is specially blessed for use in baptism. At other times, water may be blessed at each baptism by the one who administers the sacrament. The Roman Ritual provides three ritual blessings, two of which involve the symbolic touching of the water by the presider and an interchange of responses by the gathered assembly. In case of necessity, ordinary water—fresh, salt, warm, cold, clean, dirty—may be used for baptism.

Benediction of the Blessed Sacrament   A liturgical service for the purpose of acknowledging the presence of Christ in the reserved sacrament. The service consists of songs, prayers, and biblical readings, which focus the attention of the gathered congregation on the meaning and importance of the Eucharist. (See the "Divine Praises," page 154, for an example of a traditional prayer.)

The practice of Benediction dates back to the Middle Ages when people felt a desire to see the holy Eucharist, especially since personal reception of the Blessed Sacrament occurred infrequently. The popularity of Benediction was furthered by the celebration surrounding the feast of Corpus Christi (the Body of Christ), including the exposition of the host in a *monstrance* or *ciborium* and processions.

bishop   A priest who, according to the Decree on the Pastoral Office of Bishops in the Church, §15, "enjoys the fullness of the sacrament of orders." The ordination of deacons and priests within the sacrament of holy orders is exclusively the province of the bishop. Bishops are also the preferred minister of the sacrament of confirmation whenever pastorally possible.

Blessed Sacrament   This term refers to the Eucharist, the preeminent sacrament and celebration of the Lord's passion, death, and resurrection. It also refers to the reserved consecrated bread, usually kept in the tabernacle of the church, which is used most often for taking Communion to the sick in their homes.

blessing   The act of placing a person or object under the care of God or dedicating a person or thing to the service of God. A simple blessing is usually made with the sign of the cross, sometimes accompanied by sprinkling holy water. The Church has a large number of specific blessings for various times and occasions, many of which are collected in the Book of Blessings. (CCC 1671–1672)

Body of Christ   This term refers to the ways that Christ is present to humankind and to the world. It has many meanings that stem from

244

the human body of the historical Jesus. This biblical image and its extension to other images is well developed by the Second Vatican Council in its Dogmatic Constitution on the Church, §7.

Book of Blessings   The portion of the Roman Ritual which contains the blessings of persons, places, and things was published by the Holy See in 1984 as the Book of Blessings and reflects the liturgical principles declared by Vatican II. There are six parts to the book. Part I includes blessings directly pertaining to people. The blessings in Part II are related to buildings and different forms of human activity. Parts III and IV present blessings for items used in public and private prayer. Parts V and VI provide a rich collection of blessings that can be used on the parish level. See **sacramentals.**

bread, the breaking of   An ancient reference for the celebration of the Eucharist. The Acts of the Apostles, 2:42, describes the earliest Christian communities as devoting themselves "to the apostles' teaching and fellowship, to the breaking of the bread and the prayers."

bread, eucharistic   The altar bread used in the liturgy. It is an unleavened, round wafer made of wheat flour. It must be recently made so there is no danger of spoilage. It is consecrated during the eucharistic prayer and distributed during the Communion Rite of the Mass.

C

candle   A sacramental symbolizing divine life and purity. Lighted candles are carried in procession, held by the faithful when renewing their baptismal vows, and placed on the altar to indicate Christ's presence.

Canon of the Mass   A term referring to the eucharistic prayer of the Mass and containing the solemn and essential act of consecration in which the bread and wine are changed into the body and blood of Christ. The prayers of the Canon recall the great mysteries of the Christian faith and include prayers for the Church, for the living and the dead, and remembrance of the saints and martyrs. (CCC 1353)

Catechism of the Catholic Church   A universal text summarizing the doctrines of the Catholic Church that was first published in French in October 1992. It was prepared by a Vatican commission and is intended to help bishops in formulating local catechismal programs adapted to the cultural and other concerns of the local Church. It is seen as an organic presentation of the Catholic faith in its entirety. (CCC 18)

catechumen   An unbaptized person who, with other members of the faith community, is involved in the process of learning about the Catholic Church in preparation for admittance.

catechumenate   The period of instruction and involvement in the Catholic faith in preparation for the baptism of adults or for the reception of baptized non-Catholic Christians into the Catholic Church. The basic elements of the catechumenate are explained in the Rite of Christian Initiation of Adults (RCIA). (CCC 1232)

Catholic   A word taken from the Greek, meaning "universal," it is part of the official title or designation given to the body of Christian communities in union with the bishop of Rome (the pope). Saint Ignatius of Antioch first used this term in his *Letter to the Smyrnaeans* as a description of the Church. The word is now used in a variety of different ways: for example, to describe the universality of the Church as intended for all human beings; to identify a particular institution in the Church (that is, Catholic schools); to designate individual members of the Church (that is, Mary and Robert are Catholic parents).

chalice   The cup used to contain the wine, which in the eucharistic sacrifice is changed into the precious blood of Christ. It must be constructed of appropriate materials and should be blessed by a bishop or a priest. (CCC 1574)

chrism   An aromatic oil consecrated by the bishop in the Mass of Chrism on Holy Thursday and distributed to the churches for use in baptism (to signify the gift of the Holy Spirit on the newly baptized), confirmation, and ordination. Olive oil is the preferred oil for chrism, but oil pressed from other plants may be used. (CCC 1183, 1241)

chrismation   The anointing with sacred chrism during the celebration of the sacrament of baptism, which in the Eastern Church is understood and accepted as the sacrament of confirmation as well. In the Roman Catholic Church, this anointing is understood as an "announcement" of the sacrament of confirmation, which will come at a later time. (CCC 1242)

ciborium   A large cup-shaped liturgical vessel containing the bread, which in the eucharistic sacrifice is changed into the body of Christ. The ciborium must be constructed of appropriate materials and should be blessed by a bishop or a priest.

clergy   A term referring to those men who receive the sacrament of holy orders for the service of God and the Church, including deacons, priests, and bishops. A distinction may be made between diocesan clergy, that is, those ordained for a particular diocese and committed in obedience to a particular bishop, and religious clergy, that is, those who belong to a religious institute in the Church (for example, Jesuit, Franciscan, Redemptorist) and owe primary obedience to their religious superiors as well as pastoral obedience to the bishop in whose diocese they exercise this ministry. (CCC 1562–1571)

Code of Canon Law   The *Codex Iuris Canonici* is the official body of laws for Catholics of the Roman or Latin Rite of the Church. The first Code of Canon Law was promulgated in 1917 and a revised code was promulgated in 1983. The code contains laws that apply to all members of the Church, others that define and govern the hierarchy of the Church and members of religious communities, and a long section on the sacraments.

Communion, guidelines for the reception of   From the earliest days of the Church, receiving the Lord in holy Communion was seen as a sign of unity with the Church. Those preparing to join the Church did not receive Communion until they were baptized and confirmed at the Easter Vigil. Today, Communion signifies unity with the Church in sacramental life, belief, and morals. This is expressed in guidelines for the reception of holy Communion issued by the National Conference of Catholic Bishops (USA) on November 8, 1986:

For Catholics: Catholics fully participate in the celebration of the Eucharist when they receive holy Communion in fulfillment of Christ's command to eat His Body and drink His Blood. In order to be properly disposed to receive Communion, communicants should not be conscious of grave sin, have fasted for one hour, and seek to live in charity and love with their neighbors. Person's conscious of grave sin must first be reconciled with God and the Church through the sacrament of penance.

For Other Christians: We welcome to this celebration of the Eucharist those Christians who are not fully united with us. It is a consequence of the sad divisions in Christianity that we cannot extend to them a general invitation to receive Communion. Catholics believe that the Eucharist is an action of the celebrating community signifying a oneness in faith, life, and worship of the community. Reception of the Eucharist by Christians not fully united with us would imply a oneness which does not yet exist and for which we must all pray (*Origins*, January 15, 1987, vol. 16, no. 31, p. 554).

competentes   From the Latin word, meaning "those qualified," this term designates catechumens who have already been elected and admitted into the final preparations for the reception of the sacrament of baptism. They are also called "the enlightened" or "the illumined" because the sacrament of baptism has traditionally been understood as a sacrament that fully enlightens and illumines a person with the Spirit of God.

concelebration   The simultaneous celebration of Mass by more than one priest where all consecrate the same bread and wine. This practice was common in the Western Church until the Middle Ages, and was restored in modern times by Vatican II.

confessional   A designated place where the private confession of sins takes place. Confessionals are a somewhat recent development, becoming popular after the Council of Trent when Saint Charles Borromeo designed a special confession chair, surrounded by screens. Up until the Council of Trent the normal place for the individual confession of sins was before the altar rail, with the penitent kneeling at the rail, outside the sanctuary, and the priest, sitting or standing behind the rail, in the sanctuary. Today the confessional provides the option for the penitent to remain anonymous behind a screen or to walk around the screen and to sit in a chair, "face to face" with the confessor. Yet another change, after the reforms of the Second Vatican Council, is that confessionals are commonly referred to as "reconciliation rooms."

consecration   The act of making a person, place, or thing holy and sacred, setting it aside for the service of God. The bread and wine are consecrated at Mass, a permanent church building is consecrated, as are those who receive holy orders. (CCC 1377, 1538)

Corpus Christi   A word from the Latin, meaning "Body of Christ." This term designates the feast of the Body and Blood of Christ which is celebrated on the second Sunday after the Feast of Pentecost. This special feast was added to the liturgical calendar of the Church in the year 1264. Tradition has it that Saint Thomas Aquinas composed the prayers, songs, and other components of the feast.

crosier   A symbol of authority and jurisdiction, shaped like a shepherd's staff, conferred on bishops and some abbots at their consecration.

crucifix   A cross bearing the image of Christ either as suffering Redeemer or as Risen Lord. A crucifix must be on or over the altar where

Mass is celebrated. Among Catholics, a blessed crucifix is a revered object, a sacramental, and used for private and public devotion.

cruets   From the Medieval French meaning, "little jug," cruets are the small containers that hold the wine and the water used for the celebration of the Eucharist. They are usually presented to the priest during the offertory procession of the Mass.

D

deacon   A person who is ordained by his bishop for service to the people of God. In apostolic times, the ministry of deacon was to serve various corporal and spiritual needs of the people (Acts 6:1–6) and to assist in preaching the Word of God (Acts 8:40). Because of his important ministry, the deacon was expected to be a man of religious and moral integrity (1 Tim 3:8–10). In the Church, there are two kinds of deacons, transitional and permanent. Transitional deacons are those who receive the order as they advance to the priesthood, while permanent deacons are those who receive the order and remain in it permanently.

diaconate   The order of deacons, as a whole; its members.

divorce   Dissolution of the bond of marriage. The teaching of the Church, based on the teaching of Christ himself (Mk 10:2–12 and Lk 16:18), is that a ratified and consummated marriage cannot be dissolved by any human power or for any reason other than death (Canon 1141). Thus, although civil law may claim to dissolve the bond of marriage and render a person free to marry again, the Church maintains that the civil law has no power to do this. For serious reasons, such as adultery, serious danger to the spirit or body of the other spouse or the children, a spouse may have a legitimate cause for separation. (CCC 1650–1651, 2384–2386)

doxology   The ancient Trinitarian prayer that was first used in the Eastern Church, "Glory be to the Father, and to the Son, and to the Holy Spirit." In the fourth century, the second part of this traditional prayer was added, "As it was in the beginning, is now, and ever shall be, world without end. Amen." This prayer is often prayed with the psalms and with other hymns of praise and thanksgiving.

E

Eastern churches, Catholic   These are Catholic churches (whose members number approximately twelve million throughout the world) who follow the Eastern rites. Originally, they were the Patriarchates of Constantinople, Alexandria, Antioch, and Jerusalem. Today the five principal rites are the Byzantine, Alexandrian, Antiochene, Armenian, and Chaldean. Best represented in the United States, for example, is the Byzantine rite with nine dioceses serving its Ruthenian and Ukrainian rite adherents. Vatican Council II, in its Decree on Eastern Catholic Churches says, "The Catholic Church values highly the institutions of the Eastern Churches, their liturgical rites, ecclesiastical traditions, and their ordering of the Christian life. For in these Churches, which are distinguished by their venerable antiquity, there is clearly evident the tradition which has come from the apostles through the Fathers and which is part of the divinely revealed, undivided heritage of the Universal Church," §1.

Eastern churches, separated   These are the Eastern churches that are not in union with Rome. Their separation occurred in 1054 in what is often referred by historians to as the Eastern Schism. The Orthodox churches are the largest of these separated Eastern churches. They hold in common with the Eastern Catholic counterparts many matters of faith and morals, valid orders and sacraments, and a rich liturgy. They accept, however, only the doctrines decided at the first seven ecumenical councils of the Church and do not acknowledge or hold communion with the pope. Since Vatican Council II, there has been a continuing ecumenical dialogue between the separated Eastern churches and the Catholic Church. (CCC 838)

efficacious A term used in reference to the sacraments, which means that each sacrament confers the grace or the help that is intended because it is Christ who is present in the sacrament. (CCC 1127)

elevation Immediately after the words of consecration are prayed, within the eucharistic prayer of the Mass, the consecrated bread and then the consecrated wine is elevated by the priest. This ritual, with roots deep in the Middle Ages when the people had a great desire to see the consecrated elements, is today a simple gesture that expresses praise and thanksgiving. At one time in the development of the Mass the elevation was a much more dramatic and elaborate ritual.

epiclesis An intercessory prayer in which the priest asks God the Father to send down the Holy Spirit so that the bread and the wine at Mass may be changed into the body and blood of Jesus Christ. It also refers to the fact that the Holy Spirit transforms everything into divine life that it touches, not unlike fire transforms everything that it touches. (CCC 1127)

Eucharist A word from the Greek *eucharistia,* meaning "thanksgiving." Eucharist is the sacrament of the body and the blood of Jesus Christ. In the Eucharist, Jesus is present, body, soul, and divinity, under the forms of bread and wine. The Eucharist was instituted by Christ at the Last Supper (Mt 26:26–28, Mk 14: 22–24, Lk 22:17–20, and 1 Cor 11:23–25).

eucharistic adoration Devotional practices focused on Christ's presence as Lord and Savior in the consecrated bread and wine. These devotions include exposition of the Blessed Sacrament usually followed by Benediction, eucharistic processions, visits to the Blessed Sacrament, and holy hours of adoration.

Public or private devotions to the Eucharist were inspired by the desire of the thirteenth-century faithful to look at the consecrated host in order to achieve interior communion with Christ. These outside-the-Mass devotions became popular almost to the point of becoming as important as the celebration of the Mass—sometimes even replacing it in the minds of ordinary Catholics.

After Vatican II (1962–1965), these eucharistic experiences were seen as an extension of the eucharistic liturgy itself, which is the summit of the Christian Life. Thus, they provide people with additional time to contemplate and revere the mysteries celebrated in the Eucharist and to seek from Christ strength for the journey of discipleship.

eucharistic ministers Persons who preside or assist at the eucharistic assembly. Christ is always the principal agent of the Eucharist, but priests acting in his name represent him in *"persona Christi."* Other extraordinary eucharistic ministers (as opposed to the priest who is alone the ordinary minister of the Eucharist) include deacons, lectors, acolytes, those who participate in the offertory procession, and the ministers who distribute Communion.

ex opere operato The literal meaning of this Latin phrase is "by the very fact of the action's being performed" (CCC 1128); this term is one used by the Church to emphasize that the sacraments are not dependent on either the celebrant or the recipient of the sacrament, but rather on the power of God.

exposition of the Blessed Sacrament A liturgical ceremony of scriptural readings, hymns, prayers, and silent meditation in which the consecrated host is displayed, usually in a monstrance, for all the faithful to see. Exposition of the Blessed Sacrament has traditionally been part of Benediction, Corpus Christi processions, perpetual adoration, and Forty Hours devotion.

Extreme Unction   The sacrament of the anointing of the sick, celebrated when a person is very near death. Until the liturgical reforms of the Vatican Council II, the ordinary celebration of the sacrament of the anointing was almost exclusively celebrated with those who were at the point of death. However, even in this practice, there remained the hope that the sick person would recover his or her health. (CCC 1512)

F

faithful   Members of the Church who have been united in baptism to Christ and to other members of the Mystical Body. Because of their membership, the faithful have certain rights and obligations. (CCC 871–873)

fast, eucharistic   Abstention from food and drink (except water) for one hour before the reception of holy Communion. This fast may be shortened to as much as fifteen minutes for those who are sick or who have a similar compelling reason.

first Communion   The solemn observance and celebration of one who is receiving the Eucharist for the first time. For children, this usually occurs on reaching the age of reason.

font, baptismal   A container holding the baptismal water; it is usually made of durable material and properly ornamented. Every parish church is to have a baptismal font. In recent years, the baptismal font has been given a prominent and visible place in the church building.

Forty Hours   The solemn exposition of the Blessed Sacrament for a continuous period of forty hours over a three-day period. Saint Augustine in *On the Trinity* suggested that the Lord Jesus spent precisely forty hours in his tomb and it is this symbolism that may be behind the devotion. Since the Second Vatican Council the devotion has been simplified and is guided by the general norms for the exposition of the Blessed Sacrament.

Forty Hours devotion in the United States was promoted by Saint John Neumann, C.Ss.R., the fourth bishop of Philadelphia, and encouraged a sense of parish community. By 1983, the Church recommended the exposition of the Blessed Sacrament in each parish church for an appropriate period of time each year.

G

general confession   A devotional practice of confessing all serious sins committed since baptism or, in some instances, since the last general confession. This practice is sometimes chosen as a way to celebrate a significant or important occasion in a person's spiritual life, for example, before marriage or ordination. Most spiritual directors today who wish to emphasize that once a sin has been forgiven it is forgiven generally discourage the practice.

genuflection   Bending the right knee to the floor as a sign of reverence and respect for the Lord present in the Blessed Sacrament. Genuflection originated in the ceremonies of the royal court and later was extended as a way to demonstrate reverence for the cross, the altar, and the Blessed Sacrament. The practice is the norm in the Western Church while in the Eastern Church bowing is much more common.

gospel   A word taken from the Old English *godspel*, meaning "good news." A gospel is one of the four divinely inspired accounts of the life, teaching, suffering, death, and resurrection of Jesus Christ. It is customary to describe the gospels of Matthew, Mark, and Luke as "synoptic Gospels" because they give a "synopsis" or similar view of the life and teaching of Jesus; the Gospel of John reflects a different apostolic tradition. The Church holds the gospels in high esteem; passages from them are proclaimed in the eucharistic liturgy and in the formal celebration of all of the sacraments. (CCC 125–127)

H

hell   The dwelling place of Satan and the evil spirits and of all those who die deliberately alienated from God. The primary punishment of hell is the pain of loss: the deprivation of the face-to-face vision of God and eternal happiness with him. There is also the pain of sense caused by an outside agent, described as fire in the New Testament (Mt 25:41; Mk 9:43). Hell is a dire destination for one who freely chooses his or her own will against the will of God. (CCC 1033–1037)

holy hour   Devotion that involves an uninterrupted hour of prayer and meditation in the presence of the Blessed Sacrament, either exposed on the altar or reposed in the tabernacle. The custom of making a holy hour is said to derive from the query of Jesus to his apostle Peter, "Could you not stay awake with me one hour?" (Mt 26:40) and practiced further by Saint Margaret Mary Alocoque who kept a holy hour in response to a message from Christ who promised her a share in his agony in Gethsemane. Holy hours can include time for meditation on the passion of Our Lord, adoration of Jesus Christ truly present in the Eucharist, silent reflection, meditation on Scripture, reading of a spiritual book, or praying silently. Communal celebrations may include a homily, Benediction of the Blessed Sacrament, and shared prayer.

holy water   Water that is blessed by a priest for use by the people of God, ordinarily while one is blessing oneself with the Sign of the Cross; it is a symbol of spiritual cleansing and by custom is used in time of physical or spiritual dangers; it is used in all of the Church's blessings. (CCC 1668)

homily   An integral part of the Mass, it is an instruction or sermon preached after the readings from Scripture; its purpose is to explain the Word of God and also to make application of that word to the lives of people today. (CCC 2033)

host A term for the sacred eucharistic bread. The word *host* comes from the Latin word meaning "victim," and thus commemorates Christ's sacrifice for all.

I

impediments to marriage An impediment is an obstacle; according to the Code of Canon Law there are certain obstacles to a valid marriage. These are called "diriment impediments." The code defines a diriment impediment as rendering "a person incapable of contracting marriage validly" (Canon 1073). The list in the code includes the following diriment impediments: a male before sixteen years of age and a female before the age of fourteen; a person held to a bond of a previous marriage, a person who is in holy orders or bound by religious vows, and other impediments as a result of relationship (Canon 1083–1094).

incense A grainy substance made from the resins of various plants that gives off an aromatic odor when burned; used in divine worship as a symbol of the ascent of prayer to God. (CCC 2581)

intercommunion An agreement between two religious bodies that permits their respective members to receive communion in either denomination regardless of doctrinal differences.

intinction The practice of giving holy Communion by dipping the consecrated bread into the consecrated wine. Although once widely practiced immediately after the Second Vatican Council, it is generally discouraged as an ordinary way of distributing holy Communion.

J

Jansenism A particularly destructive heresy, rooted in French Pietism of the seventeenth century. Jansenism emphasized human sinfulness before God and the need to go to confession before the reception of holy Communion. As a result of this heresy, people developed the habit of going to Communion usually only once a year, typically during the Easter season, because it was perceived to be so difficult to attain the proper disposition to worthily receive the sacrament. Saint Alphonsus Liguori, the founder of the Redemptorists, was one who both struggled with this notion and also heroically preached against it.

justification   The process by which a sinner is made right with God; in the teachings of Saint Paul, God makes a person "just," free from sin and pleasing to God through grace, attested by faith (Rom 3:2–30). According to the Council of Trent, "Justification is the change from the condition in which a person is born as a child of the first Adam into a state of grace and adoption among the children of God through the second Adam, Jesus Christ our Savior." Thus, justification includes a true removal of sin by the power of God and a true supernatural sanctification through the gift of sanctifying grace or participation in the life of God. (CCC 1266)

K

keys   The symbol of spiritual power and authority conferred on Saint Peter and his successors by Jesus Christ: "I will give you the keys of the kingdom of heaven" (Mt 16:19). The "power of the keys" is an expression used to describe the authority of the bishop of Rome, the pope, over all the faithful and all the churches. It is also used to describe the Church's authority to "bind" and "loose" (forgive or retain) sins in the sacrament of penance. (CCC 551–553)

kneeling   The ordinary position of the gathered assembly during the celebration of certain parts of the Mass, from at least the Synod of Tours (831). Adoption of this posture probably developed in response to the growing awareness of the divinity of Christ and the commonly held belief that people are "not worthy" to be in the presence of the Lord. The traditional exception to kneeling has always been the proclamation of the gospel for which the even more ancient and traditional position of standing has been retained. After Vatican II, many churches instituted the custom of standing throughout the eucharistic prayer but recent liturgical discipline mandates the return to kneeling as the proper position of the gathered assembly.

Kyrie eleison Three Kyrie eleisons ("Lord, have mercy"), three Christe eleisons ("Christ, have mercy"), and three Kyrie eleisons are part of the introductory penitential rite in the eucharistic liturgy.

L

laity All members of the Church belong to the people of God, the Christian faithful. According to canon law, "The Christian faithful are those who, inasmuch as they have been incorporated in Christ through baptism, have been constituted as the people of God. For this reason, made sharers in their own way in Christ's priestly, prophetic, and royal functions, they are called to exercise the mission which God has entrusted to the Church to fulfill in the world, in accord with the condition proper to each one" (Canon 204.1). Among the Christian faithful, the laity are all the faithful except for those in holy orders (clergy) and those who belong to a Christian state approved by the Church (religious men and women). According to Vatican Council II, the Decree on the Apostolate of the Lay People, §8, the special mission of the laity is to renew the temporal order and to witness to Christ in a special way in secular affairs. (CCC 897–900)

lamp, sanctuary The light that is kept burning whenever the Blessed Sacrament is present, as a sign of reverence and respect. According to Church law, the lamp is either a beeswax candle or a lamp with olive oil; however local considerations prevail, and a bishop can give permission for some other kind of candle or oil. In some instances the lamp is electrical. The sanctuary lamp burns "to indicate and honor the presence of Christ" and "is to shine continuously before a tabernacle in which the Most Holy Eucharist is reserved" (Canon 940).

Last Supper   The traditional name given to the Passover meal which Jesus ate with his apostles in Jerusalem on the night before he died (Mk 14:22–25; Lk 22:14–20). According to Catholic teaching, it was on this occasion that Jesus instituted the holy Eucharist and the holy priesthood. The Church celebrates the Lord's Supper on Holy Thursday evening. (CCC 610–611)

laying on of hands   A ceremonial imposition of the hands on a person or a thing in order to convey some spiritual power. The laying on of hands accompanies confirmation, ordination, the anointing of the sick, as well as some sacramentals. (CCC 1288, 1507, 1538)

Lectionary   The liturgical book that contains the scriptural passages which are proclaimed during the Liturgy of the Word at Mass. The Lectionary contains a three-year cycle of readings, identified as cycle A, B, and C for the Sundays of the liturgical year and a two-year cycle identified as I and II for the weekdays of the year. Special readings are also provided for feast days and for special "votive" Masses, such as Masses in honor of the saints or the Blessed Virgin Mary.

lector   The designated person who reads scriptural and other passages (other than the gospel) during liturgical worship. (CCC 1143)

liturgical colors   A sequence of vestment colors for different seasons of the Church year which became important during the twelfth century and became standardized after the Council of Trent. Purple is used during Lent and during other penitential celebrations and sometimes during Advent, although blue is becoming more and more the preferred color for Advent. White is the color for Easter, Christmas, feast days of the saints who are not martyrs, and other special solemnities. Red is used for the feast of Pentecost, Good Friday, and for the feast of the martyrs. Green is used in ordinary time. For a long time, black was the color used for funerals, but today the chosen color for funerals is white because it reminds the faithful of the Resurrection of Jesus.

liturgy   The public worship of the Church, including the celebration of the sacrament and sacrifice of the Eucharist, the celebration of the other sacraments, and the Liturgy of the Hours (also designated as the Divine Office), which is a set form of hymns, psalms, readings, and prayers recited at particular times of the day. Vatican II, in its Constitution on the Sacred Liturgy, §2, teaches that "…it is the liturgy through which, especially in the divine sacrifice of the Eucharist, the work of redemption is accomplished and it is through the liturgy, especially, that the faithful are enabled to express in their lives and manifest to others the mystery of Christ and the real nature of the true Church." (CCC 1067–1070)

Lord's Prayer   Also known as the Pater Noster (in Latin) or the Our Father. This is the prayer that Jesus taught to his disciples. It is found in Matthew 6:9–13 and Luke 11:2-4.

M

mandatum   See washing of the feet.

major orders   A term used to refer to the priesthood and the diaconate. In 1972, Paul VI amended the grades of orders; up until that time, the term had also applied to the order of sub-deacon (which was eliminated). Paul VI also suppressed the minor orders of porter, lector, exorcist, and acolyte. The ministries of lector and acolyte have replaced them.

Mass   In Latin, *missa*, which means "to be sent or dismissed." The Mass is the center and the heart of Catholic worship. The Mass is in two parts, the Liturgy of the Word and the Liturgy of the Eucharist. In its earliest expressions, the Mass was a simple meal, but it evolved over time and with the influence of many different cultural contexts. In the sixteenth century, the Council of Trent reformed and standardized the celebration of the Mass and the directives of this council became the norm for the next four hundred years. The Constitution on the Sacred

Liturgy adopted at Vatican II implemented the renewal of the Mass as it is celebrated today.

matter and form   The matter and form of the sacraments refers to the specific material or gesture (matter) used in the sacramental rite and also the words used or significance expressed (form). This distinction is based on Aristotelian philosophy, which viewed the world, and anything of importance in the world, as being made up of matter and form. Theologians in the Middle Ages basically agreed with Aristotle and ascribed specific matter and form to each of the sacraments. (Within the text of this book, the matter and the form of each sacrament have been clearly identified for easy reference.)

medals   Metal disks imprinted with the image of Christ, the Blessed Mother, a saint, a sacred event, and so on. The Church provides a blessing for medals and has long approved the use of them as long as they are understood as an aid to devotion and prayer; there are a large number of medals approved by the Church. At the same time the Church warns against medals if the person using the medal makes them into an object of superstition. (CCC 1667–1670)

minister, sacramental   This term refers to a person who is officially commissioned by the Church to preside over or administer a sacrament. Jesus Christ is the principal celebrant of the sacrament, but Jesus acts through the ministry of the Church. The ordinary minister of baptism is a priest or deacon; however, any baptized person may administer the sacrament in the case of necessity or emergency. The bishop is the ordinary minister of confirmation but because of pastoral need priests are often delegated by the bishop to administer the sacrament. The ordinary minister of the Eucharist, reconciliation, and the anointing of the sick is a priest. The couple who are being married are the ministers of the sacrament of matrimony; the priest or deacon is the official witness that is required for validity. The minister of holy orders is the bishop.

ministry A word arising from the Latin, meaning "to render service." In the viewpoint of Catholic theology, there is one essential ministry—the ministry of Jesus Christ; his ministry is extended, however, through the members of his Body, the Church. In the Church, the term *minister* is used in a variety of ways, among which are the following:

Ordained ministry: the service of the people of God by those who have received the sacrament of holy orders (that is, bishops, priests, and deacons) and who have specific functions determined by the teaching of the Church itself.

Non-ordained ministry: the service of the people of God undertaken by baptized Catholics either (a) with a formal commission from the Church (for example, lector, catechist, acolyte) or (b) without a formal commission from the Church (for example, performing the corporal and spiritual works of mercy).

Vatican Council II calls attention to both the variety and the unity of ministries in the Church: "In the Church not everyone marches along the same path, yet all are called to sanctity and have obtained an equal privilege of faith through the justice of God (see 2 Pet 1:1). Although by Christ's will some are established teachers, dispensers of the mysteries and pastors for the others, there remains, nevertheless, a true equality between all with regard to the dignity and to the activity which is common to all the faithful in the building up of the Body of Christ" (Dogmatic Constitution on the Church, §32). (CCC 873–879, 1590–1596)

missal The liturgical book that contains all the prayers for the liturgy of the Mass according to the Roman rite. Since Vatican II, the missal consists of two books: the Roman Missal (called the Sacramentary in the United States and in Canada) which the contains the texts for the celebration of the Mass, and the Lectionary for the Mass, containing a three-year cycle of Scripture readings and chants for Sundays and a two-year cycle of first readings and gospels for the weekday liturgy. Readings for other feasts and for votive Masses are also included.

mixed marriage   A marriage between a Catholic partner and a partner who is not Catholic. The basic discipline of the Catholic Church in regard to mixed marriages is explained in the Code of Canon Law: "Without express permission of the competent authority, a marriage is prohibited between two baptized persons of whom one is baptized in the Catholic Church or received into it after baptism and has not defected from it by a formal act and the other of whom is enrolled in a church or ecclesial community is not in full communion with the Catholic Church" (Canon 1124). The express permission called for in the Canon may be granted by the local ordinary (bishop) for a just and reasonable cause; according to Canon 1125, he is not to grant this permission unless the following conditions have been fulfilled:

1. The Catholic party is to declare that he or she is prepared to remove dangers of defection from the faith and is to make a sincere promise to do all in his or her power so that all offspring are baptized and brought up in the Catholic Church; 2. The other party is informed at an appropriate time about the promises, which the Catholic party is to make, in such a way that it is certain that he or she is truly aware of the promise and obligation of the Catholic party; 3. Both parties are to be instructed about the purposes and essential properties of marriage, which neither of the contracting parties is to exclude. The Catholic party is bound to the form of marriage (that is, marriage in the presence of the local ordinary [bishop] or the pastor or a priest or a deacon delegated by either of them, who assist, and in the presence of two witnesses); but for serious reasons the local ordinary has the right to dispense from the form in individual cases. It is the responsibility of the Catholic party to request this dispensation in due time before the marriage. (CCC 1633–1637)

monstrance   A freestanding and upright liturgical container, with a closed receptacle, usually glass, that holds the consecrated host. Used during Benediction and exposition of the Blessed Sacrament.

myron   The sacred chrism used in anointings as the sacramental sign of the presence of the Holy Spirit. This sacred oil is usually reserved in a special place in the sanctuary of the church, often with the oil of the sick and the oil of catechumens. (CCC 1241)

mystagogy   The period of time, usually during the season of Easter, in which those who have been baptized at the Easter Vigil receive continued instructions and teaching. This is a period of time celebrating their new experience of the sacraments and their relationship with the Christian community.

mysteria   A word from the Greek, meaning "mysteries." It is the first name used by Greek-speaking Christians to describe the ritual actions and symbols that are known today as the sacraments.

mysterion   A Greek term used to describe an experience of something that seems to have a higher or spiritual power.

Mystical Body   A term used to describe the Church. Saint Peter speaks of the Church as the Body of Christ; Christ is the head and we are the members (Col 1:18 and 1 Cor 12:27). In 1943, Pope Pius XII wrote a complete encyclical, "The Mystical Body of Christ," in which he traced the image of the Church through the Christian centuries and in which he concluded: "If we would define and describe the true Church of Jesus Christ—which is the one, holy, catholic, apostolic Roman Church—we shall find nothing more noble, more sublime, or more divine than the expression 'the Mystical Body of Christ'—an expression that flows spontaneously from the repeated teaching of the sacred Scripture and the holy Fathers." Vatican II also explains this image of the Church at length in the Dogmatic Constitution on the Church, §7. (CCC 787–795)

N

nuptial Mass   This is the special Mass that is celebrated for weddings. The images used throughout the Mass, and in the special nuptial blessing, recall the purpose of love and the creation of new life. It is a celebration of the Christian understanding and purpose of marriage.

O

oil of catechumens   One of the three oils blessed by the bishop during the Mass of Chrism which is usually celebrated on Holy Thursday morning. This olive oil is used in the rite of the catechumenate in preparation for the sacrament of baptism and is also used in the baptismal liturgy.

oil of chrism   One of the three oils blessed by the bishop during the Mass of Chrism which is usually celebrated on Holy Thursday morning. This oil is an olive oil, mixed with a type of balsam and is used in the baptismal liturgy, and also for confirmation and for holy orders.

oil of the sick   One of the three oils blessed by the bishop during the Mass of Chrism which is usually celebrated on Holy Thursday morning. This olive oil is used in the celebration of the anointing of the sick.

ordinary, extraordinary Ministers   Each sacrament is celebrated by a specific minister, understood as the minister who would "ordinarily" celebrate it. However, a properly delegated priest can also celebrate some sacraments, which are ordinarily celebrated by the bishop, when the occasion warrants it, for example the sacrament of confirmation. The ordinary celebrant of the sacrament is a bishop but there are occasions when the bishop does not celebrate the sacrament but delegates a priest to do so (for example, during the Easter Vigil in the baptism of adults). Some sacraments cannot be delegated but only celebrated by the ordinary minister of the sacrament, for example, the sacrament of holy orders, which may be performed only by a bishop.

ordinary time   Refers to the thirty-four weeks of the liturgical calendar of the Church that is neither the Advent/Christmas season or the Lent/Easter season. During this period, four solemnities of the Lord are celebrated: Trinity Sunday, Corpus Christi, the feast of the Sacred Heart, and the feast of Christ the King.

ordination   The ritual by which candidates receive one of the three orders that are part of the sacrament of holy orders: bishop, priest, and deacon. Ordination is conferred by the imposition of the hands of the ordaining bishop(s) with the accompanying prayer of the Holy Spirit proper to the order that is received.

P

Pange Lingua   A hymn in honor of the Blessed Sacrament by Saint Thomas Aquinas. The last two verses of this hymn are known as the *Tantum Ergo*, and are frequently sung at Benediction of the Blessed Sacrament either in English or in the traditional Latin.

parish   A defined community, usually within a specific geographical territory, of the people of God, entrusted to the care of a pastor, and under the jurisdiction of the local diocesan bishop. The parish is the ordinary place where the sacraments are administered and celebrated. (CCC 2179)

paschal candle   A large candle, blessed during the Easter Vigil on Holy Saturday, that is a symbol of the Risen Christ. The candle is used during the Easter season and is also used at baptism and at the Mass of Christian Burial.

paten   The dish that is used to hold the hosts during Mass. The paten is traditionally either silver or gold but is often some other material such as ceramic or glass.

penance, sacrament of   Also known as the rite of reconciliation. It is the sacrament by which sins committed after baptism are confessed and forgiven by the absolution of a priest. Jesus Christ conferred the power to forgive sins to the ministry of the Church in John 20:21–23: "As the Father has sent me, so I send you.... Receive the Holy Spirit. If you forgive the sins of any, they are forgiven them; if you retain the sins of any, they are retained."

perpetual adoration   The continued adoration of the Blessed Sacrament for twenty-four hours a day in specific chapels throughout the world. Certain religious communities, many specifically founded for this purpose, almost exclusively celebrated the practice of perpetual adoration at one time. However, in recent times, the practice of perpetual adoration is conducted in many dioceses of the United States in certain designated parish communities.

Prayer of the Faithful   Also known as the General Intercessions of the Mass. This litany of intercessory prayers offered during the eucharistic liturgy, by a designated minister, with a sung or spoken response by the assembled congregation, such as "Lord, hear our prayer," or simply "Lord, hear us." The petitions are completed by a concluding prayer prayed by the priest.

Precepts of the Church   Obligations imposed on Catholics by the law of the Church; traditionally, six are listed: (1) to participate in Mass on Sunday and holy days of obligation; (2) to fast and abstain on days designated by the Church; (3) to confess one's sins once a year; (4) to receive holy Communion during Eastertime; (5) to contribute to the support of the Church; (6) to observe the laws of the Church governing marriage. In 1977 the National Catechetical Directory for Catholics in the United States added two other precepts, namely: "To study Catholic teaching in preparation for the sacrament of confirmation, to be confirmed, and then to continue to study and advance the cause of Christ" and "to join in the missionary spirit and apostolate of the

Church." All of the traditional precepts of the Church have been reaffirmed in the revised Code of Canon Law (1983) and in the *Catechism of the Catholic Church.* (CCC 2041–2046)

Preface of the Mass   A prayer of praise and thanksgiving, prayed by the priest, at the beginning of the eucharistic prayer. There are many prefaces from which the priest may choose. Special feasts, special events, and specific celebrations have a particular preface suitable for the occasion.

prie-dieu   A bench or kneeler suitable for kneeling in prayer. A prie-dieu usually has a place on which to rest a book.

priest   The ordained minister who presides at the Eucharist. The priest is considered one of the ordinary ministers of the sacraments, with the exception of holy orders and confirmation. The word derives from the Greek *hiereus* and from the Latin *sacerdos.*

purgatory   According to Catholic teaching, the state or condition of the elect (those who have died in sanctifying grace or in the friendship of God) still in need of purification before they see God; this purification is altogether different from the punishment of the damned. The faithful are encouraged to pray for the souls in purgatory, especially on the feast of All Souls, November 2. (CCC 1030–1032)

purificator   A linen cloth, which is used as a type of napkin during the celebration of the Eucharist. Its primary purpose is to wipe the chalice during use and to wipe the chalice clean after use. Special care is used in the washing of the purificator. See **sacrarium.**

pyx   A container used to carry holy Communion to the sick and the homebound. It resembles an old, fine, pocket watch, but it is usually carried by the minister in a leather case called a "burse."

R

Real Presence   The Constitution on the Sacred Liturgy teaches that there are five prominent means by which Christ is present. The first is in the person of the minister, the second is through the power of the sacraments, the third is in the Word of the Scripture, the fourth is in the gathered and the praying community, and the fifth is under the appearance of bread and wine in the Eucharist. It is the teaching of the Church that Christ is substantially present in the Eucharist, and as such, the Eucharist is to be understood as the Real Presence.

reconciliation   The act of reestablishing a damaged or destroyed relationship between two parties. Reconciling humankind to God was the primary work of Jesus Christ and is an essential part of the Good News (2 Cor 5:17–19). According to Catholic teaching, reconciliation with God after one has gravely sinned against him and reconciliation with the Church, which is wounded by sin, are basic results of the sacrament of penance. (CCC 1468–1469)

reconciliation room   A place in most Catholic churches which is set aside for celebrating the sacrament of penance; the person celebrating the sacrament is provided with the option of confessing anonymously behind a screen or conversing with the priest face to face. (CCC 1185)

regeneration and renewal, the washing of   Another name that is sometimes used in reference to the sacrament of baptism, indicating the action of the Holy Spirit in bringing about the new birth, which is necessary so that a person may enter the kingdom of God (Titus 3:5). (CCC 1215)

requiem   The first word in the Latin Mass of the dead meaning "rest." This was the term that was formerly given to funeral Masses that were celebrated for the souls of the dead. The Requiem Mass is now called the Mass of Christian Burial.

rites   A term used to describe the forms and ceremonies in liturgical worship; the words and actions that belong to a religious ceremony, for example, the rite of baptism. The term is also used to group various communities within the Catholic Church in accordance with their official ritual usages, for example, Roman Rite Catholics and Byzantine Rite Catholics. (CCC 1125, 1203)

Roman Missal   Another name for the Sacramentary, a liturgical book that contains the liturgy of the Mass, including introductory instructions and prayer-texts for the celebration of Mass in the Roman rite. Another book, the Lectionary, contains the Scripture readings, including the gospels, which are required for Mass.

rubrics   From the Latin term meaning "red text," rubrics are directions for liturgical actions or gestures that are printed in red in order to distinguish them from the spoken texts, which are printed in black. A specific example of a rubric would be the direction to "genuflect" after the consecration and elevation of the host at Mass.

S

sacrament   This word is derived from the Latin, *sacramentum*, which means "oath" or "pledge." Within the Catholic tradition there are seven sacraments, which are the principal liturgical rites of the Church and the primary way in which the people of God are enabled to receive the grace of God that flows from the passion, death, and resurrection of Jesus Christ.

sacramental   The Second Vatican Council, in the Constitution on the Sacred Liturgy, §60, teaches that a sacramental signifies "effects, particularly of a spiritual nature, that are obtained through the Church's intercession. By them, men are disposed to receive the chief effect of the sacraments, and various occasions in human life are made holy." Holy water, ashes, palms, candles, and other such symbols and objects are examples of sacramentals.

sacramental character According to the teaching of the Council of Trent (1545), the sacraments of baptism, confirmation, and holy orders imprint a special character on the soul, "a certain spiritual and indelible mark. It is for this reason the sacraments cannot be repeated."

sacramental form The form of a sacrament, the precise words prescribed by the rite, are the absolute minimum that must be used in the celebration of the sacrament for validity. For example in the celebration of baptism the minister must pray, "I baptize you in the name of the Father, and of the Son, and of the Holy Spirit." These words are prayed while the person is immersed in water or while water is poured over the head of the person being baptized.

sacramental grace The specific communication of a particular help or presence from God expressed by the sacrament. For example, in the anointing of the sick, the particular help from God is the healing power of Christ, continually celebrated through the ministry of the Church.

sacramental matter With the exception of the sacrament of reconciliation, each sacrament includes a recognizable material element/gesture that is essential for the valid celebration of the sacrament. For example, in the sacrament of the Eucharist, the matter is bread and wine, and in the sacrament of anointing it is the blessed oil. Reconciliation does not have a material element/gesture in the strict sense but rather the elements of the penitent's contrition, confession, and penance form the matter of the sacrament.

Sacramentary A liturgical book containing all of the prayers needed by the presider for the celebration of the Mass. The book does not contain the readings used or other material that may be required for other ministers of the liturgical rite.

sacramentum A Latin word of many meanings (military oath, something of value held in escrow at the temple) that was first used in the second century by Tertullian as a way of describing the ritual celebrations of baptism and the Eucharist. Tertullian understood sacramentum to be a necessary component of the initiation process and deemed it to be an appropriate expression for the process through which a person became a Christian. It was later applied to all ritual actions and symbols that came to be understood as sacraments.

sacrarium   A Latin word, meaning "sacristy." A sacrarium is a sink in the sacristy that drains directly into the ground, used for the cleaning of Mass linens, purificators, and chalices. The sacrarium may also be used for the disposal of blessed ashes, oil, and holy water.

sacristy   A vesting room and preparation room located traditionally near the sanctuary of the church. Many modern churches separate the vesting room (often located in the back of the church) and the preparation room (located near the sanctuary in the traditional place). The main purpose for this separation is that liturgical celebrations usually begin with a procession of the ministers, from the back of the church, through the assembly of those gathered. Before Vatican II, the priest and ministers would commonly process from the sacristy into the sanctuary without ever engaging the gathered assembly.

sanctuary   That part of the church where the priest, servers, and other ministers have places to perform their functions. This area should be large enough to accommodate the liturgical rites and should be set off from the rest of the church by a raised floor, a special decoration, or some other easily visible sign.

seal of confession   The solemn obligation of the priest in the sacrament of penance to maintain absolute secrecy about anything that may be revealed to him within the celebration of the sacrament. (CCC 1467)

Seder meal   The meal celebrated by Christ and his disciples the night before he died. The Seder meal celebrates and remembers the night that the Jewish people escaped from Egypt and were passed over (thus its other name: "Passover") by the angel of death who killed the first-born. This meal is celebrated with song, readings, and symbolic foods.

Sign of the Cross   A gesture in the form of a cross by which one professes his or her faith in the Holy Trinity; it is made in several ways: (1) one "blesses oneself," for example, at the beginning and the end of prayer, by touching the fingers of one's right hand to one's forehead, "In the name of the Father, and of the Son, and of the Holy Spirit"; (2) one forms a small cross on one's forehead, lips, and breast before the proclamation of the gospel; (3) one authorized to give blessings in the Church makes a large cross with the right hand over the person or object to be blessed. (CCC 1671–1672)

signs   Things that point to other things beyond themselves. The liturgy of the Church is constructed on signs. Jesus refers to his miracles as signs, and the sacraments are signs that manifest the special presence of God. (CCC 1145–1151)

stipend, Mass   An offering made to a priest on the occasion of requesting a Mass to be offered for one's personal intentions; according to the Code of Canon Law, "In accord with the approved practice of the Church, any priest celebrating or concelebrating is permitted to receive an offering to apply the Mass for a specific intention" (Canon 945.1), but at the same time priests are urged to "celebrate Mass for the intention of the Christian faithful, but most especially of the needy, even if no offering has been received" (Canon 945.2). The primary purpose of the Mass stipend is to support the ministers and works of the Church.

Sunday obligation   The obligation to participate in the Sunday Eucharist "is the foundation and confirmation of all Christian practice" (CCC 2181). The 1917 Code of Canon Law made attendance at Mass a serious obligation for all Catholics unless there was a serious reason present that would make it difficult to fulfill the obligation, such as the care of infants or illness.

symbol   A thing or a sign by which another reality can be experienced. In the theological sense, a symbol allows us to look behind just the messages of our senses to a belief in a greater and more mysterious reality not readily apparent. (CCC 1146–1149)

T

tabernacle   A receptacle for the exclusive reservation of the Blessed Sacrament; according to the Code of Canon Law, it should be "situated in some part of the church or oratory which is distinguished, conspicuous, beautifully decorated, and suitable for prayer" (Canon 938.2); moreover, it should be "immovable, made of solid and opaque material, and locked in such a way that the danger of profanation is avoided as much as possible" (Canon 938.3).

tradition   According to Catholic teaching, one of the sources (together with the sacred Scripture) of divine revelation; it is, as Vatican II points out, the Word of God which has been entrusted to the apostles by Christ the Lord and the Holy Spirit. Unlike many Christian communities that teach that Scripture alone is the source of divine revelation, the Catholic Church professes that "Sacred Tradition and Sacred Scripture form one sacred deposit of the Word of God, which is entrusted to the Church" (Dogmatic Constitution on Divine Revelation, §10).

transubstantiation   In Catholic theology of the Eucharist, a technical term that describes the change of the whole substance of bread and wine into the whole substance of the body and blood of Christ while only the accidents (taste, smell, and so on) of bread and wine remain. (CCC 1373–1377)

Trent, Council of   The nineteenth ecumenical council of the Catholic Church held in twenty-five sessions between 1545 and 1563; its primary work was a defense of Catholic teaching against the attacks of the Protestant reformers: in presenting this defense it also offered a comprehensive treatment of Catholic teaching on the nature of justification, original sin, grace, faith, the seven sacraments (especially the Eucharist), the veneration of saints, purgatory, and indulgences. Trent set in motion a number of Catholic reforms in regard to the liturgy, the religious education of the faithful, the training of candidates for the priesthood, and the devotional life of the Church. Its influence was, for the most part, widespread and positive, and it is considered one of the more important of the Church's ecumenical councils. (CCC 884)

U

unbaptized, fate of   If, as the Church professes, baptism is necessary for salvation (see Jn 3:5), what can be said of the salvation of those who die without baptism? This theological question has been pondered for centuries. Briefly, Catholic teaching holds that, in the case of adults, there are two possibilities: (1) baptism of blood or martyrdom and (2) baptism of desire. In the case of infants, a rather common theological opinion has been that infants who die without baptism are excluded from heaven but spend eternity in a state of natural happiness called limbo. The Church has never explicitly taught this theological explanation. Another fairly common theological explanation has been that God in his mercy can supply for the lack of baptism in ways that have not been revealed to us. (CCC 1257–1261)

V

validity   A term that entered the vocabulary of the Church with the Council of Trent. Validity concerns the conditions that have to be followed for some act to be effectual or legal. For example, reception of baptism is a prior condition for receiving any of the other sacraments.

validity of the sacraments   When applied to sacraments, validity refers to the minimal requirements of matter, form, and circumstances needed for valid administration and to recognize that an action or celebration has resulted in a true sacrament. For example, the minister must resolve to do what the Church intends in celebrating a sacrament. In marriage, since the spouses minister the sacrament to each other, their intention to celebrate the sacrament is absolutely necessary for validity.

Vatican Council II   The twenty-first ecumenical council of the Catholic Church held in Rome for four sessions: the first during the pontificate of Pope John XXIII, October 11 to December 8, 1962; the other three sessions during the pontificate of Pope Paul VI, September 29 to December 4, 1963, September 14 to November 21, 1964, and September 14 to December 8, 1965. This was the largest (2,800 members) and most productive (sixteen significant documents) of all the ecumenical councils. The teaching of Vatican II had an enormous impact on the Church in all parts of the world. Of the sixteen documents enacted by the council, four were constitutions of major importance for the whole Church, nine were decrees on particular topics for particular communities within the Church, and three were declarations. The impact of the Second Vatican Council is continuing to be experienced in the Church today.

vestments   Garments used in the celebration of the eucharistic liturgy and other sacraments. The vestments have their origin in the ordinary dress of the Roman Empire in the first centuries of Christianity, but have taken on a symbolic meaning also. The principle vestments currently in use:

   alb: a long white (*albus* is Latin for white) garment, symbolic of the total purity that should cover one's approach to God.

   amice: a square or oblong piece of linen (or similar material) to which two long tapes are attached at the upper corners. It is worn over the shoulders and is symbolic of the "helmet of salvation."

   chasuble: a long, sleeveless outer garment worn over the alb by a priest or a bishop. Traditionally, the chasuble is a symbol of charity.

cincture: a cord around the waist to keep the alb neatly in place.

humeral veil: a rectangular shawl worn around the shoulders and used to cover the hands. It is used in eucharistic processions and devotions for holding the ciborium or the monstrance.

stole: a long, thin band of appropriate material worn around the neck and shoulders, symbolic of the "yoke of the Lord"; it is worn by the priest in solemn celebration of all of the sacraments (the deacon wearing it over the shoulder only).

surplice: a waist-length, wide-sleeved, white, alb-like vestment worn over the cassock, usually in formal liturgical celebrations or in other liturgical services outside of Mass.

Viaticum   The reception of holy Communion where there is probable danger of death. According to canon law, "the Christian faithful who are in danger of death, from any cause are to be nourished by Holy Communion in the form of Viaticum" (Canon 921). It is important that Viaticum not be delayed too long but that the sick be nourished with this "food for the journey" while they are still conscious. (CCC 1524–1525)

vigil lights/votive candles   Small candles placed in glass cups, often burned before a shrine or replica of a saint as an act of devotion or for a particular intention. Vigil lights are sacramental and are symbols of the deep hope of the faithful that their prayers will be answered and that their special needs will be met. These vigil lights symbolize the light of prayer and may burn for only a few hours or as long as a week. It is believed that the flame "keeps vigil" when the person cannot be present.

votive Mass   From the *Latin* meaning "promised" or "devoted," a votive Mass is celebrated for a specific intention, such as to ask God's blessing on the harvest, or Masses celebrated in memory of the dead.

Votive Masses have their own special prayers and specific readings from Scripture, all of which contribute to a fuller explanation of the particular theme/purpose.

W

wake   This term describes the custom of remaining awake and on watch with a deceased person; it is usually a period of one or two days before the funeral when mourners pay their respects to the deceased and offer their condolences to the bereaved. According to Catholic custom, the wake should also be a time of prayer for the repose of the soul of the deceased and for strength and courage on the part of the bereaved. It is customary in the United States to have a liturgical wake service (a "vigil for the deceased") and/or praying of the rosary.

washing of the feet   A rite observed since the fifth century in parts of the Church, but certainly since the twelfth century in the universal Church; this Holy Thursday ritual imitates Jesus' Last Supper action of washing the feet of his apostles. In many parishes, it is traditional that the very poor, rejected, or marginalized are the ones who are chosen to represent the Twelve Apostles and have their feet washed by the presiding celebrant.

water, liturgical use of   A few drops of water are mingled with the wine to be consecrated at Mass. This action symbolizes the union of the two natures in Jesus, the unity of Jesus with the people of God, the pain and toil of our lives which become one with the blood of Jesus, or the commingled water and blood that came from Jesus' side at the crucifixion.

Other liturgical uses of water occur at baptism, blessing of bells, consecration of a church, washing of hands after the Offertory, and the washing of the feet on Holy Thursday. Holy water is used in fonts at the entrances of churches, for blessings, and in homes.

Water is essential for human life and has many natural qualities;

it cleanses, refreshes, purifies, cannot be confined, is flexible, is everywhere. Water is a symbol of exterior and interior purity of life and sometimes for chaos.

wine, eucharistic   The wine consecrated during the eucharistic prayer must be pure grape juice which has been naturally fermented. The wine may be white or red. A few drops of water are added to the wine at the Offertory. The consecrated wine is distributed to the faithful during the Communion rite. (CCC 1333–1334)

Word of God   An expression used to describe several different realities: notably, Jesus Christ as the Word of God (Jn 1:1, 14); and the Bible as containing "the Word of God in the words of men."

worship   The adoration given to God expresses itself in praise, thanksgiving, self-offering, sorrow, and petition. Private worship of God can occur anywhere and at any time (Jn 4:21–24). Public worship is liturgy centered on Christ.

The reverence and adoration paid to God is called *latria*. Sometimes the word *dulia* is used for the esteem paid to the saints, but is better distinguished by the word *veneration*.

Worship is an interior activity, which often expresses itself in bodily gestures or postures: singing, kneeling, prostrating, dancing, and other forms of movement. Worship is also expressed in rites and ceremonies.

Sources

Scripture quotations are taken from the *New Revised Standard Version of the Bible,* © 1989, Division of Christian Education of the National Council of Churches of Christ in the United States of America. Reprinted with permission. All rights reserved.

Translations of canons from the 1983 Code of Canon Law are taken from *New Commentary on the Code of Canon Law,* © 2000 by the Canon Law Society of America.

Prayer of Consecration for Deacons, Priests, and Bishops from *The Rites of the Catholic Church as Revised by the Second Vatican Ecumenical Council,* Volume Two. New York: Pueblo Publishing Company, 1980.

Encyclopedia of Catholicism, Richard P. McBrien, General Editor. New York: HarperCollins Publishers, 1995.

Catholicism, Richard P. McBrien, New York: HarperSanFrancisco, 1994.

Our Sunday Visitor's Catholic Encyclopedia, Rev. Peter M. J. Stravinskas, editor. Huntington, Ind.: Our Sunday Visitor Publishing Division, 1998.

Catholic Encyclopedia for School and Home, St. Joseph's Seminary and College, Dunwoodie, Yonkers, N.Y.: McGraw-Hill Book Company, 1965.

Some definitions from *The Essential Catholic Handbook,* A Redemptorist Pastoral Publication. Liguori, Mo.: Liguori Publications, 1997.

Further definitions and some prayers from *The Essential Catholic Prayer Book,* A Redemptorist Pastoral Publication, Judith Bauer editor. Liguori, Mo.: Liguori Publications, 1999.

Some prayers of Saint Alphonsus from *Manuale Presbyterorum Congregationis Sanctissimi Redemptoris.* New York: Provincial Residence, 1955.

Meditations on the Eucharist from *Meditations on the Eucharist,* Saint Alphonsus Liguori, edited by Thomas M. Santa, C.Ss.R. Liguori, Mo.: Liguori Publications, 1998.

Be Mindful of Us: Prayers to the Saints, Anthony F. Chiffolo. Liguori, Mo.: Liguori Publications, 2000.

Sacraments: A New Understanding for a New Generation, Ray R. Noll. Mystic, Conn.: Twenty-Third Publications, 1999.

Sacrament: The Language of God's Giving, David N. Power. New York: Crossroad Publishing Company, 1999.

Doors to the Sacred: A Historical Introduction to Sacraments in the Catholic Church, Joseph Martos. Liguori, Mo.: Liguori/Triumph, 2001.

The Book of Sacramental Basics, Tad Guzie, S.J. New York: Paulist Press, 1982.

A New Look at the Sacraments, William Bausch. Mystic, Conn.: Twenty-Third Publications, 1983.

Traditional examination of conscience, from *The Mission Book of the Redemptorists,* compiled by V. Rev. F. Girardey, C.Ss.R. St. Louis, Mo.: Herder Book Company, 1947.

Contemporary Examination of Conscience, adapted from *Lenten Reconciliation Service,* Daniel Korn, C.Ss.R. Liguori, Mo.: Liguori Publications, 1998.

Visit to the Blessed Sacrament from *Visits to the Blessed Sacrament and the Blessed Virgin Mary,* Saint Alphonsus Liguori. Liguori, Mo.: Liguori Publications, 1994.

Some traditional prayers and devotions from *The Raccolta.* Milwaukee, Wis.: Benziger Brothers, Inc., 1944.

A Prayer for the People of God and Their Priest, A Prayer for Letting Go of a Loved One Near Death, and other original prayers for this edition, Thomas M. Santa, C.Ss.R. 2000.

Book of Blessings, International Committee of English in the Liturgy. Collegeville, Minn.: The Liturgical Press, 1989.

"Sacramentals," excerpted and adapted from *What You Should Know About Sacramentals,* Oscar Lukefahr, C.M. Liguori, Mo.: Liguori Publications, 1998.

Excerpts from the English translation of the *Rite of Baptism,* International Committee on English in the Liturgy (ICEL), © 1976.

References from the documents of Vatican II, *Vatican II: The Conciliar and Post Conciliar Documents,* edited by Austin Flannery, O.P., Northport, N.Y.: Costello Publishing Company, 1996.

"Rights and Obligations of the Baptized" and "Rights and Obligations of the Confirmed" from *The Millennium Series,* Catechetical and Pastoral Resource Department. Liguori, Mo.: Liguori Publications, 1997, 1998.

Excerpts from the English translation of the *Rite of Confirmation,* Second Edition. International Committee on English in the Liturgy (ICEL), © 1975.

Catholic Customs and Traditions: A Popular Guide, Greg Dues. Mystic, Conn.: Twenty-Third Publications, 1993.

Signatures of Grace: Catholic Writers on the Sacraments, Thomas Grady and Paula Huston, editors. New York, N.Y.: Dutton, 2000.

"Guidelines for the Reception of Holy Communion" from *We Believe: A Survey of the Catholic Faith,* Oscar Lukefahr, C.M., Liguori, Mo.: Liguori Publications, 1990.

"Letting Go" and "A Prayer to the Holy Spirit" from *Orientations: A Collection of Helps for Prayer,* John Veltri, S.J., Guelph, Ontario, Canada: Loyola House, 1979.

Excerpts from the English translation of the *Rite of Penance.* International Committee on English in the Liturgy (ICEL), © 1974.

Daily Life in the Time of Jesus. Henri Daniel-Rops. Ann Arbor, Mich.: Servant Books, 1980.

Heal Us O Lord: A Prayer Service for Healing, Rev. James White, C.Ss.R. Liguori, Mo.: Liguori Publications, 2000.

"Pastoral Concerns," which follow the explanation of each sacrament, from *What You Should Know About the Sacraments,* Charlene Altemose, MSC. Liguori, Mo.: Liguori Publications, 1994.

"Sacraments as the Experience of Grace and Contemporary Meditations/Prayers on the Sacraments" from *Sacraments: The Presence of Grace,* Rev. Bernard Haring, C.Ss.R. Liguori, Mo.: Liguori Publications, 2000.

A Catechumen's Prayer, Elsie Hainz McGrath. Liguori, Mo.: Liguori Publications, 1997.

Communion to the Homebound, Daniel Korn, C.Ss.R. Liguori, Mo.: Liguori Publications, 1997.

Your Baptism in Christ, Francine O'Connor. Liguori, Mo.: Liguori Publications, 1997.

Excerpts from the English translation of the *Pastoral Care of the Sick: Rites of Anointing and Viaticum.* International Committee on English in the Liturgy (ICEL), © 1982.

Excerpts from the English translation of *The Ordination of Deacons, Priests, and Bishops,* International Committee on English in the Liturgy (ICEL), © 1969.

Excerpts from the English translation of the *Rite of Marriage.* International Committee on English in the Liturgy (ICEL), © 1969.

Psalm 100, adapted for married couples from *Prayer Ideas for Married Couples,* Kass P. Dotterweich. Liguori, Mo.: Liguori Publications, 1994.

"Our Humanity" from *Our Family Prayer Book,* Renee Bartkowski. Liguori, Mo.: Liguori Publications, 1994.